Knowledge Management Excellence

The Art of Excelling
in Knowledge Management

Knowledge Management Excellence

The Art of Excelling in Knowledge Management

Book 4 in the five-part series
The Five Pillars of Organizational Excellence

by
H. James Harrington, Ph.D.

and

Frank Voehl

Foreword by
Donald S. Feigenbaum, Ph.D.

Paton Press LLC
Chico, California

Most Paton Press books are available at quantity discounts when purchased in bulk. For more information, contact:

Paton Press LLC
P.O. Box 44
Chico, CA 95927-0044
Telephone: (530) 342-5480
Fax: (530) 342-5471
E-mail: *books@patonpress.com*
Web: *www.patonpress.com*

Printed in the United States of America

10 09 08 07   5 4 3 2 1

ISBN-13: 978-1-932828-11-5
ISBN-10: 1-932828-11-7

Library of Congress Cataloging-in-Publication Data
Harrington, H. J. (H. James)
   Knowledge management excellence: the art of excelling in knowledge management / by H. James Harrington and Frank Voehl.
     p. cm. — (The five pillars of organizational excellence; bk. 4)
   Includes index.
ISBN 1-932828-11-7
1. Knowledge management. 2. Organizational change. 3. Organizational effectiveness. I. Voehl, Frank, 1946– II. Title. III. Series: Harrington, H.J. (H. James). Five pillars of organizational excellence; 4.
HD30.2.H372 2006
658.4'038—dc22

                    2006013378

Notice of Liability
The information in this book is distributed on an "as is" basis, without warranty. Although every precaution has been taken in the preparation of the book, neither the author nor Paton Press LLC shall have any liability to any person or entity with respect to any loss or damage caused or alleged to be caused directly or indirectly by the information contained in this book.

Staff
Publisher: Scott M. Paton
Editors: Anna Moss, Kim Weir
Book design: David Hurst
Cover design: Caylen Balmain

CONTENTS

About the Authors ix

Other Books by H. James Harrington and Frank Voehl xiii

Dedication xv

Acknowledgments xvii

Foreword xix

Preface xxi

Pillar I—Process Management Excellence. xxiv

Pillar II—Project Management Excellence xxvi

Pillar III—Change Management Excellence xxviii

Pillar IV—Knowledge Management Excellence xxix

Pillar V—Resource Management Excellence. xxix

The Sky Is Not the Limit xxxi

Why Do You Need Organizational Excellence? xxxii

Organizational Excellence Summary xxxv

CHAPTER I

Knowledge Management—Why We Need It 1

The Value of Knowledge Management. 2

What Is Knowledge? 6

The Basics of Knowledge Management. 6

Knowledge Capital 12

Knowledge Capital and Organizational Creativity. 15

Western Versus Japanese Knowledge Capital 17

Why the Balance Sheet Won't Do the Job 18

The Knowledge Audit 25

The Knowledge Assets Map. 27

Summary 31

CHAPTER II

The Knowledge Management System................................35

The Knowledge Management Life Cycle 35
Developing the Knowledge Management System 39
Why Have a Knowledge Management System? 50
Knowledge Management Maturity Grid...........................52
Knowledge Management Vision Statement 55
Summary 56

CHAPTER III

Knowledge Management Organization Structure 59

Organizing for Knowledge Management 59
The Organization Itself 64
The Burlington Northern Railroad Story 67
Knowledge Management System Documents 75
Summary 75

CHAPTER IV

Knowledge Management Information Technology Infrastructure.......77

IT Infrastructure's Role in the Knowledge Management System 77
Knowledge Management Collaboration and Groupware Tools 79
Knowledge Management Software 87
Knowledge Management Strategic Technology Plan 88
The Knowledge Management Optimization Rollout Process....89
Building Blocks for a Successfully Implemented Knowledge Management System....96
Summary 99

CHAPTER V

Best Practices in Knowledge Management 101

Benchmarking Knowledge Management Systems 103
Organizational Change Management for Knowledge Management Systems 104
Organizational Change Management Strategies................108
FLP Case Study: The Guiding Light That Flickered 111
Simple Language 123
Summary 133

CHAPTER VI

Implementing a Knowledge Management System 135

Starting and Implementing a Knowledge Management System 135
Six Phases of Implementing a Knowledge Management System 137
Process-Based Knowledge Map 150
Knowledge Management System Budget 151
Knowledge Management System Enablers 151
Summary 152

CHAPTER VII

Knowledge Management Values 155

Valuating Knowledge Capital 155
Knowledge Valuation on the Corporate Radar Screen 158
Projecting Knowledge Management Values 165
Knowledge Management Critical Success Factors 170
Summary 172

CHAPTER VIII

Knowledge Management Excellence Summary 175

What and Why 175
Knowledge Management System Results 179
Four Knowledge Management Profiles 181

Appendix A: Glossary 187

Appendix B: Suggested Reading 199

Index 201

ABOUT THE AUTHORS

H. James Harrington

In the book *Tech Trending* (Capstone, 2001) by Amy Zuckerman, H. James Harrington was referred to as "the quintessential tech trender." The *New York Times* referred to him as having a ". . . knack for synthesis and an open mind about packaging his knowledge and experience in new ways—characteristics that may matter more as prerequisites for new-economy success than technical wizardry . . . "

H. James Harrington, Ph.D.
CEO, Harrington Institute Inc.

Present Responsibilities

Harrington now serves as the chief executive officer for the Harrington Institute. He also serves as the chairman of the board for a number of businesses and as the U.S. chairman of Technologies for Project Management at the University of Quebec.

Harrington is recognized as one of the world leaders in applying performance improvement methodologies to business processes.

Previous Experience

In February 2002, Harrington retired as the COO of Systemcorp ALG, a leading supplier of knowledge management and project management software solutions. Prior to this, he served as a principal and one of the leaders in the Process Innovation Group at Ernst & Young. He was with IBM for more than thirty years as a senior engineer and project manager.

Harrington is past chairman of the prestigious International Academy for Quality and past president of the American Society for Quality. He is also an active member of the Global Knowledge Economics Council.

Credentials

The Harrington/Ishikawa Medal, presented yearly by the Asia Pacific Quality Organization, was named after Harrington to recognize his many contributions to the region. In 1997, the Quebec Society for Quality named their quality award "The Harrington/Neron Medal," honoring Harrington for his many contributions to Canada's quality movement. In 2000, the Sri Lanka national quality award was named after him.

Harrington's contributions to performance improvement around the world have brought him many honors and awards, including the Edwards Medal, the Lancaster Medal, ASQ's Distinguished Service Medal, China's Magnolia Award, and many others. He was appointed the honorary advisor to the China Quality Control Association, and he was elected to the Singapore Productivity Hall of Fame in 1990. He has been named lifetime honorary president of the Asia Pacific Quality Organization and honorary director of the Chilean Association of Quality Control.

Harrington has been elected a Fellow of the British Quality Control Organization and the American Society for Quality. He was also elected an honorary member of the quality societies in Taiwan, Argentina, Brazil, Colombia, and Singapore. He is listed in *Who's Who Worldwide* and *Men of Distinction Worldwide*. He has presented hundreds of papers on performance improvement and organizational management structure at local, state, national, and international levels.

Harrington is a prolific author, having published hundreds of technical reports and magazine articles. He has authored twenty-eight books and ten software packages.

Frank Voehl
Present Responsibilities

Frank Voehl now serves as the chairman and president of Strategy Associates Inc. and a senior consultant and chancellor for the Harrington Institute. He also serves as the chairman of the board for a number of businesses and as a Master Black Belt instructor and technology advisor at the University of Central Florida in Orlando. He's recognized as one of the world leaders in applying quality measurement and Lean Six Sigma methodologies to business processes.

Frank Voehl, Chairman and President, Strategy Associates, Inc.

Previous Experience

Voehl has extensive knowledge of Nuclear Regulatory Commission, Food and Drug Administration, Good Manufacturing Processes, and National Aeronautics and Space Administration quality system requirements. He's an expert in ISO 9000, QS-9000, ISO 14000, and Six Sigma quality system standards and processes. He has degrees from St. John's University and advanced studies at New York University, as well as a doctor of divinity degree. Since 1986, he's been responsible for overseeing the implementation of quality management systems with organizations in such diverse industries as telecommunications and utilities; federal, state, and local government agencies; public administration and safety; pharmaceuticals; insurance/banking; manufacturing; and institutes of higher learning.

In 2002 he joined The Harrington Group as the COO and executive vice president. Voehl has held executive management positions with Florida Power and Light and FPL Group, where he was the founding general manager and COO of Qualtec Quality Services for seven years. He's written, published, and co-published more than twenty-five books and hundreds of technical papers on business management, quality improvement, logistics, and teambuilding. He's also received numerous awards for community leadership, service to third-world countries, and student mentoring.

Credentials

Voehl developed the Bahamas National Quality Award in 1991 to recognize the many contributions of companies in the Caribbean region, and he's an honorary member of its board of judges. In 1980, the City of Yonkers, New York, declared March 7th "Frank Voehl Day," honoring him for his many contributions on behalf of the youth in the city where he lived and performed volunteer work. In 1985 he was named "Father of the Year" in Broward County, Florida. He also serves as president of the Broward County St. Vincent de Paul Society, whose mission is to serve the poor and needy.

Voehl's contributions to quality improvement around the world have brought him many honors and awards, including ASQ's Distinguished Service Medal, the Caribbean Center for Excellence Founders Award, the Community Quality Distinguished Service Award, the Czech Republic Outstanding Service Award on behalf of its business community leaders, FPL's Pioneer Lead Facilitator Award, the South Florida Manufacturers Association Partners in Productivity Award, and many others.

OTHER BOOKS BY H. JAMES HARRINGTON

- *The Improvement Process* (McGraw-Hill, 1987, a best-selling business book that year)
- *Poor-Quality Cost* (Marcel-Dekker, 1987)
- *Excellence—The IBM Way* (ASQ Quality Press, 1988)
- *The Quality-Profit Connection* (ASQ Quality Press, 1988)
- *Business Process Improvement* (McGraw-Hill, 1991, the first book about process redesign)
- *The Mouse Story* (Ernst & Young, 1991)
- *Of Tails and Teams* (ASQ Quality Press, 1994)
- *Total Improvement Management* (McGraw-Hill, 1995)
- *High Performance Benchmarking* (McGraw-Hill, 1996)
- *The Complete Benchmarking Implementation Guide* (McGraw-Hill, 1996)
- *ISO 9000 and Beyond* (McGraw-Hill, 1996)
- *The Business Process Improvement Workbook* (McGraw-Hill, 1997)
- *The Creativity Toolkit—Provoking Creativity in Individuals and Organizations* (McGraw-Hill, 1998)
- *Statistical Analysis Simplified—The Easy-to-Understand Guide to SPC and Data Analysis* (McGraw-Hill, 1998)
- *Area Activity Analysis—Aligning Work Activities and Measurements to Enhance Business Performance* (McGraw-Hill, 1998)
- *Reliability Simplified—Going Beyond Quality to Keep Customers for Life* (McGraw-Hill, 1999)
- *ISO 14000 Implementation—Upgrading Your EMS Effectively* (McGraw-Hill, 1999)
- *Performance Improvement Methods—Fighting the War on Waste* (with Kenneth C. Lomax, McGraw-Hill, 1999)
- *Simulation Modeling Methods—An Interactive Guide to Results-Based Decision Making* (McGraw-Hill, 2000)
- *Project Change Management—Applying Change Management to Improvement Projects* (with Daryl R. Conner and Nicholas L. Horney, McGraw-Hill, 2000)
- *E-Business Project Manager* (ASQ Quality Press, 2002)
- *Process Management Excellence: The Art of Excelling in Process Management* (Paton Press, 2006)
- *Project Management Excellence: The Art of Excelling in Process Management* (Paton Press, 2006)
- *Change Management Excellence: The Art of Excelling in Change Management* (Paton Press, 2006)

- *Resource Management Excellence: The Art of Excelling in Resource and Assets Management* (Paton Press, 2007)
- *Making Teams Hum* (Paton Press, 2007)

OTHER BOOKS BY FRANK VOEHL

- *ISO 9000: An Implementation Guide for Small to Mid-Sized Businesses* (with Peter Jackson and David Ashton, St. Lucie Press, 1994)
- *Deming: The Way We Knew Him* (CRC Press, 1995)
- *Handbook for TQM Implementation* (St. Lucie Press, 1994)
- *Team Building: A Structured Learning Approach* (with Peter Mears, CRC Press, 1995)
- *The Executive Guide to Implementing Quality Management Systems* (with Peter Mears, CRC Press, 1995)
- *Macrologistics Management: A Catalyst for Organizational Change* (with Martin Stein, CRC Press, 1997)
- *Total Quality in Information Systems and Technology* (with Jack Woodall and Deborah K. Rebuck, CRC Press, 1996)
- *Problem Solving for Results* (with Bill Roth and James Ryder, St. Lucie Press/CRC Press, 1996)
- *SPC for Results; Facilitation for Results; Visioning for Results; Strategic Planning for Results* (Strategy Associates, 1998–1999)
- *Knowledge Management for Results* (Quality Yearbook, McGraw Hill, 2000)
- *The Roadmap to High Performance: Suggested Readings* (Strategy Associates, 2000)
- *A Guidebook for Community Building* (Recovering Prosperity Through Quality Series, ASQ, 2001); An Integrated Case Study (Recovering Prosperity Through Quality Series, ASQ, 2001)

DEDICATION

We dedicate this book to our dear friends, Rick and Kim Harrington and their three wonderful children: J.R., Julie, and Wendy. Knowing and loving them has helped make our lives better, and they've set a living example of how a modern-day family should and can live together while still pursuing their busy lives.

And to Phil Stein, who died recently while still pursuing his quality grail of measurement and metrology. Thank you, Phil, for teaching us how to persevere.

ACKNOWLEDGMENTS

We want to recognize Glen Hoffherr for all of his technical guidance and input on the knowledge management technology approach and other parts of this book. And to Candy Rogers, who converted and edited endless hours of dictation into the finished product. We couldn't have done it without her help.

We'd like to thank all of our friends at the American Society for Quality and the International Academy for Quality for their many contributions to the concepts expressed in this book.

We also want to recognize the contributions made by the team from Harrington Institute Inc. But most of all, we want to recognize the contributions made by our wives, Marguerite Harrington and Micki Voehl. They're always there when we need them, and they keep us focused on the road ahead.

FOREWORD

Jim Harrington's lifetime career of highly successful, hands-on, knowledge-based organization leadership is in itself an example of the role of knowledge in both personal and enterprise success. And it's why he's so highly qualified to write and to teach us about the critical transition that's taking place today, particularly the emphasis upon knowledge assets in the workplace.

The authors have provided us with a clear understanding of this discipline and why it's of essential importance today. It's a key to our personal and business success as we proceed into the enormously volatile world of the twenty-first century, where knowledge and its successful utilization are increasingly the ultimate competitive advantage.

"Knowledge is power" was the traditional—and today, inaccurate—phrase that an earlier business generation adhered to. Today, the very different and correct term is, "knowledge is power—when managed with excellence."

A basic principle of corporate strength is the recognition that effective knowledge management is a basic requirement in today's constantly changing global marketplace. It's a major key to business growth and profitability strength in the twenty-first century. To be effective, this requires systematic and rigorous implementation and attention.

An increasing number of today's corporate leaders recognize this. They understand that knowledge is an integral business leadership component of management and has to be organized and systematically structured as an integral component of business operations. In *Knowledge Management Excellence*, Jim Harrington and Frank Voehl clearly explain how to accomplish this successfully. In clear terms the book discusses the essential factors necessary to implement ongoing knowledge management excellence. These are supported by numerous examples that illustrate the practicality of a well-designed and implemented knowledge management system.

Know-how has long been a term used to explain the reason for the continuous success of pacesetters that are the consistent, long-term corporate leaders. *Knowledge Management Excellence* will certainly help to support that strength for its readers.

—Donald S. Feigenbaum, Ph.D.
Executive vice president and COO
General Systems Co. Inc.

PREFACE

"If only HP knew what HP knows, we would be three times more productive."

—Lew Platt
Former CEO, Hewlett-Packard

This series was written for a small group of organizations. It's not for traditionalists, the weak of heart, or for organizations that believe winning a national quality award is their ultimate objective. This series was written for organizations that aren't content with being anything less than the best they can be. It's for organizations that want to stand out from the crowd and that hunger to obtain optimum results in the five Ps:

■ *Pride*. Employees are proud of their work and their organization.

■ *Performance*. The entire organization operates at high levels of efficiency and effectiveness.

■ *Profit*. The organization is profitable, able to pay its employees good salaries, and pay higher-than-average dividends to its investors.

■ *Prestige*. The organization is considered an admirable place to work, and is known for its highly desired products and services.

■ *Pleasure*. Employees enjoy coming to work because they're doing something worthwhile in a friendly, supportive environment.

Good is no longer good enough. Doing the right thing "right" isn't good enough. Having the highest quality and being the most productive doesn't suffice today. To survive in today's competitive environment, you must excel. (See figure P.1.) To excel, an organization must focus on all parts of itself, optimizing the use and effectiveness of all of its resources. It must also provide "knock their socks off" products and services, and be so innovative and creative that customers say, "I didn't know they could do that!"

> "To compete and win, we must redouble our efforts, not only in the quality of our goods and services, but in the quality of our thinking, in the quality of our response to our customers, in the quality of our decision making, in the quality of everything we do."
> —E. S. Woolard
> Chairman and CEO, Dupont

After years of working with all types of organizations using many different approaches to improve performance, I've come to realize that five key elements must be managed for an organization to excel. I call them the "five pillars of organizational excellence." All five must be managed creatively and simultaneously. Top management's job is to keep all these elements moving ahead simultaneously. To concentrate on one or two alone is a surefire

Figure P.1   **Organizational Excellence**

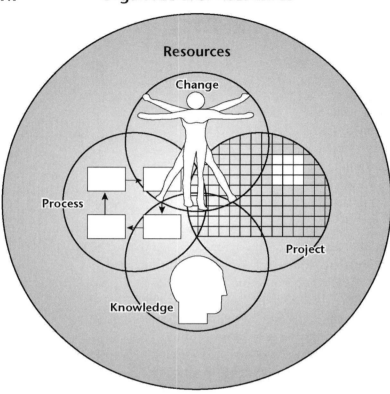

formula for failure. Priorities might shift, causing an individual pillar to move from being "very important" to simply "important," but it should never shift lower than that.

The processes discussed in this series are designed to permanently change an organization by skillfully managing its five key pillars. None of these management pillars is new by itself, but by combining them together it's possible to take a holistic approach to improving an organization's performance. (See figure P.2.)

The five pillars of organizational excellence are:

- *Process management excellence.* We must manage our processes and continuously improve them because they're the way we do business.
- *Project management excellence.* We must manage our projects because they're the way we obtain major improvements in our processes.
- *Change management excellence.* We must manage the organization so that it can cope with the chaos it will be subjected to by the magnitude and quantity of necessary changes.
- *Knowledge management excellence.* We must manage the organization's knowledge, its most valuable asset. (Knowledge gives an organization its competitive advantage, as

technology can easily be reverse-engineered and transferred to any place in the world almost overnight.)

■ *Resource management excellence.* We must manage our resources and assets because they're what drive our business results.

By effectively managing these five key pillars and leveraging their interdependencies and reactions, an organization can bring about a marvelous self-transformation. It will emerge from its restricting cocoon and float on the winds of success and self-fulfillment.

Organizational excellence is designed to permanently change an organization by focusing on the five pillars of excellence. Learning to manage the pillars together is the key to success in the endless pursuit of improved performance. To help you in this endeavor,

"These companies [excellent organizations] implement their results through effectiveness in developing and deploying management capital's intellectual, technical, human information and other resources in integrating a company's hard and soft assets."
—Armand V. Feigenbaum and Donald Feigenbaum Authors of *The Power of Management Capital*

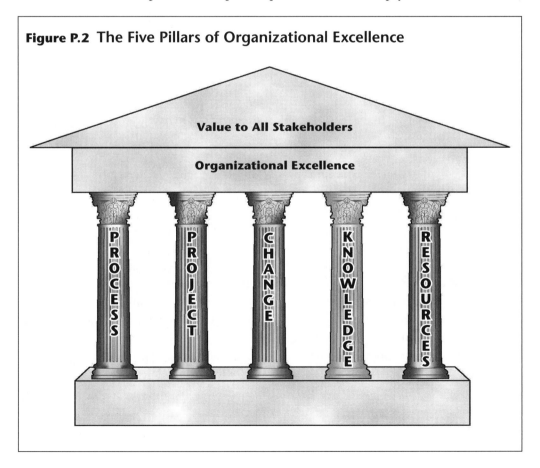

Figure P.2 The Five Pillars of Organizational Excellence

each volume in this five-book series addresses one of the pillars. The series consists of the following books:

- *Process Management Excellence: The Art of Excelling in Process Management*
- *Project Management Excellence: The Art of Excelling in Project Management*
- *Change Management Excellence: The Art of Excelling in Change Management*
- *Knowledge Management Excellence: The Art of Excelling in Knowledge Management*
- *Resource Management Excellence: The Art of Excelling in Resource Management*

None of the five pillars can individually support organizational excellence. All of them must be present and equally strong to support the weight of success with all of its stakeholders. The challenge that excellent organizations face today is how to nurture an innovative learning culture while maintaining the procedures and structures that ensure optimum performance as well as customer and investor satisfaction. The Five Pillars of Organizational Excellence series was designed to help solve this dilemma.

Because it's important to understand how the five pillars interact with and support each other, a short discussion about each of them follows.

PILLAR I—PROCESS MANAGEMENT EXCELLENCE

"Your processes manage the organization, not your managers."
—HJH

The process management concept certainly isn't new to management professionals; it's the basis of most improvement methodologies.

A *process* is a series of interconnected activities that takes input, adds value to it, and produces output. It's how organizations do their day-to-day routines. Your organization's processes define how it operates.

To manage a process, the following must be defined and agreed upon:

- An output requirement statement between process owners and customers
- An input requirement statement between process owners and suppliers
- A process that can transform suppliers' input into output that meets customers' performance and quality requirements
- Feedback measurement systems between process and customers, and between process and suppliers
- The method by which people are trained to understand the process
- A measurement system within the process

These six key factors should be addressed when designing a process. However, the problem facing most organizations is that many of their support processes were never designed in the first place. They were created in response to a need without understanding what a process is.

> **"Most individuals, teams, and groups within an organization will take the path of least resistance. Inevitably, over time, they will function at the lowest level of acceptability."**
> **—William J. Schwarz CEO, CEO Alliance and the Center for Inspired Performance**

The Two Approaches to Process Management

There are two basic approaches to managing processes:

- The micro-level approach, which is directed at managing processes within a natural work team or an individual department
- The macro-level approach, which is directed at managing processes that flow across departments and/or functions within the organization

Most of the work that quality professionals do is related to continuously improving processes. Some of the tools they use include design of experiments, process capability studies, root cause analysis, document control, quality circles, suggestion systems, Six Sigma, Shewhart's cycles, ISO 9001, and just-in-time manufacturing and supplier qualification.

In excellent organizations, management requires each natural work team (i.e., department) to continuously improve the processes it uses.

Refining a process is an ongoing activity. If the refinement process is working as it should, the total process' efficiency and effectiveness should be improving at a rate of 10 to 15 percent a year. In most cases, the project team focuses on the major problems that reflect across departments and reap such a harvest within three to twelve months. At that time, the project team can be disbanded and the process-refinement

> **"If you [management] create an expectation of continuous product or service improvement, but fail to deliver on that expectation, you will see a build-up of fear and negative forecasting."**
> **—Stephen R. Covey, Ph.D. Author, *The Seven Habits of Highly Effective People***

Figure P.3 What Different Types of People Have to Say About a Half-Full Glass

- The optimist: It's half full.
- The pessimist: It's half empty.
- The process manager: We have twice the number of glasses as we need.

activities turned over to the natural work teams involved in the process. Area activity analysis methodology, which is discussed later in this book, is the most effective approach to process refinement.

By focusing on its processes and working with its suppliers, IBM reported that, "Between 1997 and 2001, the hardware reliability of our high-end servers improved by more than 200 percent while computing power increased by a factor of four."

PILLAR II—PROJECT MANAGEMENT EXCELLENCE

"How can you compete when more than 70 percent of your improvement efforts are unsuccessful?"

—HJH

According to the Chaos Report compiled by the Standish Group International:
- Only 26 percent of all projects are successful.
- Forty percent of all information technology (IT) projects fail or are canceled.

A *project* is a temporary endeavor undertaken to create a unique product or service.

Projects in most organizations are mission-critical activities, and delivering quality products on time is non-negotiable. Even for IT projects, things have changed. Benchmark organizations are completing 90 percent of their projects within 10 percent of budget and schedule. Information systems organizations that establish standards for project management, including a project office, cut their major project cost overruns, delays, and cancellations by 50 percent (Gartner Group, August 2000).

Process redesign and process reengineering are two of the most important projects that organizations undertake. These types of projects have a failure rate estimated to be as high as 60 percent. The two main causes for these high-cost failures are: poor project management and poor change management. IBM launched eleven reengineering projects that addressed everything from the way the company manages internal information systems to the way it developed products and serves customers. IBM reported, "We have reduced IT spending by 31 percent for a total savings of more than two billion dollars. Since 1993, cycle time for large systems development has been slashed from fifty-six months to sixteen months. For low-end systems, it's seven months—down from two years."

The Professional Project Manager

We liken project management to quality management. Everyone thinks he or she knows what quality is, so organizations assume that anyone can manage quality. This same thought

Figure P.4   **Integrated Management Tools**

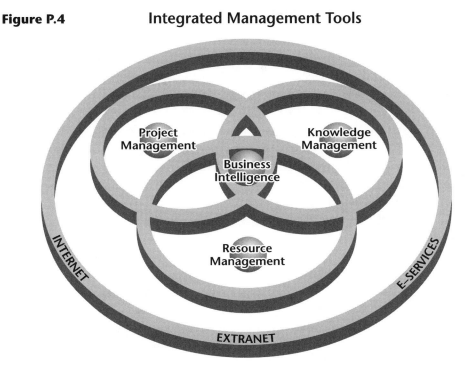

pattern applies to project management, but just as a quality manager is a special type of professional with very special skills and training, so is a project manager. Project managers require skill, training, and effective leadership specifically related to project management.

The Project Management Body of Knowledge (PMBOK) defines sixty-nine tools that a project manager must master. Few project managers have mastered all of these tools. In today's complex world, most organizations have numerous projects going on at the same time. Many of them are interlinked and interdependent. Their requirements and schedules are continuously changing, which causes a chain reaction throughout the organization. For this reason, organizations can't afford to manage each project in isolation. They must instead manage their project portfolios, making the appropriate trade-offs of personnel and priorities.

Project Management Excellence: The Art of Excelling in Project Management, book two in this series, focuses on how to use project management tools to effectively manage an organization's projects and integrate them into the total operations. This requires the effective integration of projects, resources, and knowledge to obtain business intelligence.

PILLAR III—CHANGE MANAGEMENT EXCELLENCE

We all like to think of ourselves as change masters, but, in truth, we're change big-ots. Everyone in the management team supports change. They want to see others change, but when it comes to the managers themselves changing, they're reluctant to move away from past experiences that have proven successful for them. If an organization is going to change, top management must be the first to do so.

Change is inevitable, and we must embrace it if we're going to be successful in the challenging world in which we live. In *Change Management Excellence: The Art of Excelling in Change Management*, book three in this series, we discuss a change management system that's made up of three distinct elements:

- Defining what will be changed
- Defining how to change
- Making the change happen

Most of the books written to date about change management have been theoretical in nature. They talk about black holes, cascading sponsorships, and burning platforms, but these are only the last phase of the change process. Most organizations don't understand or follow a comprehensive change management system. An effective change management system requires that the organization step back and define what will be changed. It's not about reducing stock levels, increasing customer satisfaction, or training people; it's about the fundamentals. Which of the key business drivers must be changed, and how do they need to be changed?

"Research confirms that as much as 60 percent of change initiatives and other projects fail as a direct result of a fundamental inability to manage their social implications."
—Gartner Group

An organization must develop crisp vision statements that define how key business drivers will be changed over time. This requires that the organization have an excellent under-standing of what its business drivers are and how they're cur-rently operating. Then the organization must define exactly how it wants to change these key business drivers over a set period of time. Once the organization has defined what it wants to change, it can then define how to change. During this stage, the organization looks at the more than 1,100 different improvement tools that are available today, determines which tools will bring about the required changes to these key business drivers, and schedules the implementation of these tools and methodologies. This schedule makes up a key part of the organization's strategic business plan.

The last phase in the change management process is making the change happen. This is the area where behavioral scientists have developed a number of excellent approaches to break down resistance and build up resiliency throughout the organization. It's this phase that most change management books have concentrated on, but it's the last phase in the total change management system. Book three of this series focuses on all three phases of the change management system, discussing in detail how to define what will be changed, defining how to change it, and how to make the change happen.

PILLAR IV—KNOWLEDGE MANAGEMENT EXCELLENCE

"When a person dies, a library is lost."
—HJH

Today more than ever before, knowledge is the key to organizational success. To fulfill this need, the Internet and other information technologies have provided all of us with more information than we can ever consume. Instead of having one or two sources of information, the Internet provides us with hundreds, if not thousands, of inputs, all of which must be researched for that key nugget of information. We're overwhelmed with so much information that we don't have time to absorb it.

To make matters worse, most of an organization's knowledge is still undocumented; it rests in the minds and experiences of its employees. This knowledge disappears from the organization's knowledge base whenever an individual leaves an assignment. This book will discuss knowledge management in detail.

PILLAR V—RESOURCE MANAGEMENT EXCELLENCE

"Even the best ideas need resources to transform them into profit."
—HJH

Nothing can be accomplished without resources. They lie at the heart of everything we do. If we have too few, we fail; if there are too many, there's waste—hindering the organization's competitive ability. Too many organizations limit their definition of resources to people and money. These are important, but they're only a small part of the resources an organization must manage. In *Resource Management Excellence: The Art of Excelling in Resource Management,* book five in this series, we look at all of the resources available to an organization and how to manage them effectively.

When resource management is discussed, it's in the broadest sense—all the resources and assets that are available to the organization. This includes stockholders, management, employees, money, suppliers, inventory, boards of directors, alliance partnerships, real estate, knowledge, customers, patents, investors, goodwill, and brick and mortar. When all of these are considered, it quickly becomes apparent that effective resource management is one of the most critical, complex activities within any organization. Managers and employees must examine their own performances to be sure they're doing the best they can.

Jack Welch, former CEO of General Electric, has created the following "Six Rules for Self-Examination":

1. Face reality as it is, not as it was or as you wish it were.
2. Be candid with everyone.
3. Don't manage; lead.
4. Change before you have to.
5. If you don't have a competitive advantage, don't compete.
6. Control your own destiny, or someone else will.

Each resource must be managed in its own special way to assist in building an excellent organization. The big question is, "How do you pull all these different activities and improvement approaches together and prioritize them?" To answer this, we'll present a thorough, total involvement approach to strategic planning, one that involves everyone—from the chairman of the board to the janitor, from sales to personnel, from development engineering to maintenance. Yes, this is a total-involvement approach to strategic planning; it's both bottom up and top down.

A total strategic planning process (i.e., business plan) has three main objectives. (See figure P.5.)

Eleven documents are needed in a comprehensive, strategic business plan:
- Mission statement
- Value statements

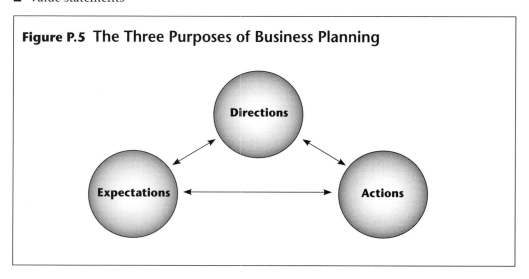

Figure P.5 The Three Purposes of Business Planning

- Organization's vision statements
- Strategic focus
- Critical success factors
- Objectives
- Goals
- Strategies
- Tactics
- Budgets
- Performance plans

"We expect a lot—highly motivated people consciously choosing to do whatever is in their power to assure every customer is satisfied . . . and more. Every day. Without this concentrated effort, attempting a flawless service is really quite futile."
—Fred Smith
Founder and CEO,
Federal Express

Resource management can't be an afterthought; all executive decisions must be based upon it. It requires a lot of planning, coordination, reporting, and continuous refining to do an excellent job. Too many organizations manage operations by simply throwing more resources into the pot. They may be successful with this approach as long as they have little competition, but even the giants fail if they don't do an outstanding job of resource management.

THE SKY IS NOT THE LIMIT

"You are only limited by what you can envision."
—HJH

We used to say, "The sky's the limit" when we were thinking of the limits of possibility. Today there's no limit—if you can dream it or imagine it, then you can do it, or there's someone out there who can do it for you.

We need to start thinking differently. The word "impossible" should be stricken from our vocabularies. Thinking outside of the box isn't good enough; we must tear down the walls of the box and build a culture without walls.

Our workforce is becoming more mobile. Organizations are cutting back by outsourcing all but their core capabilities and competencies. Business offices are shrinking as increasingly large numbers of people are working from their homes. No organization can afford to pay its employees to do one-of-a-kind jobs when consultants can do it faster, better, and at reduced risk.

WHY DO YOU NEED ORGANIZATIONAL EXCELLENCE?

Times have changed, and our thinking about the way we manage our improvement activities must change with them. Only the very best organizations will attract customers in today's competitive environment. Producing excellent products isn't enough today; we must excel in all parts of our organization. Piecemeal approaches such as TQM, Six Sigma, and customer-relationship management must give way to a holistic view of the organization and its improvement efforts. An organization should wow its customers, not just satisfy them. Customers should rate the total organization as outstanding, not just very good.

Customers remember an organization's name for two reasons and for two reasons only:

- If it produces a poor product or service
- When it produces an exceptional product or service that makes them say, "Wow! That was a great experience."

> **"We must simply learn to love change as much as we have hated it in the past."**
> **—Tom Peters**
> **Author, *Thriving on Chaos***

If you simply meet your customers' requirements, you don't build customer loyalty. They can be lured away from you if your competition undercuts you by a few cents. Your organization must radiate excellence in everything it does.

For the last fifty years, the quality professional, management professional, and consultant have tried—unsuccessfully—to impose improvement systems on business, government, and academia. Consider the following attempts:

- Quality control—failed
- Total quality control—failed
- Zero defects—failed
- Total quality management—failed
- Process reengineering—failed
- Six Sigma—failing
- ISO 9001:2000—added little real value

The question is, "Why, after great spurts of success, do these sound improvement systems fall into oblivion?" They're much like an old toy that gets put back in the dark corner of the closet when a new toy is found under the Christmas tree.

These exercises in futility stem from applying improvement initiatives to an organization as if they were bandages. What's really needed is fundamental organizational change. Treating symptoms usually doesn't affect a cure; it just prolongs the agony.

These approaches failed because the initiatives were applied as separate activities instead of with the intention of making a total organizational transformation. It's similar to giving a person who has pneumonia an aspirin for his or her headache, thinking it will cure the disease.

From decade to decade, our business focus continually changes:

■ 1970s—people
■ 1980s—teams
■ 1990s—processes
■ 2000s—knowledge and adaptability

In keeping with these changes, the approaches to performance improvement have also changed:

■ ISO 9001 and ISO 14001—process-driven, lacking in business focus
■ Total quality management (TQM)—process-driven, with statistical analysis and teams that are customer-focused
■ National quality awards—quality-driven, plus results
■ Six Sigma—problem/solution-driven, with a customer focus
■ Total improvement management (TIM)—performance-driven/total organization-driven sales, marketing development, personnel, and production. It included organizational change.
■ Organizational excellence—performance-driven, including processes, projects, organizational change, information technology, resources, and knowledge management

> "Only 5 percent of the organizations in the West truly excel. Their secret is not what they do, but how they do it."
>
> —HJH

The following gives a point score to the effectiveness of these approaches to improve organizational performance.

■ Casual—no recognized system (0 points)
■ ISO 9001 and ISO 14001—minimum requirements (200 points)
■ Six Sigma—problem-focused (400 points)
■ TQM—"womb to tomb" quality and teams (500 points)
■ National quality awards—result-based (600 points)
■ TIM—combined quality, reliability, performance, and results (800 points)
■ Organizational excellence—five pillars (1,000 points)

> "You can win the National Quality Award with 600 points out of a maximum of 1,000 points. That's 60 percent of the way to the goal."
>
> —HJH

"We want to operate far more efficiently. We want to operate at a new level of excellence."
—**Robert J. Herbold**
Former COO, Microsoft

You might ask, "Where are we today?" A survey conducted by Dow Corning provides us the 2003 status. It included sixty-nine executives from a wide range of industries in the Americas, Europe, and Asia. This survey revealed that TQM was the most important business innovation for these organizations during the last three years. Although Six Sigma has received a lot of press during the past eight years, it didn't rate in the top three most important business innovations. The top three, in descending order, are:

- TQM
- Process engineering
- Supply chain management

The American Society for Quality recently sponsored a survey of 600 executives from manufacturing, service, government, health care, and education. The survey reported that 99 percent of the executives surveyed believe that quality contributed to the bottom line.

"The sizeable gap between usage and awareness leads me to believe that businesses and organizations either don't use quality methodologies to improve their operations or they just don't realize that the processes they have in place are attributable directly to the quality discipline."
—**Ken Case**
Former president,
American Society for Quality

Also, it indicated that 92 percent of the executives believe that an organizationwide effort to use quality techniques provides a positive return. Figure P.6 gives a breakdown of the most frequently used quality techniques.

The survey indicates that a wide gap exists between the executives' awareness of quality improvement processes and implementation. Again, the survey reveals that TQM is used over 300 percent more than Six Sigma. The quality profession suffers by constantly changing the name of its activities despite little change in content.

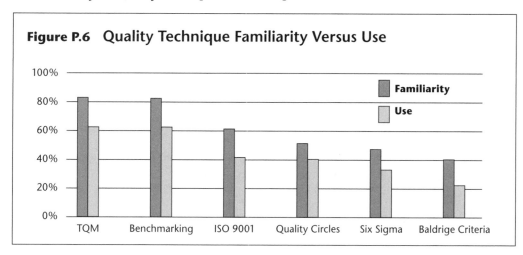

Figure P.6 Quality Technique Familiarity Versus Use

ORGANIZATIONAL EXCELLENCE SUMMARY

"Being good is good. Being the best is great!"
—HJH

When we look at the five pillars that must be managed to achieve excellence, we see common threads that run through all of them:

- Communication
- Teamwork
- Empowerment
- Respect for one another
- Honesty
- Leadership
- Quality
- Fairness
- Technology

> **"The essence of competitiveness is liberated when we make people believe that what they think and do is important—and the get out of the way while they do it."**
> **—Jack Welch**
> **Former CEO, General Electric**

All of these key factors are built into the word "management." They turn an employee into an individual who owns his or her job, thereby bringing satisfaction and dignity to the individual for a job well done.

In today's worldwide marketplace, customers don't have to settle for second best. Overnight mail brings the best to everyone's doorstep. The Internet allows people to shop internationally, making it easy for them to get the best quality, reliability, and price, no matter who offers it. Customers are concerned about the products they buy, but they're equally or more concerned about dealing with organizations that care, are quick to respond, and that will listen and react to their unique needs. This means that to succeed in the 21st century, organizations must excel in all parts of their businesses. Your organization must excel at what it does, but its stakeholders must also recognize your efforts as excellent. This will win over today's savvy customers.

CHAPTER I

KNOWLEDGE MANAGEMENT—
WHY WE NEED IT

"My people are destroyed for lack of knowledge."
—Hosea 4:6

Once upon a time, we put a man on the moon. It was July 1969. Just eight years earlier, President John F. Kennedy had pointed to the celestial outfield like Babe Ruth, and the United States summoned all of its intellectual and industrial muscle to knock one out of the park. And what a home run it was. More than 400,000 of the country's best and brightest—engineers, scientists, technicians, and managers—united in the largest scientific and industrial achievement in the history of mankind, invested their lives and $150 billion to turn the dream into reality.

> **"Knowledge is the only instrument of production that is not subject to diminishing returns."**
> **—John Maurice Clark**
> **American economist**

Then, three-and-a-half years after Neil Armstrong first kicked up moon dust, two other astronauts parked their lunar rover in a four-billion-year-old lava-flooded valley southeast of the Sea of Serenity, climbed into the Apollo 17 lunar module, secured the air hatch, and blasted back to earth. Back to the laboratories, the factories, and the new opportunities launched as a result of the investment in putting man on the moon.

Today, that investment in space is lost. The terrestrial side benefits remain, but we can no longer put a man (or woman) on the moon.

> **"The organization of the future is held together by information."**
> **—Peter Drucker**
> **Author and consultant**

We forgot how.[1]

We're living in a knowledge economy. The value of most organizations is defined by their intellectual capital rather than by their physical assets, often by more than 600 percent. The Mecca for knowledge in organizations today is located in Northern California's Silicon Valley. Today, knowledge is king. In the late 1800s, Andrew Carnegie was the wealthiest man in the world. His wealth was made up of assembly plants, steel mills, raw materials, equipment, and the finished goods of Carnegie Steel. Today, Bill Gates' wealth comes from the "heads of his programmers." Knowledge is such an important organizational asset that the Financial Accounting Standards Board is working on establishing standards for measuring intangibles.

"The big measure of competitive advantage will be how quickly you can share the right knowledge."[2]
—Donnee Ramelli
President, General Motors University

"The fundamental building material of a modern corporation is knowledge," according to Valery Kanevsky and Tom Housel in their article "The Learning-Knowledge-Value Cycle: Tracking the Velocity of Change in Knowledge to Value" (from *Knowing in Firms: Understanding, Managing and Measuring Knowledge*. Sage Publications, 1999). All organizations have it, but most of them don't know what they know, don't use what they do know, and do not reuse the knowledge that they do have. In today's knowledge economy, knowledge is power and power brings success. The difference between failure, survival, and success is the way the organization uses its knowledge.

Knowledge management isn't new. Peter Drucker was talking about the "knowledge worker" forty years ago. He points out in *Post-Capitalist Society* (HarperBusiness, 1993) that the knowledge evolution has been divided into three eras:

- *Enlightenment.* During this era knowledge was pursued for the sake of learning, to gain wisdom, and to obtain understanding. This was the period before the Industrial Revolution.
- *Industrial.* Knowledge was applied to invention of technology; it led to systematic and organized knowledge being applied to products.
- *Knowledge.* This era started around 1880 when Frederick Taylor introduced the scientific approach to organizing work.

THE VALUE OF KNOWLEDGE MANAGEMENT

Not too long ago, back in the dark ages of the 1970s, a coffee machine or water cooler was the only technology needed to facilitate in-house knowledge sharing. But as the information needs of the modern business organization grew ever more demanding, formal systems and practices were needed to encourage the transfer of knowledge between the workers, other departments, and other organizations. With the advent of the knowledge revolution, once-digital networks emerged as the central resource for communication and information retrieval, and many companies are discovering that making individual knowledge common property has the potential to significantly improve operational efficiency and decision quality.

The workers in a company with a high corporate IQ collaborate effectively so that all of the key people on a project are well informed and energized. The goal is to have the organization develop the best ideas from throughout and then act with the same unity of purpose and focus that a single, well-motivated person would bring to a situation. Digital information flow can bring out the organization's cohesiveness.

According to Peter Drucker, the recognized organizational development guru on all things called knowledge and management, we need to be careful about putting the words "knowledge" and "management" together. His advice is to talk about things called "knowledge people" instead. His reasoning is simple: Books and other systems meant to capture knowledge only capture information, which becomes knowledge only if someone knows what to do with it. "And that's between our ears, not in books," states Drucker. "Because of that, the knowledge people own the means to production again. If one of them walks out the door and takes knowledge with them, or the knowledge is somehow lost, it takes 20 to 30 times that person's salary to replace it."[3]

The importance of knowledge has expanded exponentially in the twentieth century, and successful organizations have made learning and applying it a core competency. More than sixty years ago Winston Churchill declared, "The empires of the future are empires of the mind." Today even the U.S. government has recognized the importance of knowledge; it's spending $820 million on KM products and services. By 2008 that number will rise to $1.3 billion. It looks like the events of September 11, 2001, could have been avoided if the U.S. government had just combined the information it had and turned it into knowledge.

> **"Knowledge management can be compared to the Industrial Revolution, where the work shifted from hand-centric labor to machine-centric processes leading to an explosive rise in production and new technologies. In the same way, KM drives the shift from the manual generation of information (paperwork, which is still common today) to complete electronic processing (with the ability to effectively use and apply information). This KM revolution leads to faster rates of producing knowledge assets, and new technologies for adapting knowledge faster."**
> **—Matthias Leibman**
> **Project manager, Microsoft**

Here are some additional statistics to show the value of knowledge in today's economy:

- I estimate that Buckman Laboratories, Cap Gemini Ernst & Young, and McKinsey & Co. spend about 7 percent of their respective revenues on knowledge management.
- Silicon Graphics reduced sales training costs from $3 million to $200,000 by managing its product information communication process. (Source: B. Manasca)
- The cost of information technology (IT) support in producing a car is more than the cost of the steel needed to build it.

A survey of knowledge management executives conducted by Arthur Andersen and the American Productivity and Quality Center found that:

- 79 percent agreed that managing organizational knowledge was central to the organization's strategy.
- 50 percent believed they were doing a bad job at knowledge management.
- 88 percent felt that openness and trust were critical to knowledge sharing.

More information has been produced in the last thirty years than during the previous 5,000 years. We can't go back to what we used to do, for this "old world" has changed. "The information supply available to us doubles every 5 years," writes Richard Saul Wurman, in his book *Information Anxiety* (Doubleday, 1989). He also notes that the weekday edition of

Profile 1.1 Buckman Laboratories

"Communication is human nature; knowledge sharing is human nurture."
—Alison Tucker, Buckman Laboratories

Background

Buckman Laboratories, headquartered in Memphis, Tennessee, with twenty-two offices in nineteen countries and operations in more than eighty countries, is a manufacturer of specialty chemicals.

Buckman Laboratories maintains a unique Web site (*www.knowledge-nurture.com*) for knowledge management. Its goal is to establish a resource to help people learn about it, and Buckman's audience isn't just customers and associates, but also the worldwide knowledge management community—practitioners, newcomers, academics, students, and thinkers. The Web site includes the Buckman Room—Buckman's knowledge management awards—and the useful Starter Kit, a listing of recommended materials for those interested in learning about knowledge management. The site's Library offers books, articles, journals, Web sites and other references, and the Events Board lists upcoming conferences and other events. For what's new, there's the "What's New" link.

Knowledge Management Strategy and Structure

Buckman associates use K'Netix, an interconnected system of knowledge bases, to share solutions and to ensure that their customers get fast and accurate responses to their questions or concerns. Company lore holds that CEO Bob Buckman conceived of K'Netix when he was bedridden with a bad back. Frustrated at being out of touch with his company, Buckman drafted a prototype of the perfect information-sharing network.

Although that makes a good story, according to Melissie Rumizen, assistant to the chairman for knowledge sharing at Buckman Laboratories, "our KM efforts predated that incident." The need to collect and distribute best practices across the corporation before those practices were out of date was the actual impetus for K'Netix. Seeking a better way to share knowledge, Buckman's engineers designed a network that could tap the knowledge of all employees and provide a means to share that information as quickly as possible in response to customer needs. That was the true beginning of K'Netix.

Success Story

In March 1992 Buckman Laboratories introduced K'Netix, accelerating the concept of knowledge transfer and knowledge sharing within the company. For the four previous years, the average sale of products less than five years old was 22.2 percent of total sales. For the four years following the introduction of K'Netix, the average sale of products less than five years old was 32.9 percent of total sales. Buckman attributes this acceleration in the sales growth of newer products to its improved ability to communicate and share knowledge across the organization.

"As our people became more comfortable with the very significant cultural change, collaboration increased and is now part of the fiber of the company," Rumizen explains. And all levels of Buckman Laboratories participated. "Culture change takes significant chunks of time, and it has to involve top management if it is going to be successful. You cannot delegate it."

(Source: Michelle Delio, "Keys to Collaboration," *Knowledge Management*, October 1998. Used with permission. For more information, see the profile on the Ark Group, the magazine's publisher, on page 32.)

the *New York Times* contains more information than the average person was likely to come across in a lifetime in seventeenth-century England. There's a thousand times more information available through the computer on your desk than there is in anyone's personal home library.

Horsepower has given way to brainpower. Knowledge has become more precious than equipment in our quickly changing world. In the 1950s, organizations and their employees were searching for information; today they're drowning in it. No one has time to sponge up the information relevant to their interests, let alone sort through the mountains of available information to find what's relevant. And as many of us have experienced, you can get lost for days just surfing the Internet looking at interesting information.

The gap between developed and developing countries in intellectual capital presents a major problem. There's a big gap in both ideas and objects (infrastructure). To reduce these gaps, the developing countries need to have the following:

- Functional legal systems
- Stable monetary policy
- Emphasis on education
- Low level of pay

> **"You need to operate under a start-up mentality in which information and knowledge is accessible to all employees and the environment supports and promotes constant innovations."**
> **—Joe W. Forehand**
> **Chairman, Accenture**

Today's workforce is different than it was fifty or even twenty years ago. It's changed from a labor-intensive to a knowledge-intensive base. The personal characteristics of today's knowledge workers are very different. They want to develop a career through life-long learning, experience, and socialization. They relate more to other professions, networks, associations, and peers than to the organization that employs them. They're more interested in their employability than being employed. Their focus is on career growth rather than position growth. They're more motivated by challenging tasks and recognition than by financial incentives. Knowledge workers place a greater priority on individual goals than group goals.

Interestingly, these fundamental changes in organizational intelligence have emerged during recent years, and each of these changes has implications for providing knowledge management planning and feedback to leaders. There's been a major shift in how we think about management and leadership. At the same time, people's careers have taken on new roles and responsibilities. Also, organizations have been investing considerable energy in improving their cultures through knowledge sharing and information systems.[4]

These three paradigm shifts—from manager to leader, dependency to self-responsibility in knowledge planning, and traditional hierarchy to culture-focused change—require the organization and its leaders to develop knowledge management processes, measures, and feedback systems to guide future development, innovation, and improvement efforts.

WHAT IS KNOWLEDGE?

Knowledge is information transformed into capabilities for effective action. In effect, knowledge is action. It's actionable information. And, in fact, a good part of our current knowledge isn't stored in databases, but in people's minds.

Definition: Knowledge is a mixture of experiences, practices, traditions, values, contextual information, expert insight, and sound intuition that provides an environmental framework for the evaluation and incorporation of new experiences and information.

"An investment in knowledge pays the best interest."
—Benjamin Franklin

Definition: Knowledge management is a strategy that turns an organization's intellectual assets—both recorded information and the talents of its members (tacit and explicit knowledge)—into greater productivity, new value, and increased competitiveness.

Definition: Knowledge management system (KMS) is a proactive, systematic process by which value is generated from intellectual or knowledge-based assets and disseminated to the stakeholders.

THE BASICS OF KNOWLEDGE MANAGEMENT

Knowledge management (sometimes called intellectual capital[5]) is a strategy that consists of:

- The practice of adding actionable value to information by capturing, filtering, synthesizing, summarizing, storing, retrieving, and disseminating tangible and intangible knowledge
- Developing customized profiles of knowledge for individuals so they can access the kind of information they need when they need it
- Creating an interactive learning environment where people share what they know and apply it to create new knowledge

A company's competitive advantage, which involves capitalizing on technology, coping with organizational changes, and securing employment flexibility, makes managing knowledge an imperative issue. With technology becoming a commodity, the key enterprise resources are people and information. Workers have important company-relevant (tacit) knowledge in their heads that could provide their co-workers with insight if it's made available to them in some way.

Information is a source for good decision making, but a piece of information is more effective when presented in a context, together with other pieces of related information that make the original information more meaningful and actionable. In other words, a quarterly report by region may provide significant information, but it's much more meaningful and actionable when analyzed in conjunction with the company's business plan and the industry trends for the past three years.

> **"Knowledge management can be a hard field to grasp, but organizational success depends on sharing knowledge. However, unless the transfer system is a good fit for the task, KM may be abandoned or ignored."**
> —Lt. Gen. Steven W. Boutelle CIO/G6, U.S. Army

Companies that "don't know what they know" are bound to "reinvent the wheel" many times.[6] KM can improve corporate efficiency by providing a framework of tools and techniques to expand underutilized intellectual assets. By marshaling resources to respond to opportunities and threats, the company's responsiveness can be vastly improved by bringing people together across time and geography to share ideas, allowing innovation to flourish faster and bear richer fruits.[7]

The three essential aspects of KM are discovery, organization, and sharing. We discover knowledge where it is—in the heads of people, workflow diagrams, procedure manuals, or mined from transaction output stored in databases. We organize the knowledge according to the company's preferred classifications, and we share the knowledge among those employees who are authorized to know about it and can benefit from its availability.

According to the "father" of knowledge management, Karl Erik Sveiby, companies usually take one or more of the following approaches to knowledge management to achieve their objectives:

- Capturing, storing, retrieving, and distributing tangible knowledge assets, such as copyrights, patents, and licenses
- Gathering, organizing, and disseminating intangible knowledge, such as professional experience, creative solutions, and the like
- Creating an interactive learning environment where people readily transfer and share what they know, internalize it, and apply it to create new knowledge[8]

To become a true "knowledge-creating company," an organization must create a "knowledge spiral." Knowledge must be articulated and then internalized to become part of each individual's knowledge base. The spiral starts all over again when completed, only at higher and higher levels, extending the knowledge application to other areas of the organization.[9]

Knowledge management teaches corporations, from managers to employees, how to produce and optimize skills as a collective entity. It's the leveraging of collective wisdom to increased responsiveness and innovation. Or as Kirk Klasson, vice president of strategy for Novell, simply put it, "KM is the ability to create and retain greater value from core business competencies."

"Knowledge is more compact, factual, rich, and useable than information."

—HJH

Richard Morse, in the report "Knowledge Management Systems: Using Technology to Enhance Organizational Learning" (IRMA Conference 2000) defines three different ways people create knowledge:

■ Action-based learning that involves working on problems and implementation of solutions

■ Systematic problem solving, which requires a mindset disciplined in both reductionism and holistic thinking, attention to detail, and a willingness to push beyond the obvious to assess underlying causes

■ Learning from past experiences, which reviews a company's successes and failures to define what will be of maximum benefit to the organization

"Information is data endowed with relevance and purpose. Don't overlook the part about relevance and purpose when you design and implement your information requirements."
—Peter Drucker
Author and consultant

Organizations today are challenged to progress through four wisdom filters. (See figure 1.1.)

■ *Collect data.* Data are bits and pieces that aren't put into organized patterns and analyzed.

■ *Information.* Used to draw a conclusion (e.g., reports, white papers, budgets, or bills)

■ *Knowledge.* At this level, information is screened to identify trends and best practices. Duplications and obsolete material are discarded.

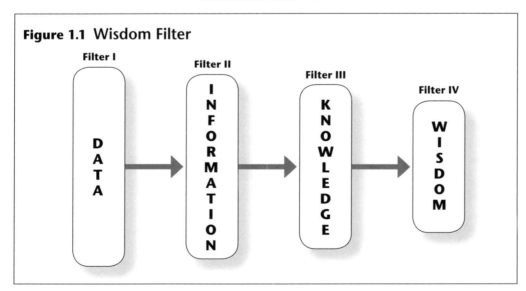

Figure 1.1 Wisdom Filter

■ *Wisdom.* At this level, knowledge is based upon experience, impact studies, and results analysis, validating its worth. It can be applied to future projects, and you'll get very predictable results.

Knowledge isn't like a tangible product. If you have five apples and you sell one, you have four left. However, knowledge is intangible; it can be sold, given away, or traded, and you still have the knowledge. In fact, the more you use knowledge, the more valuable it becomes. But knowledge is also perishable. If it's not renewed and replenished, it becomes worthless. Yes, knowledge has a shelf life. Someone with an MBA who does nothing to renew his or her knowledge finds that knowledge obsolete within four years. Knowledge is always changing and this requires every organization to either become a learning organization or an obsolete organization.

 "A vital asset of today's organization is knowledge. Organizations that are able to get the right knowledge to the right person at the right time will prosper—those that don't—won't."

—HJH

Every individual possesses at least four kinds of knowledge:
■ *Theoretical.* Formal education is an effective way of obtaining theoretical knowledge.
■ *Professional.* This type of knowledge is obtained through professional societies, conferences, and contact with thought leaders.
■ *Technical.* This type of knowledge is gained through experience. It's knowing how to get things done and how to perform well in one's chosen field, and in related fields. It's the collection of experiences and data related to an assignment, and the use of special equipment.
■ *Moral.* This type of knowledge is gained through the application of individual and organizational values and how they're applied.

Two Categories of Knowledge

There are two categories of knowledge: explicit and tacit. (See figure 1.2.) Explicit knowledge is defined as knowledge that's stored in a semi-structured content, such as documents, e-mail, voice mail, or video media. It can be articulated in formal language and readily transmitted to other people. Explicit knowledge is usually known as hard or tangible knowledge. It's conveyed from one person to another in a systematic way.

"Humans, left to their own devices, will build isolated fiefdoms, and pretty soon it is hard to pull the information together that you really need on an ongoing basis to manage the organization."
—Robert J. Herbold
Former COO, Microsoft

Tacit knowledge is knowledge that's formed around intangible factors. It's personal, content-specific knowledge that an individual gains from experience or skills that he or she develops. It often takes the form of beliefs, values, principles, and morals. It guides the individual's actions. Tacit knowledge is usually known as soft knowledge. It's only accessible through the direct corroboration and communication with the individual that has the knowledge.

Unfortunately, up to 80 percent of an organization's knowledge assets is the soft knowledge that's retained by the individual. Just ask yourself how much of what you know would be classified as hard knowledge. The big challenge that organizations face today is how to convert as much of the soft knowledge as possible into hard knowledge. Here's a recent example of how IBM handled this problem. IBM held an electronic "WorldJam," which ran for three days, for the purpose of converting soft knowledge into hard knowledge. More than 52,000 IBM employees participated by logging in from offices, hotel rooms, homes, and airports. They discussed ten key subjects, ranging from building customer relationships to how to keep the employees on the road feeling like they're part of IBM. This proved to be a very successful means of converting soft knowledge into hard knowledge, as more than 6,000 ideas and comments were posted.

Figure 1.2 Explicit Knowledge Versus Tacit Knowledge

Explicit (or Hard) Knowledge	Tacit (or Soft) Knowledge
■ Based on documented skills, competencies, experience and expertise, policies, procedures, instructions, standards, and results	■ Based on undocumented experience and expertise. Reflects ways of doing things.
■ Exists as part of an organization	■ Personal to owner
■ Often well documented	■ Rarely documented
■ Held within an organization	■ Held within individuals
■ Accessible and easy to share	■ Not easily accessible and difficult to share
■ Accessed and enabled through collection and codification	■ Accessible only through personal exchange, learning, and practice

(Source: Van der Velden, Maja. "Knowledge Facts, Knowledge Fiction: The Role of ICTs in Knowledge Management for Development." *Journal of International Development,* Vol. 14, No. 1. Manchester, UK: Institute for Development Policy and Management, 2002.)

Profile 1.2 British Petroleum—The Knowledge Spiral in Action

British Petroleum (BP) is one of the most advanced practitioners of knowledge management. One example is the reduced cost of constructing European BP retail sites by sharing knowledge among project engineers. The program started formally in 1994 and was called "virtual teamwork." Under the visionary lead of top management, the program evolved and became a formal process. The objective was to make the use and reuse of existing knowledge a routine way of doing work, and to create new knowledge to radically improve business performance.

BP's knowledge management spiral encompasses a cycle of learning processes before, during, and after any event. When the learning processes result in business lessons, peers distill them and define the best practices. Finally, both specific and generic lessons are incorporated into knowledge assets on the corporate intranet.

(Source: Strategy Associates Inc. Used with permission. For more information, contact Frank Voehl at *fvoehl@aol. com.*)

Organizations tend to focus on one of the two types of knowledge strategies—a hard knowledge or a soft knowledge strategy. The knowledge strategy you select will define how you select, train, and reward your employees.

If you select a hard knowledge strategy such as the one embodied in the knowledge management spiral, you'll want to hire individuals who are trained to reuse knowledge and are effective implementers. You'll train them in groups or through distant learning techniques and reward them for contributing to the common database.

If your organization selects a soft knowledge strategy, you'll want to hire people who can live in turmoil and like to solve problems (i.e., independent thinkers). They'll require a lot of personal one-on-one training. They'll learn by experience, not reading. You should reward these people based upon how effectively they share their knowledge with others. Organizations shouldn't select only one strategy; they need both soft and hard knowledge strategies or they'll be left behind. Using only one strategy will only get you 30 percent of the way to your knowledge goal. However, when you effectively combine them, you hit a home run and will be positioning yourself as a leader.

> **"KM is information or data management with the extra practice of capturing the tacit experience of the individual to be shared, used, and built upon by the organization, leading to increased productivity."**
> **—J. Starr**
> **"The Rules of the Game,"**
> ***Journal of Business Strategy***

> **"Managers need to develop a system that encourages people to write down what they know and get those documents into the electronic repository . . . Companies that are following the personalization (soft) approach need to reward people for sharing knowledge directly with other people."**
> **—Morten T. Hansen, Nitin Nohria, and Thomas Tierney**
> **"What's Your Strategy for Managing Knowledge?"**
> ***Harvard Business Review***

KNOWLEDGE CAPITAL

Knowledge capital can be divided into three categories:

■ *Customer capital.* Customer base, trademarks, and brands
■ *Human capital.* Know-how, creativity and innovation, knowledge, competencies, education and training, and experiences
■ *Structure capital.* Information systems, processes, databases, and operating procedures

The five points of the knowledge capital star represent the five key knowledge-asset areas. (See figure 1.3.)

"If you have an apple and I have a pear and we exchange fruit, you end up with just a pear and I end up with just an apple. But if we exchange ideas, we both end up with two ideas."

—HJH

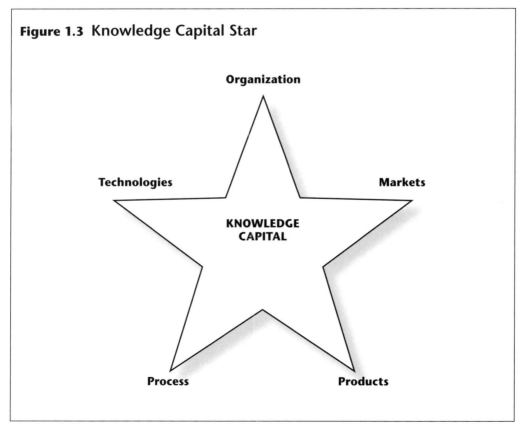

Figure 1.3 Knowledge Capital Star

Knowledge capital (i.e., intellectual capital) is the intellectual material, knowledge, information, intellectual property, and experience that can be put to use to create wealth. It's collective brainpower.

A knowledge artifact is a specific instance of a knowledge asset.

Knowledge is part of the social process. In Ikujiro Nonaka and Hirotaka Takeuchi's book, *The Knowledge Creating Company* (Oxford University Press, 1998), the authors point out that knowledge is passed on through four different modes of knowledge conversion:

- *Conversion process*. Knowledge change
- *Socialization*. From tacit knowledge to tacit knowledge
- *Externalization*. From tacit knowledge to explicit knowledge
- *Combination*. From explicit knowledge to explicit knowledge
- *Internalization*. From explicit knowledge to tacit knowledge

Accumulating tacit knowledge is one of the biggest challenges for any organization. IBM, with its 320,000 employees and 30,000 managers scattered over six continents, makes for a confusing place to work. Add to that the difficulties it's facing as its workforce becomes increasingly mobile, resulting in many managers not getting face-to-face meetings with their employees. (The internal definition of IBM is "I am By Myself.") To offset these potential problems, Samuel Palmisano, chairman and CEO of IBM, launched a new two-year program exploring the role of managers in the twenty-first century. To get this program started, IBM held what it called a "Manager Jam." This was a forty-eight-hour, real-time Web event in which managers from more than fifty different countries exchanged ideas on how to deal with the problems that remote management presented. More than 8,000 managers actively participated in this Internet discussion. John Rooney, head of the development team in Cambridge, Massachusetts, pointed out that he received some great suggestions from managers in India and the Asia-Pacific region. His comment related to the Manager Jam was, "This was a really nice global water cooler."

The result of this exchange was a long list of new and creative ideas that will help prepare IBM's managers for the challenges facing them with their mobile workforce.[10]

A survey conducted by *PM Network* magazine in 2004 asked, "What is the biggest barrier to increasing the amount of information available to decision makers?" The response was:

- 75 percent—Corporate culture, no tradition of information sharing
- 21 percent—No clear business benefit or driver
- 4 percent—Technical difficulties
- 0 percent—IT budget and staffing limitations

According to GE, "KM has to do with locating or creating useful knowledge and transmitting it throughout the company." GE stated that its biggest challenge to its KMS is making an effective knowledge portal. Today, technology enables masses of information to be delivered to more portals than ever before. However, few organizations understand how to break the obsolete, academic model of supplying the same amount of data and information to everyone. Historically, content has been the focus. Today, the user or client is critical and the context of knowledge provides the winning edge. Individuals don't need to spend long hours learning out-of-date information. Instead, what they need to know to succeed is changing so fast that it's wasteful to spend long hours in theoretical training. Using just-in-time, short interventions and simulations provides significantly better benefits at a lower cost.

More than ever, due to the growing speed of change, downsizing, reengineering, the growth in organizational scope, globalization of markets, proliferation of networked organizations, the growing intensity of knowledge, and the advancement of IT, including the Internet, organizations have found it necessary to understand and manage their unique business knowledge. Organizations that successfully capture and focus their knowledge assets (both individual and corporate) will survive and prosper.

The increasing role that knowledge plays in creating economic value and the recognition of the importance of knowledge-based systems has been in the forefront of the strategic management debate for some time now. Recent studies show that the only thing that's sustainable is what the organization knows, how it uses what it knows, and how fast it can know something new.

"Information acts like a force of gravity that pulls the decision-making power lower into the organization."
—Richard Danzig
Former U.S. secretary of the Navy

The knowledge management methodology was developed so that intellectual capital can be managed as an organizational asset. Knowledge management is designed to capture the flow of the organization's data, information, and knowledge, and deliver it to the knowledge worker that uses it on a day-to-day basis. Dow Chemical developed a six-step approach to managing intellectual assets (knowledge capital) as follows:

1. *Strategy.* They defined the role that knowledge would play in Dow Chemical.
2. *Competitive assessment.* They studied the competition to define their knowledge strategy and assets.
3. *Classified portfolio.* They determined what their core competency knowledge base was, how they used it, and where it should be used.
4. *Evaluation.* They studied their knowledge assets to define their worth and maximize their total value.
5. *Investment.* They invested additional effort to fill any identified weaknesses or voids.
6. *Assemble their knowledge portfolio.* They continuously refined and identified their knowledge assets. This was their continuous improvement phase.

KNOWLEDGE CAPITAL AND ORGANIZATIONAL CREATIVITY

Creativity is, by implication and design, the product of a single mind, while innovation is the collective process of making money from creativity. Although others may stimulate a creative act, a single human brain must always synthesize facts or impressions, even in a group or team environment. Much of the work done in research laboratories, however, requires group effort, so it makes sense to evaluate how colleagues improve or impede the creativity of individuals through the management of knowledge capital.

Anyone who has ever worked in a group has probably seen how group thought can hamper creativity. Personality problems and animosities arise, adrenaline starts flowing, and, before long, group members are arguing instead of engaging in constructive dialogue. Because when it comes to behavior, we're often not that far removed from animals, and just as almost all animals jealously guard their turf, humans zealously protect theirs. In many cases, two people with similar capabilities, training, and equipment who are working on the same problem can become obsessed by friction and rivalry.

On the other hand, science is generally considered to be a field that often transcends national, racial, religious, family background, gender, and even language boundaries. Although scientists can transcend the more obvious boundaries, their work is often circumscribed by cultural boundaries in more subtle ways. These boundaries often cause problems, but, on the other hand, they can be turned into advantages. New employees and hires have always been a source of vitality, fresh thinking, new ideas, and resiliency for research systems. European immigrant researchers certainly were a big boost to U.S. science and technology earlier in the twentieth century. During today's overall transformation of national and global systems, new entrants represent an important opportunity.

Diversity helps when marketing internationally, as well as when launching a campaign to a new population, whether at home or abroad. In situations like these, it's an asset to have someone from that population on your planning team. If we can set aside our differences, we might find just the right perspective needed to achieve our goals. Studies have shown that team members work more amicably when they bring unique backgrounds, capacities, or attitudes to the group. If we reduce turf-consciousness and promote a spirit of mutual assistance, the knowledge capital of such a group can be uncovered, thus unleashing a new wave of creativity. People's culture, age, and gender help them use knowledge and see the world in different ways. These perspectives are a key to knowledge management and creative thinking, and, in turn, the key to successful research and development. Organizations must stop seeing diversity as a problem, and start seeing it as an advantage. To succeed, we must understand and use the skills, traditions, and backgrounds of a diverse workforce. In other words, diversity gives businesses added knowledge capital, which is one of the key advantages in the "global village of tomorrow." The wider range of knowledge

---

Profile 1.3 W. R. Grace and Co. Moves Knowledge Capital Using Technology

Background

W. R. Grace's corporate research center, Washington Research Center (WRC), in Maryland, performs one-third of its research. This facility provides a vantage point to see how technology can be moved from one W. R. Grace business operation to another. Every business at W. R. Grace has access to the full range of technologies at WRC, allowing all of its business groups to have the equivalent of a critical mass of technologists. The research and development (R&D) budget is approximately $180 million, with about 1,800 people in 40 laboratory locations around the world. These researchers work in 30 fields, as diverse as electronic shielding, polymer chemistry, human health, and agriculture. In terms of functionality, activities range from discovery research, through process engineering, to designing manufacturing plants.

Knowledge Management Strategy and Structure

With such a diversity of technical skills and interests, there exists great potential for valuable interactions among those 1,800 researchers. W. R. Grace management thinks of the corporate research center as being the center of a wheel with 30 spokes, each spoke leading to the different technology functions. The businesses take what they need from the center. This allows corporate research to stay abreast of these businesses, and frequently it uncovers new business opportunities. For instance, polyvinylchloride technology cuts across W. R. Grace's packaging, health care, container, and battery-separator businesses. WRC undoubtedly knows what's going on in most of those applications, and is expected to understand where there's a potential for using a technology developed in one area for transfer to another field. Researchers can call someone at WRC who is knowledgeable about a specific area. If that person doesn't have the answer, he or she may network and eventually find someone at another Grace laboratory, or provide the name of an outside consultant or university lab.

The key hurdle is to balance exploring new ideas with completing assignments. It's a cycle. W. R. Grace had a tremendous number of new ideas in the mid-1980s, for example, in catalysts for environmental control, membranes in health care, the discovery of the gene gun, ceramics, and so forth. Today the company is tightly focused on trying to succeed with those projects by bringing them through advanced development, and the results show that it has had a good success rate. Also, W. R. Grace must determine which projects are ready for the go/no-go decision, because it can't possibly spend major dollars on each and every project.

Success Story

To increase cross-fertilization among the businesses along the circumference of its organization wheel, W. R. Grace holds a companywide technical forum every year or two and invites 100 of its top researchers to meet in an off-site location for three to four days to discuss their interests.

This structure allows them to pursue an idea that seems valuable, but doesn't directly affect any of W. R. Grace's current businesses. For example, W. R. Grace has the resources in WRC to pursue an idea that's outside of its core businesses. If the company believes the idea will succeed, it will invest in developing it. This structure is not an obvious or easy thing to deploy, because some companies will only do R&D in areas that are closely allied with their core. W. R. Grace management believes that if they continue to address only the stated needs of their core businesses, it could be at a disadvantage in the future.

> History has certainly shown that businesses that look good can quite suddenly start to mature and turn sour within a few years. To decide to focus only on core businesses can leave you in a trap if it turns out that you missed something important, such as a paradigm shift. W. R. Grace has enough variety that it can shift its knowledge capital to new non-core areas, and this has proved to be an asset in the past. But such shifts can also be a detriment, as well as a loss of focus. When management believes that they have more great ideas than they can possibly handle internally, they look for strategic alliances to move some knowledge capital out.
>
> (Source: Strategy Associates Inc. Used with permission. For more information, please contact Frank Voehl at *fvoehl@aol.com.*)

viewpoints offers a more complex and complete spectrum of talents, which can improve many aspects of product and process research.

The remarkable achievements of U.S. scientists during World War II demonstrate that success also depends on the knowledge capital inherent in group loyalty and cohesion. Because members recognized the goals as vital, and energies were focused on clear objectives, egotism was blended and often suppressed. These groups were able to achieve in a few short years what otherwise would've taken decades. Groups also become more cohesive when they have the prospect of profiting from success. Recently, some biotechnology firms have made exemplary achievements, aided by the rewards and recognition that they received from reaching their research goals. Industrial research laboratories have begun putting such concepts of group dynamics into practice. When developing a new product, they assemble a team and assign it a knowledge value, consisting of cost, production, and marketing components. These teams may be highly interdisciplinary, with team members specializing in theory, materials, and process engineering. Sometimes marketing people are included. The team spirit that often develops nourishes knowledge capital contained in imagination and creativity.

WESTERN VERSUS JAPANESE KNOWLEDGE CAPITAL

According to Rudolph J. Marcus, Ph.D., retired ethics consultant for the Office of Naval Research, the science of Western knowledge capital is based on principles of root cause analysis. "Japanese science, by contrast, is holistic—problems are viewed as entire entities," Marcus explains. "I have traced differences in Western and Japanese science to different cultural and behavioral patterns in Japan, and those in turn are reactions to Japan's population density and its distribution of natural resources." The Japanese themselves refer to their "template mentality," a preference for following an existing pattern rather than create a new one. Science in the Western manner is goal-oriented, and can be expressed alphabetically, and the holistic Japanese approach "is multi-valued and process-oriented, emphasizes the long term, executes experiments only physically, and can be expressed in ideograms." Yet Marcus believes working together "across paradigms" can be fruitful. "Some behaviors and practices on both sides help this process, while others are a hindrance. It takes a concerted effort to appreciate—and take advantage of—team members brought up in different cultures. Good communication and a positive learning attitude are required." Mutual adaptation and respect are key elements of success.

Quoting President Linda Wilson of Radcliffe College, Marcus concludes: "In this 'Age of Knowledge' . . . we will develop not just more knowledge, but also better and broader knowledge, more connections among knowledge areas, and much better assimilation and accommodation of knowledge. . . . "[11]

As we start taking cultural diversity seriously, we're embarking on a two-way learning process. Just as we need to learn about the culture of newcomers, they must learn about ours. Coaching and mentoring thus become indispensable—also a two-way street: As the newcomer learns what's expected and how to succeed, the mentor gains insight into other cultures and customs. Terminology must be understandable. If daily parlance is full of clichés and slang, your staff's communications will be barely comprehensible to foreigners. (Will all of your employees understand when you "up the ante" on or "deep-six," a project?) Remember that some people who seem to understand are just trying to save themselves the embarrassment of asking a lot of questions.

WHY THE BALANCE SHEET WON'T DO THE JOB

An organization's balance sheet doesn't reveal the real value of the organization. Abraham Briloff, the accounting guru, stated decades ago, "What it [balance sheet] reveals is interesting, but what it conceals is vital. Knowledge management is an evolving broad umbrella of topics and viewpoints, which takes a comprehensive look at the subject differences." (Source: *The Subjective Side of Strategy Making: Future Orientations and Perceptions of Executives*. Greenwood Publishing Group, 1986.) Most current knowledge management networks promote the creation of entire networks to manage knowledge. These usually don't easily interface with other critical elements of the organization. Their focus is on the technology to capture and manage knowledge.

"Knowledge has become the key economic resource and the dominant—and perhaps even the only—source of competitive advantage."
—Peter Drucker
Managing in a Time of Great Change

These implementations present significant problems because knowledge is ill-defined and it's captured haphazardly and used indiscriminately. Data, information, and knowledge usage are chaotic and lack defined success metrics. The most important thing is that data, information, and knowledge be employee-driven to improve both efficiency and effectiveness, thereby increasing organizational competitiveness.

Today, we talk about the new types of capital worth of an organization. There are three categories of capital worth:

- *Structural capital.* The speed that an organization can convert customer capital and intellectual capital into a product or service—the shorter the cycle time, the greater the value of structural capital.

- *Customer capital.* Its value is based upon how well the organization understands its customers' needs and expectations.

- *Intellectual or knowledge capital.* It's the value of the organization's people, knowledge, skills, interpersonal and customer relationships, and their understanding and use of the organization's infrastructure and its abilities. It provides a way to establish the organization's real value by measuring its hidden value.

> **"What can be measured is not always important and what is important cannot always be measured."**
> **—Albert Einstein**

Leif Edvinsson and Michael S. Malone defined educational capital in their book, *Intellectual Capital* (HarperBusiness, 1997) as, "The sum of human capital and structural capital. It involves applied experience, organizational technology, customer relationships, and professional skills that provide an organization with a competitive advantage."

The following are some key definitions that need to be understood to discuss the true worth of an organization's knowledge:

- *Book assets* are the tangible assets plus financial assets.

- *Knowledge capital* is the present value of all future knowledge earnings, discounted at an appropriate rate.

- *Knowledge earnings* are the portion of normalized earnings over and above expected earnings attributable to book assets.

> **"All of the people in this company, right down to the manufacturing line workers, are, in a large sense, knowledge workers. For that role in our strategic plan, employee retention is one of the key metrics by which we measure our success or failure."**
> **—Patrick H. Nettles**
> **Chairman and CEO, Ciena**

Calculating knowledge capital and earning values each year provides management with a better view of the actual value of the organization. (See figure 1.4.) The actual value and yearly changes in the actual value are one of the best measurements of progress. Intel Corp. has long been a leader in growing knowledge capital. For example, in 1999 it had a $1.1 billion knowledge growth. According to Baruch Lev, "For the first time [in 1997] we validated the usefulness of the [knowledge] scoreboard's measures by establishing them as superior measures of value creation." Knowledge earnings are more useful when compared with the more traditional performance measurements. High levels of knowledge earnings are more statistically associated with market returns than net earnings or cash flow are. The growth in knowledge earnings shows the strong connection with market returns.

Today, CFOs are realizing that the intangible knowledge assets are dwarfing the value of tangible book assets. Is it any wonder that leading organizations around the world are looking at knowledge management systems as key to their long-range success? One of the major problems is how to reliably quantify the value that an organization derives from knowledge

Figure 1.4 The Scope of Knowledge

Industry	Knowledge Capital ($ Millions)	Market Value ($ Millions)	Knowledge Capital/ Book Value	Market Value/ Book Value
AlliedSignal	$27,652	$33,122	5.2	6.3
American Standard	$6,786	$2,730	-9.7	-3.9
AMR/DE	$9.618	$8,071	1.4	1.2
AT&T	$89,346	$194,045	3.5	7.6
Avon Products	$8,900	$6,012	31.2	21.1
Boeing	$14,861	$38,397	1.2	3.1
Caterpillar	$17.416	$19,489	3.4	3.8
Coca-Cola	$58,481	$119,168	7.0	14.2
Dell Computer	$86,566	$106,204	37.3	45.8
DuPont	$40,912	$59,006	2.9	4.2
Eastman Kodak	$26,064	$23,868	6.5	6.0
Exxon	$64,139	$184,528	1.5	4.2
Ford Motor Co.	$72,097	$61,406	3.1	2.6
GE	$112,160	$388,607	2.9	10.0
General Motors	$51,769	$40,409	3.5	2.7
Intel	$170,487	$248,278	7.2	10.5
IBM	$113,269	$218,900	5.8	11.3
Lockheed Martin	$22,478	$12,879	3.7	2.1
Merck	$109,749	$151,502	8.6	11.8
Microsoft	$210,893	$466,216	12.7	28.0
Monsanto	$21,681	$22,648	4.3	4.5
Motorola	$12,025	$53,600	1.0	4.4
Oracle	$42,423	$64,777	11.5	17.5
Pepsico	$40,179	$44,530	6.3	7.0
Sears Roebuck	$21,090	$11,858	3.5	2.0
United Technologies	$20,951	$28,395	4.3	5.9
Wal-Mart Stores	$70,073	$211,593	3.3	10.0
Xerox	$32,850	$27,848	6.3	5.4

(Source: Mintz, S. L. "The Second Annual Knowledge Capital Scoreboard," *CFO* magazine, February 2000.)

assets like capital expenditures, patents, brands, trademarks, and research-and-development programs. Brad Goodwin, while serving as vice president of finance at Genentech, stated, "In our business, research and development—particularly development—[knowledge] is a big component of our economic investments and of our expenses. Yet the asset does not get reflected in our balance sheet."

> **"People, the knowledge they have and the new knowledge they create, are the corporate assets that impact our performance more than any other form of capital."**
> **—Gene Tyndall**
> **Founding partner, Supply Chain Executive Advisors LLC**

Although there are a number of suggested ways to measure knowledge assets, there's still a lot of debate about which system is best. It's best to just select one and get started. Don't wait for all the professors and consultants to agree on the standard. It's more important that you measure your organization's knowledge assets; you can always refine the methodology once there's a common agreement on the method. Figure 1.6 shows typical values. Paul A. Strassman, author and information systems advisor, uses the term, "knowledge value-added." He believes that the annual returns realized from knowledge capital can be defined by subtracting the cost of sending the financial capital from profits.

Knowledge Management magazine published an article called "The State of KM" in 2001 about the International Data Corp. (IDC). It reported that the knowledge deficit for the Fortune 500 companies was $12 billion in 1999 and would be over $31 billion by the end of 2003. The IDC defines knowledge deficit as a "metric that captures the inefficiency and cost associated with intellectual rework, substandard performance, and employee inability to find knowledge resources."

> **"Companies that embrace the BSC [balanced score card] are clearly taking a step toward knowledge management."**
> **—Marcos Ampuero**
> **Vice president, Cap Gemini Ernst & Young**

In one of Paul A. Strassmann's regular columns in *Knowledge Management*, he provides a good insight to what the knowledge capital per employee runs in five well-known organizations. (See figure 1.5.)

There are two primary reasons for measuring knowledge capital. The first and most important is to identify the knowledge components within the organization so that they can be managed and improved. It's the internal perspective of knowledge management. The second reason is to be able to identify the true value of the organization so that it can be communicated to the marketplace. This is the external perspective. Both are important, but focusing on the internal perspective provides

Figure 1.5 Disparity in Employee Value

Company	Employees	Employees Capital/Employee
Merck & Co.	57,300	$1,423,916
Glaxo Wellcome	54,350	$784,215
Abbot Laboratories	56,236	$702,468
Johnson & Johnson	93,100	$582,568
Warner-Lambert	41,000	$261,847

the biggest value to the organization because it provides management with the insight needed to project the organization into the future. The external perspective, on the other hand, is particularly important as it converts the organization's intangible assets into values that accountants can use. The organization's value can't truly be determined if things like culture, market access, knowledgeable workers, brand recognition, and competitive position aren't considered.

The need to measure the intangible assets of the organization led to Robert S. Kaplan and David P. Norton developing the concept of the "Balanced Scorecard," which they published in a 1992 *Harvard Business Review* article titled "The Balanced Scorecard Measures that Drive Performance." But even this didn't provide good guidelines on how to measure the knowledge assets of the organization. In 2001, A. Neely and C. Adams published "Performance Prism Perspectives" in *The Journal of Cost Management*, which reflected the need to include knowledge capital with the traditional asset measurements, but it fell short in telling how to do it.

In the late 1990s there were a number of models developed to measure knowledge assets. The most used were:

- IC Audit Model
- Skandia Navigator
- Intangible Assets Monitor
- IC-Index
- Knowledge Assets Map

IC Audit Model

Annie Brooking developed the IC Audit Model in 1996 as she tried to put a dollar value on intellectual capital.

This approach is very externally focused. It starts with an intellectual capital audit questionnaire consisting of twenty questions. It's followed by a much more detailed audit of the organization's intellectual capital looking at:

- Infrastructure assets
- Market assets
- Human-centered assets
- Intellectual property assets

Once the data's collected, three approaches are used to calculate the value of intellectual capital. They are:

- *Cost-based.* Defining the replacement cost value
- *Market-based.* Defining the market value of the asset
- *Income-based.* Defining the income-producing capability of the asset

There are a number of problems related to this approach, as Brooking has already agreed. It needs further refinement to be used effectively. (Source: "Intellectual Capital: Designing Key Performance Indicators for Organizational Knowledge Assests," *Business Process Management Journal,* October 2004.)

Skandia Navigator

Skandia Navigator was published by Leif Edvinsson and Michael S. Malone in 1997. It divided assets into financial capital and intellectual capital. Intellectual capital was further subdivided into human capital and structural capital (other intangible assets). Structural capital was again subdivided into customer capital and organizational capital. Organizational capital was subdivided into innovation capital and process capital.

As a result of these subdivisions, Skandia Navigator ended up with four categories:

- Human capital
- Customer capital
- Innovation capital
- Process capital

This approach is very similar to the Balanced Scorecard, with the addition of the fifth focus measurement—the human perspective. The five focus assets are:

- Financial
- Customer
- Process
- Innovation
- Human

In this approach, the classification of assets was externally focused. It was really designed to meet the needs of one company, Skandia. Here again there are a number of problems with the approach. The major problem is the equation that sums the intellectual capital and financial capital data because the variables aren't separable in a way that they interact with each other.

Intangible Assets Monitor

Karl Erik Sveiby published the Intangible Assets Monitor in 1997. It focused on intangible assets as opposed to intellectual capital. Sveiby divided the concept into three intangible asset categories:

- Competence of employees
- Internal structure of the organization
- External structure

Figure 1.6 Intangible Assets Monitor Measurement

	Employee Competence	Internal Structure	External Structure
Growth and Renewal			
Efficiency			
Stability			

Sveiby's approach was internally focused to provide management with a way to monitor progress and define corrective action. To accomplish this, each of the three intangible asset categories was measured in three ways:

- Growth and renewal
- Efficiency
- Stability

This allowed a 3 × 3 matrix to be developed. At each of the nine intersecting points, two to three measurements were developed. (See figure 1.6.)

This methodology provides management with the tools needed to develop and control the intangible assets of the organization, but it doesn't integrate well into the total measurement framework, which is very important in today's world.

IC-Index

The IC-Index approach was originated by Johan and Goran Roos in 1997 in an attempt to look at the total intellectual capital situation. It was designed to allow management to compare changes in IC with changes in the market. This approach divides total value into financial capital and intellectual capital. (See figure 1.7.) It then divides IC into human capital and structural capital, each of which is then divided into three subcategories.

This approach separates the knowledge assets assimilated by the employee from the structural assets of the organization. It consolidates all of the intellectual capital measurements into a small number of indices, sometimes as few as one. To accomplish this, the organization lists the most important intellectual capital measurements for each of the six intellectual capital categories. These are then ranked based upon impact. This should reduce the number of intellectual capital measurements to no more than three per intellectual capital category. Now each measurement is expressed as a dimensionless number. To help select the intellectual capital forms, indicators, and weights for each indicator, a 3 × 3 matrix is developed. Listed along the top of the matrix are the capital forms, weights, and indicators. Listed along the side of the matrix is the strategy, company (the characteristics

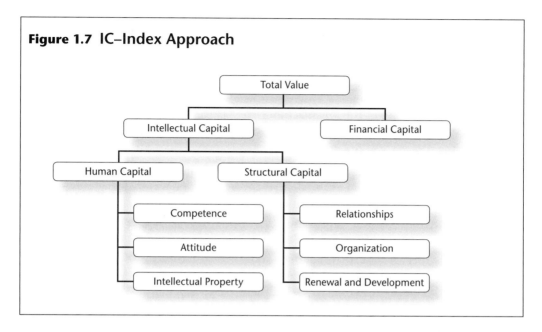

Figure 1.7 IC–Index Approach

of the company), and business (the characteristics of the business the company's in). When selecting a capital form, strategy is the driving force, which is why it's given the highest rating. When selecting weights, you need to understand the relative value of each capital form as related to the business the company is involved in. When selecting indicators, the primary consideration is the industry that the company is competing in.

Like other measurement approaches, there are good and bad features. It does provide the organization with a way to see how changes in the other performance indicators reflect in changes in the IC-Index. But using it makes it difficult to define what the key business drivers are. For more information on the IC-Index, read *Intellectual Capital: Navigating in the New Business Landscape* (New York University Press, 1998), by Goran Roos, Nicola Carlo Dragonetti, Leif Edvinsson, and Johan Roos.

THE KNOWLEDGE AUDIT

The unpredictable and often informal nature of knowledge sharing in an organization defies structured measurement. Some factors in an organization that can't be objectively measured are:

- Awareness of core competencies
- Ability to build effective teams
- Ability to leverage responsiveness and innovation based on external sensitivity to the market

There are many efforts under way that approach knowledge audits from a financial standpoint, but since they measure the result and not the causes of good knowledge management, they offer little in the way of specific insights to help enhance an organization's knowledge management practices.[12, 13]

A successful knowledge audit accomplishes several things. It provides an overview of the strengths and weaknesses of the organization's knowledge, it offers a scientific analysis of the organization's potential for competitive advantage, and it uncovers the benchmarks of successful knowledge management within an organization. Thus, the knowledge audit:

- Provides a broad view of the organization's use and practice of knowledge
- Enables a rapid and focused evaluation of an organization's knowledge management activities and attitudes
- Identifies potential areas for improvement and opportunities to leverage knowledge

Knowledge audits are most useful in organizations that have a broad awareness of their need for knowledge management, but that wish to focus on exploring more specific needs and establishing a master plan of action. In 1998 Lee Mantelman reported, "The Knowledge Management Consortium International (KMCI), created last year [1997] to develop professional and technical standards in the emerging KM field, has begun to make headway in the elusive but critical area of quantifying KM program successes. The organization's Metrics Task Force is applying two approaches to measurement, balanced-scorecard and complex adaptive system metrics."[14]

In an age when information is abundantly available to everyone, it's no longer enough to possess knowledge. You have to act on it. It's not enough to accumulate knowledge in libraries or databases. You have to apply it by making better decisions, coordinating company operations, and advancing competitive strategies. Businesses today have ample incentive for putting knowledge into action. In an aggressively competitive, knowledge-driven economy supported by lightning-fast networks and powerful software tools for capturing, transforming, and distributing knowledge, every market is up for grabs. Established leaders can falter, while start-ups come from nowhere to redefine whole industries.

In addition, our understanding of knowledge and how to manage it has grown as leaders in business and academia have built on each other's insights. A substantial body of research and practical working experience gives guidance on how to successfully manage knowledge for business advantage. Second, advancing technologies are enabling these new understandings to be put into practice more rapidly than ever before. In a very real sense, technology is the lever that translates knowledge into action. And while technology alone doesn't guarantee a successful knowledge program, the absence of technology would most likely guarantee failure.[15] In fact, of the companies surveyed, 8 percent said they've augmented customer satisfaction levels, 60 percent said they've improved employee satisfaction, and 59 percent said they've led to product or service innovations. Only 36 percent said they lowered customer costs, 30 percent said they've helped reduce the company's time to market, and 60 percent said intangible assets are reflected in their market value. So knowledge management does bring financial value.[16]

THE KNOWLEDGE ASSETS MAP

The year 1997 was an active time for trying to define how knowledge could and should be measured, but let's skip ahead four years to 2001 when Marr and Schiuma published their Knowledge Assets Map (KAM) approach. This approach was a breakthrough as it addressed both the internal and external perspective in an effective manner. It effectively built upon the work related to knowledge measurement that had been done in the 1990s. This approach divides knowledge assets as follows:

- Stakeholder resources
  - ☐ Stakeholder relationship
  - ☐ Human resources
- Structural resources
  - ☐ Physical
  - ☐ Virtual infrastructure
    - ▲ Culture
    - ▲ Routine to practice
    - ▲ Intellectual prosperity

The KAM ends up with six classifications of knowledge assets. They are:

- *Stakeholder relationship.* The primary connection between the organization and its stakeholders. It includes:
  - ☐ Brand image
  - ☐ Customer relationships
  - ☐ Distribution assessments
  - ☐ Alliance partnerships
  - ☐ Contracts
  - ☐ Licensing agreements

- *Human resource.* This is the knowledge asset that resides in the employees. It includes:
  - ☐ Loyalty
  - ☐ Competence
  - ☐ Problem-solving capabilities
  - ☐ Attitude
  - ☐ Creativity

□ Motivation
□ Commitment

- *Physical infrastructure.* This not only includes the facilities layout, but also the way information is communicated. It includes:
  □ Databases
  □ Networks
  □ Workflow

- *Culture assets.* This addresses the foundation that the organization is to build upon. It includes:
  □ Vision
  □ Values
  □ Behaviors
  □ Management philosophies
  □ Beliefs
  □ Past performance

- *Practices and routines.* This defines how work gets done in the organization. It includes:
  □ Operating instructions
  □ Management styles
  □ Informal communications
  □ Written and unwritten rules

- *Intellectual property.* This is the resulting knowledge asset from human resource activities. It consists of:
  □ Operating processes
  □ Copyrights
  □ Patents
  □ Trademarks

As you can see, there are many measurements that could be used related to each of these six categories. It's very important that management define those that are key to their specific organization and limit those they're measuring and tracking. Management must select those that relate to their specific organization's competencies and strategies. To understand what knowledge assets are important to the organization, you must first understand what core capabilities and competencies are essential to execute the organization's present strategies. Then management can identify what knowledge assets are essential to maintaining and improving them.

The Knowledge Culture

Rudyard Kipling's feeling in the quote to the right isn't much different than the way many employees feel today, but that's a culture that's a sure formula for failure.

> "They copied all that they could follow but they couldn't copy my mind, and I left 'em sweating and stealing a year and a half behind."
>
> **—Rudyard Kipling**

Knowledge sharing is first and foremost a cultural issue. When employees start to share knowledge, the organization's culture will change, becoming much more open. And so it's understandable that installing a KMS is more of a cultural challenge than a technological challenge. In fact, cultural resistance is the most significant barrier to knowledge management implementation.

To reiterate, the major problem we face in implementing a KMS is the culture of the organization. This stems from the fact that knowledge is power and as you make more and more knowledge available throughout the organization, there's a decided shift in power away from management to the staff. There's also a major problem at the staff level with sharing the individual's tacit knowledge. For years we've paid and promoted people based upon their knowledge and the way they use it. Individuals look upon their tacit knowledge as their competitive advantage.

> "The climate we create as leaders has a major impact on our ability to share knowledge across time and space."
>
> **—Robert Buckman Chairman, Buckman Laboratories**

To share it with others is viewed as taking away this advantage. This means that as you go about implementing a KMS, the culture and rewards structure has to undergo major changes. We need to reward people based upon the way they share their knowledge, as well as how they create and use the knowledge that's available.

One of the basic objectives of an effective KMS is to convert as much tacit knowledge into explicit knowledge as possible. This is because explicit knowledge is much easier, cheaper, and effective to disseminate throughout the organization. To establish a knowledge culture, we need to understand the type of people we have in the organization and their approach to obtaining knowledge. Karen Stephenson, a social scientist at Harvard's Graduate School of Design, performed a study to define the informal pathways by which knowledge is communicated. She points out that there are three types of people:

> "Evangelizing knowledge management and then not following up with tangible rewards can be extremely demoralizing. Organizations need to adjust the ways in which employees and teams are rewarded. Focusing on people's ability to lead within their sphere of influence creates buy-in across groups, develops personal skills, integrates other groups' thinking, and creates a reinforcing rewards system which are all needed for successful knowledge management initiatives."
>
> **—Robert S. Kaplan and David P. Norton**
> *The Balanced Scorecard: Translating Strategy into Action*

- *Hubs.* People who collect and share data
- *Pulse-takers.* People who build relationships that keep them informed about what's going on in the organization
- *Gatekeepers.* People who control the flow of information that's communicated to a specific part of the organization

Profile 1.4 Levi Strauss & Co. Takes Its Knowledge Management Information Systems Seriously

Background

Levi Strauss & Co. produces Levi's jeans, Dockers pants and shirts, and other apparel. The company has manufacturing and sales operations in many countries, and competes in a mature market. Levi Strauss employs creative, talented, and committed individuals and teams that have worked hard—and with great pride—since 1853 to build the company into the industry leader it is today. Levi Strauss is all about building its brands—a portfolio of the most powerful and relevant clothing brands in the world. (The Levi's trademark is registered in more than 160 countries.) To achieve this, the company is always looking for top talent—knowledgeable people who are energized, innovative, and entrepreneurial in spirit.

Knowledge Management Strategy

As a company, Levi Strauss & Co. employs knowledge management systems that help it strive for sustained and responsible commercial success. As a culture, the company operates with a common set of core values—empathy, originality, integrity, and courage—that distinguishes it and provides great pride of association. Ultimately, a strong corporate reputation is the collective perception of a company's knowledge, brands, values, and financial performance, which comes from the knowledge capital of individual employees and teams. At Levis Strauss this knowledge capital is maintained through a series of databases—including the company intranet, which is used for internal knowledge sharing and management—and an in-house knowledge network, a customized internal system that shares information about employees, services, and skills.

Structure

Each of the 2,500 employees at Levi Strauss & Co. has a workstation and access to information in the firm's mainframe computer. To empower employees, management decided to create an open-system knowledge architecture with complete systems access. Employees are trained to access various knowledge networks to obtain specific types of information. Employees even have read-only access to their personnel files. Through an interactive knowledge management system called OLIVER (On-Line Interactive Visual Employee Resource), employees can review their total compensation, pension, and employee investment plans; check disability, health care, and beneficiary details; and access other personal information. Customers and suppliers are linked to the Levi Strauss organization through LeviLink, an electronic data interchange system.

Success Story

All knowledge management information systems at Levi Strauss, from purchasing and personnel to logistics, are interconnected. The desire to support this open communication capability is a priority in all of the company's technology purchases. The company has also created a special position, Director of Quick Response, to deal with electronic services to retailers and suppliers. Expert systems are used in several areas, such as inventory management. Finally, the globalization of its business has caused the organization to install international communications networks that enable its far-flung operations to stay connected and in touch with each other.

(Source: Strategy Associates Inc. Used with permission. For more information, please contact Frank Voehl at *fvoehl@aol.com*.)

These three types of people transmit tacit (soft) knowledge throughout the organization and, in most cases, they do this more effectively than the formal organization structure does it. (Karen Stephenson's *Quantum Theory of Trust*, Financial Times Prentice-Hall, will be available in 2008.)

Different people will take the same information and reshape it to their own thinking pattern. Each person has a different background that has shaped his or her beliefs,

"At the bottom, it's all about culture. If the culture isn't well put in place, all of what we're talking about is for naught."
—Hubert Saint-Onge
"Tacit Knowledge: The Key to Strategic Alignment of Intellectual Capital,"
Knowledge Management

prejudices, hopes, needs, wants, reactions, and interpretations. It's normal for a person to embrace some parts of the information presented to them, ignoring other parts. A good KMS will help to offset these misconceptions and draw the correct conclusions from the information that's available to them.

SUMMARY

There seems to be an agreement among most experts that there's no standard definition of knowledge management; or, as one person put it, if you have ten experts in a room, you're likely to get a hundred definitions. If there's anything experts do agree on, it's that knowledge management isn't about managing people in the traditional sense of the word; nor is knowledge management really about managing knowledge. Experts prefer terms such as knowledge sharing, information systems, organizational learning, intellectual capital, and asset management. Let's use this definition by Steve Barth as a starter: "Knowledge management is the practice of harnessing and exploiting intellectual capital to gain competitive advantage and customer commitment through efficiency, innovation, and faster and more effective decision making."[17]

Knowledge management is ultimately just another way of looking at the world of business, because it's a realization that who and what you know are assets of the organization. And just like the factory and the machines in it, the people who operate them, the inventory they build, and the cash put into the bank, an organization's knowledge assets need to be managed for the greatest possible return on investment. These knowledge assets include transaction data on all of the organization's processes, projects, customers, and vendors. Add to that all of the research logs, patents, trade-

"There is an optimal balance between social networks and organizational hierarchy and there are correlations between these networks that show when an organization is ready for change."
—Karen Stephenson
Professor, Harvard Graduate School of Design

marks, marketing strategies, and business plans; competitive insights accumulated daily by each employee; and the competitive intelligence available through the Internet and other information sources that also contribute to this accumulation of knowledge. Then

Profile 1.5 Ark Group

A United Kingdom-based consulting firm with branches in the United States and around the world, Ark Group concurs with foremost knowledge-management theorist Karl-Erik Sveiby, who defines the concept as "the art of creating value from intangible assets." Knowledge management can help organizations create, discover, exploit, disseminate, and retain the expertise, understanding, and practical know-how that individuals and organizations possess. Ark's contribution to the profiles in this book are a testimonial to that fact.

The rise of information management as a core organizational function has turned the spotlight onto roles and concepts that were previously barely acknowledged, let alone valued. The power to comply with new legislative demands and meet increased customer expectations and corporate information needs today lies in the hands of librarians, taxonomy specialists, and information managers.

The skills and tools required to manage information continue to change as new technologies, media, and communication channels become embedded in our everyday lives. Document and records management, Web site content management, knowledge sharing and information-architecture design are just some of the functions that can fall under the information manager's responsibilities.

During the past eight years, Ark Group has followed the rapid evolution of information management and with a goal of sharing the latest developments, profiling the exponents of good practice, and investigating the emerging trends through its events, publications, and reports.

For some time now, organizations have harnessed knowledge management to stimulate innovation while delivering tangible improvements in operational efficiency and productivity. Knowledge management programs now lie at the heart of many organizations' efforts to secure competitive advantage and adapt to their economic environments. Ark Group believes that these trends point to the necessity of every organization developing an effective knowledge management strategy.

Through its industry-leading publications and events, Ark Group examines all aspects of knowledge management in full, including:

- How companies can facilitate innovation and foster knowledge creation
- What companies can do to get the most from the knowledge they possess
- How companies can ensure that their most valuable knowledge sources don't walk out of the door

By bringing together the latest thinking from world-renowned knowledge experts and the lessons learned by practitioner firms at the forefront of the field, Ark Group has put theory into practice and demonstrated how knowledge management relates to every type of organization.

For more information, contact Ark Group at *www.ark-group.com*.

(Source: Original material developed by Ark Group. Used with permission.)

add the knowledge contained in every e-mail, word document, spreadsheet, and fax that zaps its way through your electronic infrastructure.

> **"The general causes of troubles arise from wrong knowledge and incorrect operations."**
> **—Hitoshi Kume**
> *Statistical Methods for Quality Improvement*

Yet these things still account for only a fraction of the real value of your knowledge assets. Much of the real value of intellectual capital is in the heads and hearts of your knowledge workers—their skills, experience, hard-won insight and intuition, and the trust they've invested and earned in relationships both inside and outside of the organization. This knowledge is even harder to evaluate, share, and leverage.

Tens of millions of dollars can be spent on tools to enable collaboration, data warehousing, data mining, document management, and Internet searches, but if only executive management gets the big salary and a bonus, very few workers are going to willingly share what they learn. To understand something about knowledge management, you first have to understand knowledge, which isn't the same thing as information, just as information isn't the same as data. But as many experts are fond of pointing out: It's silly to pretend knowledge management doesn't involve the manipulation of all three. You often see a hierarchy that looks like this: Data becomes information when it's organized; information becomes knowledge when it's placed in actionable context. And none of the amazing technology that makes knowledge sharing possible works without addressing the social system of corporate culture.

REFERENCES

1. Petch, Geoff. "The Cost of Lost Knowledge," *Knowledge Management,* October 1998.
2. Bartlett, Jeffrey. "Learning to Change," *Knowledge Management*, August 2001.
3. Drucker, Peter. *The Age of Discontinuity* (Harper & Row, 1969). This isn't one of Drucker's best-known works, but it's where he first wrote about knowledge workers and a future knowledge society.
4. O'Dell, Carla and C. Jackson Grayson. *If We Only Knew What We Know: The Transfer of Internal Knowledge and Best Practice* (The Free Press, 1998). This work is based upon an examination of the best practices of more than seventy leading companies.
5. Stewart, Thomas A. *Intellectual Capital: The New Wealth of Organizations* (New York: Currency Doubleday, 1997).
6. Barth, Steve. "Heeding the Sage of the Knowledge Age," *CRM*, May 2000.
7. Allee, Verna. *The Knowledge Evolution: Expanding Organizational Intelligence* (Newton, MA: Butterworth-Heinemann, 1997). This book is one of the first full treatments of knowledge management and the broad implications of the field.
8. Sveiby, Karl-Erik. *The New Organizational Wealth: Managing & Measuring Knowledge-Based Assets* (San Francisco: Berrett-Koehler Publishers, 1997). One of the few authors with hands-on experience of running a business, Sveiby was one of the first to emphasize the importance of the physical office environment and the impact of information overload.

9. Nonaka, Ikujiro and Hirotaka Takeuchi. *The Knowledge-Creating Company: How Japanese Companies Create the Dynamics of Innovation* (New York: Oxford University Press, 1995).

10. *American Way*, American Airlines. November 1, 2002.

11. Marcus, Rudolph. "Harvesting the Advantages of Cultural Diversity," *R&D Innovator*, November 1992.

12. Kjoulopoulos, Thomas M., Richard Spinello, and Wayne Toms. *Corporate Instinct: Building a Knowing Enterprise for the 21st Century* (New York: Van Nostrand Reinhold, 1997). In this book, the means by which to measure the basic intelligence and capacity of an organization to leverage knowledge is called "Corporate IQ."

13. Higgins, James M. *Innovate or Evaporate: Test & Innovate Your Organization's IQ: Its Innovation Quotient* (Winter Park, FL: New Management Publishing Co., 1995). In this book, the basic intelligence and capacity of an organization to leverage knowledge is called "Intelligence Quotient."

14. Mantelman, Lee. "Task Force Tackles Measurement," *Knowledge Management*, October 1998.

15. Applegate, Lynda M., F. Warren McFarlan, and James L. McKenney. *Corporate Information Systems Management: Text and Cases* (fifth edition) (New York: Irwin/McGraw-Hill, 1999). The fifth edition of this classic text for IT managers includes a strong focus on technology strategy for senior executives.

16. Based upon a 1998 knowledge management study conducted by Arthur Andersen on behalf of its clients. Arthur Andersen researched the leadership qualities of the future and one of the top-ten core skills is self-awareness. Generating innovative ideas faster than the competition will require agile brains working intelligently as a collective force of energy. Thus, highly reflective CEOs and team leaders will be stronger knowledge creation leaders.

17. Barth, Steve. "Heeding the Sage of the Knowledge Age," *CRM*, May 2000.

CHAPTER II

THE KNOWLEDGE MANAGEMENT SYSTEM

THE KNOWLEDGE MANAGEMENT LIFE CYCLE

Installing a knowledge management system (KMS) isn't easy; it requires the total organization to undergo a transformation that includes its culture, structure, and management style, but the results are well worth the effort. However, before we talk about the KMS, let's look at the knowledge management life cycle. In its simplest form, it's made up of six phases. (See figure 2.1.)

> "It used to take years to deliver a turnaround. It's now a question of days and weeks and months, so knowledge sharing has become critical to being effective and efficient."
> —Anne M. Mulcahy
> Chairman and CEO, Xerox Corp.

Phase I—Creating Knowledge

Creating information and knowledge can and does occur at any place, which includes all parts of the organization and the outside world. Knowledge is the result of an individual's

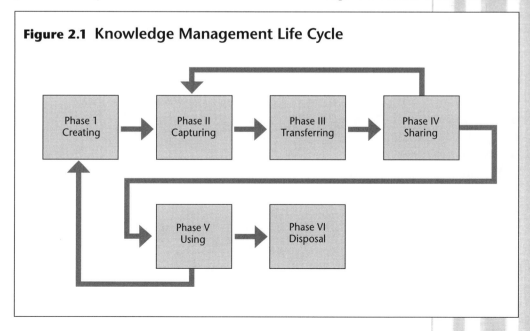

Figure 2.1 Knowledge Management Life Cycle

creative thoughts and actions. All individuals can be encouraged to contribute to, and increase the availability of, information and knowledge.

> **"Capabilities are underpinned by knowledge. Therefore, organizations that seek to improve their capabilities need to identify and manage their knowledge assets."**
> **—Bernard Marr, Gianni Schiuma, and Andy Neely**
> **"Intellectual Capital—Defining Key Performance Indicators for Organizational Knowledge Assets"**
> ***Business Process Management Journal***

Phase II—Capturing Knowledge

To effectively capture knowledge, its value must first be identified. This includes both hard (explicit) and soft (tacit) knowledge. Achieving this goal was so crucial to IBM that it hired outside journalists to interview its own people, to capture how they made the decisions that led to successful outcomes.

Phase III—Transferring Knowledge

To transfer knowledge, captured information must be transformed into a standard format that can be accessed and addressed by the stakeholders. This phase includes organizing knowledge by subject matter or other category, to meet the needs of the users. Furthermore, processes must be put in place to prompt the system to update knowledge.

> **"Consequently, human factors, the main driver of knowledge management success, has come second to information technology in many of the real world practices."**
> **—C. Carter and H. Scarbrough**
> **"Toward a Second Generation of KM? The People Management Challenge"**
> ***Education & Training***

Phase IV—Sharing Knowledge

Sharing knowledge refers to distributing knowledge that's already been collected. This phase often takes place using a portal but also includes social aspects of sharing knowledge, such as phone and other personal communications, face-to-face meetings, and virtual chat rooms.

The knowledge-sharing phase is the most important phase of the knowledge management life cycle. People throughout the organization must be willing to share their knowledge and experiences for the KMS to succeed. However, there are many reasons why people don't want to share their knowledge. These include:

- "I'm valuable because I know something that no one else knows."
- "I'm not rewarded for sharing."
- "Sharing is a waste of time."
- "People should be able to think it out themselves."
- "I'm too busy to share information."
- "The timing isn't right."
- "It takes too long to find out where to go to get the information."

The truth of the matter is that many people fear they'll lose their personal competitive advantage if they share their knowledge.

"Share your knowledge.
It's one way to achieve immortality."
—HJH

Phase V—Using Knowledge

This is where the KMS pays off. Sharing past experiences and other knowledge helps prevent errors and creates new and better responses to the organization's opportunities. Also during this phase, new knowledge is created and fed back to phase I.

Phase VI—Disposal of Knowledge

As new ideas are created, better ways to work are developed and best practices change. It's important to purge the knowledge system of obsolete information and past best practices. This must be done with care, of course, because historical data are very valuable should new approaches prove to be unsound.

When Christopher Columbus arrived in Jamaica out of supplies, the tribal chief wouldn't allow his crew to pick up anything they needed. Being a navigator, Columbus knew that a complete eclipse of the moon was going to occur. Taking advantage of this knowledge, he told the chief that God would punish the tribe if they didn't give him the required supplies. He said that God would turn off the moon's light. When the eclipse occurred right on schedule, the tribe was horror-stricken and gave him all the supplies he asked for.[1]

An Englishman trying to take advantage of the same natural event in the 1900s told a Sudanese chief that if he didn't follow his orders, he would turn off the moon's light. The chief replied, "If you're referring to the lunar eclipse, it should happen the day after tomorrow." The bottom line is that your knowledge base needs to be updated on a regular basis to be a competitive advantage, even for an explorer, as this story clearly demonstrates.[2]

> **"Intellectual workers enrich human knowledge both as creators and as researchers; they apply it as practitioners, they spread it as teachers, and they share it with others as experts or advisors. They produce judgments, reasoning, theories, findings, conclusions, advice, arguments for and against, and so on."**
> **—R. Cuvillier**
> **"Intellectual Workers and Their Work in Social Theory and Practice"**
> ***International Labour Review***

> **"Success depends on a clear strategic logic for knowledge sharing and it really depends on culture, that an organization should share and use knowledge automatically, and overcome the hoarding and trust issues."**
>
> **—J. Starr**
> **"The Rules of the Game,"**
> ***Journal of Business Strategy***

Profile 2.1 Rewriting the Unwritten Rules at Rutgers University

Background

Rutgers University (State University of New Jersey) has 50,000 students and 5,000 researchers and faculty scattered among a number of campuses around the state.

Knowledge Management Strategy and Structure

Rutgers University is spending $100 million to lay high-speed fiber optic lines to link all of its classrooms, offices, laboratories, and dormitories. Professor Wise Young, director of the Neuroscience Center at Rutgers, is establishing a new collaborative university research facility—a center designed for knowledge sharing among Rutgers' laboratories in conjunction with more than 60 other research laboratories around the world. Every part of the laboratory is specialized for efficient communication and sharing of visual, audio, and numerical data, as well as real-time personal interactions. Many laboratory instruments are designed to allow user-groups to access them remotely.

The center will use primarily two types of software for remote collaboration: Timbuktu Remote and CU-SeeMe. Timbuktu allows people to work on computers as if they were physically sitting in the central lab. CU-SeeMe allows individuals at up to eight locations to video-conference with each other. "Both programs are cheap and powerful, and are flexible enough to accommodate a variety of Internet bandwidths," Young explains.

Success Story

State-of-the-art microscopes and facilities, costing millions of dollars, are beyond the means of individual scientists, most universities, and many private researchers. Using facilities around the clock, to make the most of the investment, is the wave of the future even for Rutgers' collaborative laboratory.

Plans for future purchases include a microscope (the Zeiss 510) with state-of-the-art video cameras to collect and store slide images in the form of movies. "Instead of throwing a slide on the wall to show an image, a lecturer can access a server over the Internet to play a high-resolution video movie," says Young. And in Osaka, Japan, there is a high-voltage electron microscope that can be used over the Internet. Such cutting-edge technological advancements require people to work together in new ways.

"Because our academic and business organizations are predicated on competition, there is a natural reluctance to share and to give," Young says. "But it can and does happen. As a member of a team, you begin to realize that the whole is greater than the sum of the parts. You realize that being part of the team allows you to do things that you would never otherwise think of."

(Source: Michelle Delio, "Keys to Collaboration," *Knowledge Management* magazine, October 1998. Used with permission. For more information, see the profile on the Ark Group, the magazine's publisher, in chapter I.)

DEVELOPING THE KNOWLEDGE MANAGEMENT SYSTEM

The processes to develop the KMS include:

- Using, enacting, executing, and exploiting
- Communicating, deploying, disseminating, and sharing
- Compiling, formalizing, standardizing, and explicating
- Appraising, evaluating, validating, and verifying
- Acquiring, capturing, creating, and discovering
- Evolving, improving, maintaining, and refreshing
- Storing, securing, conserving, and retaining[3]

> "Organizational capabilities are based on knowledge. Thus, knowledge is a resource that forms the foundation of the company's capabilities. Capabilities combine to become competencies and these are core competencies when they represent a domain in which the organization excels."
> —C. K. Prahalad and G. Hamel "The Core Competence of the Corporation," *Harvard Business Review*

There's an overwhelming amount of knowledge within most organizations. To manage all of a company's knowledge would be too time consuming and costly. When adding a KMS, most organizations define their most important knowledge management categories then concentrate on those. Often the KMS is designed to bring together the knowledge related to an organization's core capabilities and competencies.

The KMS depends upon people using its technology to effectively share knowledge and experiences. However, it's important to remember that people are the source of all knowledge. The IT system manages information to create knowledge, yet technology is merely the enabler for accessing, analyzing, updating, and disseminating knowledge.

The following is a list of KMS-enabling modules, as Microsoft defines them:

- Communities, teams, and experts
- Portals and search
- Content management (publish and metadata)
- Real-time collaboration
- Data analysis (data warehousing and business intelligence)

> "There is no finish line."
> —Nike Inc. motto

A Workplace Neural Network

Five major components are required for a workplace neural network (WNN). In a consumer-driven marketplace it's essential that accurate information is available when required, to satisfy the needs of customers, so a WNN system must be designed to meet an organization's unique needs. Successful organizations offer multiple incentives for both sharing and seeking knowledge.

At a minimum, a WNN must provide accurate information. It should also offer the opportunity for individuals to acquire additional coaching or help from subject matter experts. In addition, this information, coaching, and support must be captured and made available in real time, or as close as possible. Further enhancements should include the ability to track and test the validity of knowledge, the frequency of its use, and its relevance. Knowledge that's no longer relevant or useful should be purged.

The five major components of a knowledge management system are:

- *Content.* Includes subject matter experts, governing body, data, information, knowledge in any form from any source, and vetting process
- *Availability.* Includes formatting, media, design, authoring, style, and usability measures
- *Collaboration management.* Includes interaction, storage, gap analysis, delivery tracking, and measurement
- *Generators.* Includes platforms, systems, and applications
- *Delivery style.* Includes locations, methods, pipes, hardware, and software

Content

Large consulting firms like Ernst & Young were early adopters of KMS. Such companies hope to capture the practical knowledge and experience of senior staff to benefit less experienced consultants. Because knowledge is useless unless it's relevant to the user's needs, one of the biggest challenges is defining exactly what knowledge needed to be captured. It's difficult to predict what knowledge will be relevant and worth capturing unless an organization anticipates specific applications. Without taking time to accurately define how the knowledge will be applied, the KMS can quickly become an all-encompassing yet useless database.

The content of any organization's KMS should consist primarily of the data, information, and knowledge that provide the organization with its competitive advantage. The KMS should be regularly reviewed by an organization's subject matter experts, and measured against the requirements of appropriate governing bodies. All WNN content should be assessed for currency, relevance and other key details.

Everyone in the organization should be able to submit information for review and assessment. This doesn't mean that everyone should be able to access any information he or she wants. However, it does mean that anyone with a legitimate business need should have access to essential information as needed. It's important to develop appropriate security for the KMS. Biometrics may provide more realistic security protection than most network security systems today.

A KMS should also include content from outside the organization, as appropriate. This often includes packaged training courses, white papers, and other pertinent data and information. The desire to enhance the organization's wisdom makes this additional content meaningful; how it's used in the organization may provide a competitive edge.

Availability

Once an organization has defined the knowledge it needs to collect and disseminate, it should then decide who will use the KMS and how they'll access the information—often a more difficult task than one would assume. It's usually quite easy to define who KMS users will be, but more challenging to determine just how they'll use the system. In other words, "who" defines where and how you'll communicate with stakeholders, and "how" determines the database makeup and the content within each knowledge silo. These classifications affect how knowledge within the KMS is organized, searched for, and located. The classification taxonomy or schema is the most important part of the technology application.

Meeting this major challenge requires agreement about how KMS output will be presented, and about what information the system needs to contain. The KMS implementation will result in a new culture of information management throughout the organization. This cultural change will be smoother if the company reminds stakeholders that the goal is to create a knowledge-driven information network to solve organizational problems effectively and to gain a significant competitive advantage.

Availability refers to how the knowledge is made available. This may be via intranet, extranet, Internet, or other network. To be useful, the information network must be easily available to all employees who need access to knowledge in their daily work. An effective KMS includes easy-to-use content authoring and publishing solutions. It should accept all needed formats such as HTML, Flash, PowerPoint, and streaming video. Custom content should be developed to the Aviation Industry CBT Committee (AICC), Sharable Content Object Reference Model (SCORM), or other standard, so that the system "plays nicely" with others. In addition, easy-to-control templates should provide a consistent look and feel. A robust KMS includes interactive simulations, case studies or games, online skills practice, and testing and feedback systems. Content publishing must be simple and require no programming or other special skills.

An effective KMS is a significant investment, but it will more than pay for itself as it increases an organization's competitive advantage. The system must be able to track who's participated and what they've learned or taught, give feedback on individual job performance, and calculate return on investment. The KMS must be able to provide reports and tools that define a comprehensive and dynamic tracking system, one that evaluates how the KMS is being used and the value it delivers.

Collaboration Management

A KMS requires collaboration, interaction, online learning, and coaching on an as-needed basis. This aspect of system management may include small group meetings, virtual training, working sessions, and knowledge growing sessions, to name a few. Collaboration management must be usable, manageable, and scalable. The KMS provides an infrastructure for managing, tracking, sharing, archiving, and delivering strategic business knowledge across an organization. Knowledge must appropriately link to organization-specific resources, including human resource and enterprise resource planning systems. Both individual knowledge gaps and organizational resource gaps need to be identified.

In addition to cataloging the organization's data, information, and knowledge, a robust KMS tracks all access, how well business needs are being met, and return on investment. The KMS also enables skill searches, employee assessments, applicant screening, and more.

Generators

A robust KMS will be accessible from any appropriate platform and operating system. It will incorporate multiple forms of content, including PowerPoint, multimedia, Web-based material, streaming video, shared whiteboard, and other shared software. Furthermore, it will provide voice-over Internet protocols, audio conferencing, live application demonstrations, polling, real-time feedback and response, Web touring, text chat, and more. In addition, AICC and SCORM standards should be accommodated. The knowledge system will also accept proprietary formats, as required.

Delivery Style

A KMS easily and conveniently delivers appropriate network access. In addition, it must easily capture data, information, and knowledge from face-to-face encounters. The knowledge system must be configured to work under actual network circumstances, from very narrow bandwidth to very high-speed lines. An organization must have the ability to communicate to its audience when and how it's most appropriate, to support and continue rich interaction and sharing among employees.

Tacit (Soft) Knowledge Flow

A most important yet difficult part of any KMS is improving the way tacit (soft) knowledge flows through the organization to its target audience. Although one of the key objectives of every KMS is to transform soft knowledge into hard (explicit) knowledge, it's rare for a KMS to transform more than 20 percent of soft knowledge into hard knowledge. One problem with soft knowledge is that it's often misinterpreted.

Verbal communication is the most common way that soft knowledge is transferred from person to person. But frequently, the target audience either misunderstands or misses the main point of what's being communicated. To develop an effective, soft KMS, the verbal communication process and its risks must first be understood. A major challenge for KMS designers is error-proofing the communication process. (See figure 2.2.)

To more fully understand this process and its complexity, consider the nineteen steps of a simple communication cycle:

1. Verbal communication process starts with a person having a thought, a thought that's greatly influenced by that individual's culture, education, past experience, feelings, and environment at the moment the thought was generated.
2. This thought now has to be transformed into words.
3. The individual finds another person that he or she wants to share the thought with, to make a verbal connection. In figure 2.2, the communication is made by way of a

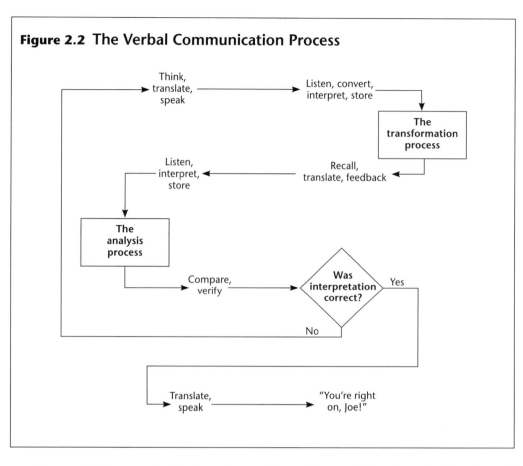

Figure 2.2 The Verbal Communication Process

phone call. Communicating by phone reduces the possibility that the thought will be transmitted correctly, because the person receiving the communication can't see the sender's facial expression or body language. Communications by phone are never as good as face-to-face communications, but the phone is usually better than e-mail, unless the communication needs to be documented.

4. The communicator expresses the thought in a language that he or she believes the targeted individual (receiver) will understand.

5. Sound waves travel through the communication medium, which downgrades the sound by reducing volume and/or distorting the sound quality.

6. The "receiver" receives the sound waves and converts them into electrical pulses that travel through the nervous system to the brain where they're stored.

7. The stored electronic pulses are then interpreted by the receiver based upon his or her culture, education, past experience, and feelings as well as the individual's immediate environment at the moment these sound waves are received. The individual's interpre-

tation, in the form of thoughts, is then stored in the brain. (Note: the environments of the sender and receiver can be, and often are, very different. The sender's environment may allow him or her to be very focused, but the receiver may be distracted by the TV, noisy children, or the needs of someone who can't be kept waiting.)

8. In a good verbal communication system, the receiver then communicates back to the sender his or her understanding of the communication. To do this, the receiver needs to transform the stored thought into words that she or he communicates in a language that the sender will understand.

9. Sound waves travel back through the communication medium, which again degrades the sound by reducing volume and/or distorting the sound quality.

10. The original sender receives the sound waves and converts them into electronic pulses that travel through the nervous system to the brain where they're stored.

11. These stored electronic pulses are then interpreted by the original sender based upon his or her culture, education, past experience, feelings, and environment, and are then stored in the brain in the form of a thought.

12. The sender then compares the original thought to the one just received from the receiver, to determine if the receiver interpreted the original thought correctly.

13. If the thoughts were interpreted incorrectly, the processes revert back to step one and start over.

14. If the thoughts were interpreted correctly, the sender must translate the concluding thought into words.

15. The original sender expresses the thought in a language that he or she believes that the target individual will understand.

16. Sound again travels through the communication medium, which degrades the sound by reducing volume and/or distorting the sound quality.

17. The receiver receives the sound waves and converts them into electronic pulses that travel through the nervous system to the brain where they're stored.

18. The stored electronic pulses are then interpreted by the receiver based upon his or her culture, education, past experience, feeling, and environment, and then stored in the brain.

19. The receiver takes appropriate action based upon his or her interpretation of the feedback.

One thing that makes effective verbal communication so difficult is that it's more than just the words being transmitted to individuals or groups of individuals; it also includes tone of voice, inflection, and delivery. To add to the complexity of verbal communication, much of it occurs face-to-face. In that situation additional complexity is added, as nonverbal communication often tells more about the content of the communication than the words themselves. Nonverbal communication is a completely separate communication system, one that everyone needs to understand and use. Every KMS, then, must include training in how to communicate, to effectively transmit knowledge from one source to another, including nonverbal communication techniques. With the technologies available today, including conference calling, cell phones, and e-mail, people often assume that communication is getting better. Yet the truth of the matter is, the quality of most communication is actually much poorer than when people typically spoke face-to-face. Today we have quantity and endless options in our communications, but also decreased quality and understanding.

Explicit (Hard) Knowledge Flow

"We are drowning in information but starved for knowledge."
—John Naisbitt
Megatrends: Ten New Directions Forming Our Lives

The KMS (figure 2.3) is a filtering and analysis system. The raw materials that go into this system are data from the many measurement points within and outside the organization. These materials are accumulated and stored in a data warehouse. The data in the data warehouse are then analyzed and distilled into information—reports, statements, bills, and the like—that is then typically stored in an information warehouse. The information warehouse also receives information from many other sources, like minutes of meetings, external reports, books, literature reviews, conferences, papers, and from tacit knowledge that's converted into explicit information. Never underestimate the excellent information that can be collected from external sources (outside information).

As figure 2.3 indicates, information in the information warehouse is far less than data contained in the data warehouse, even with the addition of outside information, because

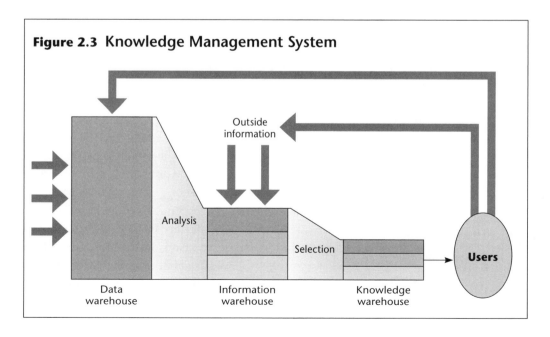

Figure 2.3 Knowledge Management System

data included here is distilled data. The information warehouse is then organized into information silos that separate information into specific knowledge subjects. This is usually done electronically using intelligent agents and/or network mining.

The five Cs that differentiate data from information are condensation, calculation, contextualization, correction, and categorization.

- *Condensation.* Data is summarized in a more concise form.
- *Calculation.* Data is analyzed, similar to condensation of data.
- *Contextualization.* The reason for collecting the data is known.
- *Correction.* Errors have been removed.
- *Categorization.* The unit of analysis is known.

> "Books are not lumps of lifeless paper but minds alive on the shelves. From each of them goes out its own voice . . . and just as the touch of a button on your stereo set will fill the room with music, so by taking down one of these volumes and opening it, one can call into range the voice of a man far distant in time and space, and hear him speaking to us, mind to mind, heart to heart."
> —**Gilbert Highet**
> **Literary critic**

Information within each silo is then reviewed to determine if it represents new or added-value information that should be added to the knowledge warehouse. This review is often undertaken by subject matter experts. These same experts will maintain the knowledge warehouse, updating it with new information and removing obsolete information. (Raw data are never stored in the knowledge warehouse.) For example, best practices for an individual knowledge area are continuously changing, so previous best practices need to be removed and replaced by current best practices.

Access to output from the knowledge warehouse is usually via a restricted portal set up for users of a given knowledge category. The warehouse contains structured electronic repositories of knowledge—document-based knowledge and informative, discussion-type knowledge—or repositories of "who knows what." The knowledge warehouse can be considered the "bank" of an organization's intellectual capital, given its constant deposits and withdrawals. (See figure 2.4.)

Explicit knowledge may not communicate the true meaning of an experience. Without rich cultural and conversational content, documents lose much of their real value. The

> "The need to acquire knowledge from outside—which you may call benchmarking—and the need to acquire knowledge from inside—the sharing of best practices—and then make it portable is a universal concept that will remain long after modern metaphor has changed."
> —**Steve Kerr**
> **Chief learning officer,**
> **Goldman Sachs**

inflection in a voice, the twinkle in an eye, an expression on someone's face, and gestures and body movements are all part of a total communication. Face-to-face communication is always more effective than phone calls, e-mails, or reports. For this reason, the knowledge community increasingly uses video conferencing. The problem with video conferencing is that it often produces tacit (soft) knowledge rather than explicit (hard) knowledge. Visual Communicator Studio, by Serious Magic Inc. (*www.seriousmagic.com*), addresses this problem. This simple tool captures and shares multimedia

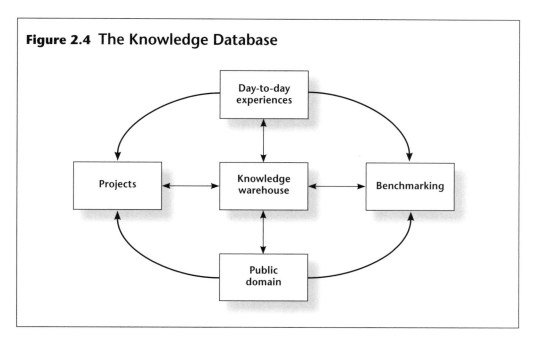

Figure 2.4 The Knowledge Database

presentations in a way that enriches personal knowledge. To use this tool an organization needs only one or two video cameras, a microphone, and a laptop to document the meeting. Visual Communicator Studio combines PowerPoint, whiteboard, and screenshot images. If a PowerPoint presentation is selected, for example, recipients can hear all conversation related to the presentation and see any notes recorded by participants.

KMS Technology Framework

Information and knowledge can enter the KMS from many different sources after it's filtered. Some of them are:

- Books
- Classes
- Conferences
- Communities of practice
- Document management
- Groupware (informal capture, document exchange, and collaboration)
- Independent thought (mind maps and visual thinking tools)
- Data warehouse (data mining, data cleansing, and validations)
- Intranets
- Water coolers
- Problem-solving sections
- Project management

- Telephones
- Web conferencing expertise pointers (dialogue conversation)
- Whiteboards
- Workflow

A typical KMS technical strategy can be divided into five elements: information sources; information mapping; a knowledge flows framework; intelligent agents and network mining; and knowledge exchanges. These elements can be subdivided into further knowledge elements, as follows:

- Information sources
  - ☐ Books
  - ☐ Bulletin boards
  - ☐ Distributed search and retrieval
  - ☐ Level controls
  - ☐ Multimedia content
  - ☐ Operational data
  - ☐ Project management tools
  - ☐ Reports
  - ☐ Transaction reports

- Information mapping
  - ☐ Check in/out
  - ☐ Communities of practice
  - ☐ Distribution channels
  - ☐ External networks
  - ☐ Informal discussions
  - ☐ Metadata
  - ☐ Models
  - ☐ Organizational data
  - ☐ Repository

- Knowledge flows framework
  - ☐ Collaborative tools
  - ☐ Databases
  - ☐ Discussions
  - ☐ File systems
  - ☐ Legacy systems
  - ☐ Messaging
  - ☐ Portals

☐ Web sites and pointers
☐ Workflow

■ Intelligent agents and network mining
   ☐ Data and text mining
   ☐ Information classification
   ☐ Information clustering and lumping
   ☐ Information indexing
   ☐ Push/pull agents
   ☐ Web-farming technologies

■ Knowledge exchanges
   ☐ Collaborative annotation
   ☐ Conferences
   ☐ Context addition
   ☐ Legacy integration
   ☐ Messaging integration
   ☐ Platform independence
   ☐ Viewing tools

> **"Having the right technology to support the right vision is essential. But the drawback of knowledge management initially was actually too much reliance on technology. Somehow people thought that technology alone was going to solve this problem."**
> **—Jim Murphy**
> **Research director,**
> **AMR Research**

The KMS architecture is made up of seven layers:
■ Repositories (knowledge warehouse)
■ Middleware and legacy integration
■ Transportation (e-mail, Web, audio, and video)
■ Application (collaborative work tools, electronic conferencing)
■ Collaborative intelligence (search, logging, and indexing tools)
■ Access/security (firewall and recognition systems)
■ Browser interface

It's important to point out that a KMS isn't an IT system. IT enablers do play an important part in the total KMS, but it's a small part—the easiest part to put in place. The IT solutions are well known and widely used. Most organizations have little problem with this part of the KMS. The real challenge—and cost—is the required culture change.

World-Class KMS

The organizations we rate as having a world-class KMS are:
■ Cap Gemini Ernst & Young
■ British Petroleum
■ The World Bank

- Intel
- The American Quality and Productivity Center
- Lucent Technologies
- 3M
- Xerox
- Monsanto
- Nokia

We believe that government is leading the way when it comes to KM, with worldwide policing and other knowledge-capturing systems. However, the health care industry lags far behind. There's a lot that KM systems could do to improve the quality of health care and health care delivery.

WHY HAVE A KNOWLEDGE MANAGEMENT SYSTEM?

It's important to understand that information systems and knowledge acquisition are two very different processes.

Knowledge acquisition is the process of developing and creating insight, skills, and relationships, and is the primary job function of a knowledge engineer. According to Brian R. Gaines and Mildred L. G. Shaw in their article "Eliciting Knowledge and Transferring It Effectively to a Knowledge-Based System" (*IEEE TKDE*, February 1993), knowledge acquisition traditionally consists of "the reduction of a large body of information to a precise set of facts and rules" and is associated with expert systems. Recently, these functions (and this job description) seem to be making a transition from addressing specific project requirements to meeting broad organizational objectives.

> **"Knowledge itself cannot be managed, only the processes or systems through which we share knowledge can be managed."**
> **—Nina Platt**
> **Director of library services, Faegre & Benson**

The user of an information system needs to be able to ask the right questions to get the information that he or she needs. We've all known the frustration of going to the Web for information and not being able to find it because we're not using the correct search words.

> **"Information is data endowed with relevance and purpose."**
> **—Peter Drucker**
> **Author and consultant**

A KMS shifts this burden to the system. This explains why organizations around the world, already facing hard times, are willing to invest in, install, and operate a KMS. According to a survey conducted by *Knowledge Management* magazine and International Data Group (IDC),[4] the reasons for adopting a KMS, in order of preference, are as follows:

- Retain expert personnel.
- Increase customer satisfaction.

- Improve profit and grow revenues.
- Support e-business initiatives.
- Shorten product development cycles.

Many organizations don't start to develop their KMS because they don't have a way to evaluate where they are today. Roger E. Bohn, in "Measuring and Managing Technological Knowledge" (*Sloan Management Review*, 1994), defined a KM maturity grid. He called it "Bohn's stages of knowledge growth." (See figure 2.5.) We find this to be an excellent way to define the as-is status of an organization's KMS.

According to Greg Dyer and Brian McDonough's article "The State of KM" (*Knowledge Management*, May 2001), organizations use their KMS in the following order:

- Capture and share best practices.
- Provide training and corporate learning.
- Manage customer relationships.
- Deliver competitive intelligence.
- Provide project workspace.
- Manage legal and intellectual property.
- Enhance Web publishing.
- Enhance supply chain management.

> **"We think there is a correlation between the transfer of knowledge among caregivers and customer satisfaction."**
> **—Bill Roberts**
> **"A Balanced Approach,"**
> ***Knowledge Management***

Figure 2.5 Bohn's Stages of Knowledge Growth

Stage	Name	Comment	Typical Form of Knowledge
1	Complete ignorance	Nothing known	Does not exist anywhere
2	Awareness	Resembles pure art	Knowledge is primarily tacit.
3	Measure	It's pretechnological	Knowledge is primarily written.
4	Control of the mean	A scientific method is feasible.	Written and embodied in hardware
5	Process capability	A local recipe exists.	Hardware and operating manuals
6	Process characterization	Tradeoffs to reduce costs are known.	Empirical equations (quantitative)
7	Know why	Takes on the form of science	Procedures, methodologies, scientific formulas, and algorithms
8	Complete knowledge	Nirvana	Never happens, but you can always hope for it!

As you can see, there are many good reasons to start a KMS and many different ways that it can be used. A knowledge management strategy isn't just an IT strategy, but also a well-balanced mixture of technology, cultural change, new reward systems, and a new business plan.

Knowledge management combines a diversity of knowledge sources—information from Web sites, databases, employees, partners, and stockholders. While capturing content, the KMS generates greater value by relating this to others' information. It fuels what Bill Gates calls the "thinking worker."

In the past fifty years, the world of economics has been transformed from a production-based value system to a knowledge-based value system. With this change, technology's ability to capture information and data has far outstripped people's ability to absorb it. A KMS helps individuals and organizations prepare for constantly shifting demographics and customers' needs by sorting through masses of information and providing just the knowledge needed to problem-solve or take advantage of business opportunities.

> **"Let facts speak for themselves."**
> **—Hitoshi Kume**
> *Statistical Methods for Quality Improvement*

Basic economic theory suggests that most assets are subject to diminishing returns, but this doesn't apply to knowledge. Knowledge assets grow in value as knowledge becomes the standard used by more and more organizations. When you sell a book (a physical asset), you lose it. Conversely, you can sell the same knowledge again and again. This is what economists call "the law of increasing returns." Many universities offer classes on knowledge management, but Jackson State now applies knowledge management to the way it runs the university.

People and organizations assume they know what they need to know, but this isn't possible in a rapidly changing world. One is reminded of a story of the blind men touching an elephant, each offering a different description of what the elephant is. One blind man touches the trunk and believes he knows what an elephant is; another touches the tail and describes the elephant based on that experience. Each believes his experience to be correct. Words can't always describe facts, and discussions can't determine the facts. What's white may turn out black. Discussions alone can't determine whether something is white or black.

KNOWLEDGE MANAGEMENT MATURITY GRID

Before implementing a KMS, it's wise to step back and think about the system already in place. Every organization has some type of KMS. It may not be the most advanced system and it may not be working well, but it's working. No organization can exist without the ability to transfer knowledge to its employees in some way or another. One quick and common way is through the internal "grapevine" inherent in every organization. However,

Profile 2.2 Air Products Uses CHEMREG to Measure Compliance

Background

With more than 2,000 active products and several hundred new products each year, Air Products was very concerned about measuring its compliance to U.S. Department of Transportation (DOT) requirements concerning shipping hazardous materials. Air Products used a manual process to generate shipping descriptions for bills of lading, labels, and materials safety data sheets (MSDS), which was very labor intensive, time consuming, and error prone. Its business partners were getting impatient, and constant government scrutiny required continuous improvements in safety, health, and environmental performance.

Knowledge Management Strategy

In 1993, Air Products appointed a special knowledge management task team to create a system for measuring compliance to new regulations. This was the birth of CHEMREG, an internally developed software system with two separate but integrated applications:

- A rational product database containing physical characteristics on all of the commercial products and many experimental ones in the Chem group, with data supplied by various business and lab personnel
- A knowledge-based system that generates information, such as shipping descriptions and instructions, based upon product data and regulatory rules, in much the same way that an expert system would.

Success Story

All appropriate regulatory information has been incorporated into the knowledge-based portion of CHEMREG, allowing it to produce accurate shipping descriptions for the U.S. DOT, the International Air Transport Association (IATA), and the International Maritime Organization (IMO).

The CHEMREG team also developed a new process to print document instructions that assist shipping locations with proper labeling, placarding, and packaging instructions. A new global information system was added in 1994, to gather data more quickly and to inform individuals of shipping descriptions for new products. This reduced the shipping cycle time to two days for the entire process. The measurement system also includes a query capability that allows users to perform 'what-if' analysis on product data and regulatory compliance.

Air Products recently modified its KMS to accommodate another cycle of regulatory changes by DOT, IMO and IATA, and also developed automatically generated MSDS. Using product databases, this expert system determines appropriate phraseology and content for the MSDS. The CHEMREG system will soon address generating MSDS based upon European regulations, including ISO 14001 and related quality system standards.

CHEMREG is expected to become the worldwide focal point for regulatory issues related to distribution and environmental health and safety.

(Source: Strategy Associates Inc. Used with permission. For more information, contact Frank Voehl at *fvoehl@aol. com*.)

the grapevine has a tendency to distort information, particularly if it's disseminating bad news. Employees also get information from other sources, including managers and people working outside the organization. Even if information received isn't accurate, it may be accepted as factual.

Figure 2.6 Twelve-Level Knowledge Management Maturity Grid

Key Change Area: Knowledge Management

Scale
1. Knowledge management is not part of the organization's activities.
2. Knowledge management is part of the organization's vision, but no documented plan has been developed.
3. Knowledge management has been included in the three-year approved budget, but there is no implementation plan or measurement system in place.
4. Management is doing post-mortems of all projects to define lessons learned, but there is no documented approach to be sure that everyone benefits from the analysis. A plan for implementing a full knowledge management system has been prepared and is being implemented.
5. At the end of each project, lessons learned are defined, documented, and used to determine how every future project will be implemented.
6. A central warehouse of best practices used in the organization's projects has been established, and all employees have been trained on how to use it.
7. All clients are required to include best practices as defined in the data warehouse before a project is submitted for consideration. The approval of a project is contingent upon the inclusion of best practices.
8. A benchmarking clearing house has been established and data are collected from outside of the country.
9. The benchmarking clearing house includes international best practices and is used extensively throughout the organization.
10. Best practices are statistically correlated to their impact upon countries' capacity improvement.
11. Knowledge is stratified to reflect how best practices differ based upon an area's development status.
12. The organization is recognized as a center of competency for knowledge management systems and is frequently "best marked" by other organizations.

An organization first needs to define the as-is status of its present KMS. It's usually best if an independent consultant does an assessment. However, the twelve-level maturity grid in figure 2.6 is a quick way to assess an existing KMS.

To perform a quick analysis, first read all twelve statements. Then read each one again separately, to decide if your organization is "equal to or better than" the description given. If it is, proceed to the next statement and repeat the process. Do this until you come to a statement that you don't believe your organization is equal to or better than. Then go back to the statement just prior to this; that is the level that defines the as-is status of your KMS.

> **"A company grows because it has hidden values. To keep growing, you must surface them, care for them, and transfer them through the business . . . if managers can measure it, they will value it."**
> **—Leif Edvinsson**
> *Intellectual Capital*

This approach isn't exact. Neither general statements nor individual views can accurately reflect an organization's true knowledge status. For this reason we recommend that a complete independent assessment be conducted. (See the Harrington Institute, *www.harrington-institute.com*, for more details.) Alternatively, use Bohn's Stages of Knowledge Growth, presented earlier in this chapter (see figure 2.5), to get an estimate of as-is status.

KNOWLEDGE MANAGEMENT VISION STATEMENT

"It isn't hard to come up with a new idea;
what's hard is giving up what worked in the past."
—HJH

Once as-is status is defined, it's time to determine how an organization's future KMS will be required to perform. If there's no difference between as-is status and future-state performance, then there's no need to change the KMS.

The KMS vision statement should define how the organization would like its personality (culture) and actions to change over the next three years, as related to knowledge management. The vision statement should be brief—no longer than three sentences (two would be even better). It should clearly describe how the organization will be operating three years from now. For example, an appropriate vision statement would read: "We *are* effectively converting soft knowledge into hard knowledge as it relates to all approved projects," rather than, "We *should be* effectively converting soft knowledge into hard knowledge, as it relates to all approved projects." The statement should define *what* you're doing in order to correct today's problems, not *how* you're doing it.

The following is a typical KMS statement generated by one of our clients:

"We are recognized as a sustainable international knowledge management center providing value to our stakeholders in our core competencies."

Another client's knowledge management vision reads:

"All our staff and managers frequently use and contribute to the KMS. Each employee has a personalized portal and it is their preferred source of knowledge accession. The employees are rewarded based upon how they share information."

SUMMARY

Most valuable knowledge today is *about* technology, though it shouldn't actually be confused *with* technology. Every organization in the knowledge age needs to take advantage of the Internet. The adoption of technology for the Web-based lifestyle is happening faster than the adoption of electricity, cars, TV, and radio. As consumers rapidly move online, one of the most fundamental shifts will be the degree to which consumers will manage knowledge of their finances online, including banking, mortgage, utilities, and credit cards. By the end of 1998, about half of all U.S. households had PCs, and about half of those PCs were connected to the Web. The Web allows us to join communities across the globe and provides the opportunity to strengthen knowledge connections in our own backyard. It connects colleges, friends, and families in new ways, forming knowledge-based communities with members from all over the world. The Internet is becoming the town square in the global village of tomorrow.

Today, the Web's delivery platform is the browser. If an organization or community is geographically dispersed, its intranet becomes the critical link to effective knowledge sharing.[5] Web technologies have helped transform the lowly PC into a humming portal to a global, twenty-four-hour sphere of communication and education. The physical infrastructure supporting these new capabilities has evolved too, becoming quick, robust, and secure enough to support commerce and other sensitive transactions online.

For companies engaging in KM, breakthrough thinking about how to leverage the Web emphasizes how to serve new and existing customers with added value and currency. Companies are also opening up their intranets and sharing information and knowledge more widely than ever before. In addition, Web sites are being recast to provide support for virtual organizations, teams, partnerships, and strategic alliances with customers and suppliers.[6]

W. Edwards Deming always said that the customer defines quality. He also preached that as quality increases, costs go down. Yet the Internet allows a home-based Web-based business to achieve quality and low costs with few employees and no mention of the word quality. Variation in administrative tasks such as order processing and accounting is essentially eliminated with computers. There's no need for inspection because these tasks are embedded into software. Complex algorithms check and recheck figures. Distribution and shipping are so advanced that packages can be tracked to their exact location by logging onto the shipping company's Web page. Inventory control procedures have progressed from "just in time" to "exactly on time." Today's customer is much more informed about—and accustomed to—this level of quality than ever before.

The U.S. economy is in the greatest shape ever, and e-commerce has become the epitome of capitalism, an accomplishment beyond Deming's wildest dreams. For decades, Peter Drucker has written about the coming knowledge-based economy, which has clearly arrived. But what will this mean for quality focused organizations?

A colleague recently attended an American Society for Quality meeting where a representative from Blue Cross Blue Shield spoke about its impressive quality department. However, she wasn't seeing the big picture. Blue Cross Blue Shield provides a service, and people who buy health insurance want quality insurance at a low cost. Blue Cross Blue Shield has thousands of employees and hundreds of buildings, a costly enterprise. They also have a quality department.

The point is this: If two people working out of a cramped garage build an Internet site that provides a level of service far beyond what Blue Cross Blue Shield can deliver, then which has the better quality program? Is it Blue Cross Blue Shield, because it has a quality department and "knows" what quality is? Or is it those two people in the garage who never heard of quality or knowledge management but have met and exceeded the expectations of customers?

Using real examples, Amazon.com provided better quality and service than Barnes & Noble, Dell did it to IBM, and eToys is doing it to Toys R Us. New ventures such as Yahoo!, and YouTube.com will run right over NBC, CBS, and ABC once the Internet fully utilizes broadband access. Entire industries—telecommunications, cable, and stock trading—are changing so fast that if a company isn't paying attention to what its customers want, it could be taken out of the marketplace as quickly as the typewriter. The music and video industry is now fighting changes brought by the Internet. But if a customer can download favorite music or a movie at a fraction of the cost of a CD or DVD, which will she or he choose?

Is this what Deming and other quality experts envisioned? To some people—and as quality gurus have been teaching—quality means flowcharting, surveys, teams, and Six Sigma. Possibly, this is what your organization is teaching. But many companies have forgotten that quality is ultimately defined by the customer. Many Internet companies have already proven that they can meet the needs of customers with just a Web page and a few employees. Friendly cashiers and informed sales representatives may be moot on the Internet.

An Internet site offers each customer the ultimate personal shopping experience, whether that consumer lives in northern Maine, New York City, or Paris. Shoppers don't have to drive, park, or deal with sales people. They can dash from store to store in seconds, so comparison-shopping is a breeze. Through knowledge management interfaces, the Internet shopping site greets them by name and makes suggestions based on prior searches and purchases.

Clearly, customers want their products at the lowest possible cost. The bar for online customer service has reached such a height that it's difficult for land-based stores to compete. Additionally, the Internet reaches limitless demographics and locations. How will quality professionals respond? Similar wake-up calls have been issued before, to stimulate visionary discussions about how the Web is changing the quality profession. If quality departments don't begin to see "outside the box," they may be leading their organizations down the wrong path.

REFERENCES

1. Miles, Kathy. "Christopher Columbus and the Lunar Eclipse," *www.starryskies.com*, 2003.
2. Zimmerman. Alan. From his Web site, Dr. Zimmerman's Tuesday Tips; Tip No. 292 on cooperation and teamwork, January 2002 (*www.tuesdaytip.com*).
3. Macintosh, Ann, Ian Filby, and Austin Tate. "Knowledge Asset Road Maps," Proceedings of the Second International Conference on Practical Aspects of Knowledge Management, 1998.
4. Dyer, Greg and Brian McDonough. "The State of KM," *Knowledge Management*, May 2001.
5. Stein, Martin and Frank Voehl. *MacroLogistics Management: A Catalyst for Organizational Change* (Boca Raton, FL: CRC Press/APICS, 1998).
6. Gates, Bill. *Business @ the Speed of Thought: Using a Digital Nervous System* (New York: Warner Books Inc., 1999).

CHAPTER III

KNOWLEDGE MANAGEMENT ORGANIZATION STRUCTURE

ORGANIZING FOR KNOWLEDGE MANAGEMENT

Typical knowledge management system (KMS) organizational structures consist of the following:

- Chief knowledge officer
- Cultural change agent
- Subject matter experts (knowledge analysts)
- Knowledge engineer
- Knowledge manager
- Knowledge steward
- Thematic networks
- Information technology (IT) support

> "The goal should merely be to facilitate the creation, distribution, and use of knowledge by others. Furthermore, the knowledge managers themselves should not imply by their words or actions that they are more 'knowledgeable' than anyone else."
> —**Tom Davenport**
> **President's chair in IT and management, Babson College**

To get the KMS started at Dow Chemical, an eleven-member team undertook a five-year, $15 million effort to manage knowledge throughout the organization's twenty-three business groups. This team assigned information stewards to oversee each business group.

Chief Knowledge Officer

It's critical for someone to champion the knowledge management project and take a leadership role in managing the organization's knowledge. A common title for this role is chief knowledge officer (CKO). The chief executive officer (CEO) is responsible for coordination of all the organization's knowledge systems. The CKO will usually report to the CEO. Typical CKO assignments are:

> "We're starting to talk about information the same way we talk about plants or products. This is an asset of Dow Chemical Company and we established that awareness."
> —**Cynthia Flash**
> **"Personal Chemistry,"**
> *Knowledge Management*

- Leading the design of the organization's KMS
- Assessing the organization's knowledge resources and requirements
- Communicating the value of knowledge management
- Establishing a knowledge management infrastructure

- Communicating best practices
- Building a knowledge culture
- Measuring the effect of the KMS
- Preparing or approving the KMS plan and budget

> **"As a chief learning officer, my job is to facilitate the move toward the boundaryless organization by integrating best practices within GE."**
> **—Steve Kerr**
> **Chief learning officer,**
> **Goldman Sachs**
> **(previously at General Electric)**

The CKO is the steward of the organization's most valuable asset—knowledge. In their book, *Smart Things to Know About Knowledge Management* (Capstone, 1999), Thomas M. Kouloupoulos and Carl Frappaolo state that CKOs are needed "because most organizations are as naïve about knowledge leadership today as they were about organizational leadership in the days of Adam Smith."

Allen Reed, an associate for the global executive search and assessment company Russell Reynolds Associates, has helped many organizations find CKOs or the equivalent. The primary skills that he looks for is the candidate's ability to develop a knowledge-sharing culture that's accepted by all the employees. In her article, "Who is the CKO?" (*Knowledge Management*, May 2001), Cynthia Flash observes that a chief knowledge officer needs a wide range of skills. According to Flash, "Someone in that role will find these attributes indispensable, according to CKOs and consultants:

> **"Most of my stress is related to handling the cultural aspects of KM, the people issues. You can get into a bind not knowing where your work as the champion ends."**
> **—Wise Young**
> **Research scientist,**
> **Rutgers University**

- Interpersonal communication skills to convince employees to adopt cultural changes
- Leadership skills to convey the KM vision and passion for it
- Business acumen to relate KM efforts to efficiency and profitability

> **"My focus is on improving productivity, profitability, and customer value."**
> **—Kent Greenes**
> **CKO, Science Applications International Corporation (SAIC)**[1]

- Strategic thinking skills to relate KM efforts to larger goals
- Collaboration skills to work with various departments and persuade them to work with each other
- Ability to institute effective educational programs
- Understanding of information technology and its role in advancing KM."

Notable organizations that have established the position of CKO include:

- Hewlett-Packard
- Coca-Cola
- PricewaterhouseCoopers
- Cap Gemini Ernst & Young

The Knowledge Management Consortium International (KMCI) in Vernon, Connecticut, offers a two-level knowledge management and innovation certification program. The level-one certification consists of a thirty-two-hour formal class, but certification isn't given until the student has a completed business plan for a KM initiative that's approved by a review board. Following the week-long class, students go back to their jobs but keep in touch with the class and KMCI as part of an online community of practice. This network provides support to students as they develop their business plans. This certification program is geared toward people who plan to become CKOs in government organizations.

Cultural Change Agent

As mentioned earlier, incorporating the technology for knowledge management is simple. The challenge is making the necessary changes in an organization's culture to transform knowledge hoarding into knowledge sharing. The cultural change agent is a person who has the special organizational change management (OCM) skills to make this transformation happen. He or she knows how to develop OCM maps, obtain cascading sponsorships, avoid black holes, and break down resistance to change. This individual or individuals provide the second most important activity on the KM team.

> **"The goal should merely be to facilitate the creation and distribution and use of knowledge by others. Furthermore, the knowledge managers themselves should not imply by words or actions that they are more 'knowledgeable' than anyone else."**
> **—Tom Davenport**
> **President's chair in IT and management, Babson College**

Subject Matter Experts (Knowledge Analysts)

If the organization itself is the heart of the KMS, the subject matter expert is the digestive system. The system's raw information is a smorgasbord of related and unrelated facts, half-truths, and unsubstantiated and false information. The subject matter expert provides the filtering system that separates the "wheat from the chaff." He or she is also the catalyst to encourage continuous KMS input from various internal and external sources. At the World Bank each of the many knowledge silos has a subject matter expert assigned to maintain the portal and to insure that questions and inquiries from system users are answered in an expeditious manner. Subject matter experts also maintain ongoing communications with users (communities of practice) to help transform tacit knowledge into explicit knowledge. In some organizations, subject matter expert teams (led by a chairperson) are assigned to each knowledge silo instead of an individual.

> **"Subject matter experts are beginning to share best practices pretty readily."**
> **—Ron Raborg**
> **Associate commissioner, Social Security Administration**

Knowledge Engineer

The knowledge engineer converts explicit knowledge into procedures, instructions, programs, or videos. He or she helps prepare the organization to accept necessary changes.

Knowledge Manager

Knowledge manager is a title used in organizations when the KMS isn't centralized. The knowledge manager coordinates knowledge systems within an organization. Knowledge managers are typically used in large organizations with many knowledge warehouses or those just starting the knowledge management journey. The knowledge manager role is similar role to that of corporate director of quality.

Knowledge Steward

The knowledge steward is responsible for ongoing support to knowledge users, and typically provides training and advice on knowledge tools, practices, and methods. The term "steward" indicates that the individual is responsible and willing to help and guide others in their area of expertise.

Thematic Networks

The heart of a successful KMS is comprised of conversations between people who share common interests. A KMS thrives on the unrestricted exchange of thoughts, ideas, and experiences. Thematic networks make up a key element in this exchange. These networks consist of individuals and groups sharing common interests and skills. Thematic networks can take many forms, the most common being communities of practice. These are defined as "communities that form where people assume roles based on their abilities and skills instead of their titles and hierarchical structure." A community of practice is sometimes called a community of interest.

> **"Great minds discuss ideas. Average minds discuss events. Small minds discuss people."**
> **—Eleanor Roosevelt**

Communities of practice communicate directly with one another, with members using each other as sounding boards. Communities of practice are interest-driven and their members are loosely associated. Teams, by contrast, are task-driven and their members usually work together on a regular basis.

> **"Communities of this sort are difficult to construct and easy to destroy. They are among the most important structures of any organization where thinking matters, but they almost inevitably undermine its formal structure."**
> **—Thomas M. Koulopoulos and Carl Frappaolo**
> *Smart Things to Know About Knowledge Management*

Think of knowledge networks as clusters of people that band together to share or gain knowledge, then disband once their needs have been satisfied. Members of knowledge networks then move on to join other knowledge networks, to obtain a different type of knowledge. Often, strategic centers are established as the hub of major thematic networks. Organizations including Apple, Nike, Sun Microsystems, and Toyota are using strategic centers. Each strategic center has a well-defined vision and mission, and clearly states its area of interest or expertise. Typically, strategic centers are created to cover each core competency and capability. This approach acknowledges that collaborative problem-solving conversations and teamwork are the best approaches for tapping an organization's knowledge base.

The KMS enabling software helps knowledge workers to join thematic networks, by allowing them to subscribe to subject matter sources. Building thematic networks, communities of practice, and teams is characteristic of the KMS software, whether the process is driven by system information or administered by the KMS architect.

> **"We have the human relations resources groups that have certain responsibilities for development of competencies and how groups can better share and network."**
> **—Jim Allen**
> **Former KM director, Dow Chemical**

Interest Networks

Interest networks support and strengthen communities of practice in managing development programs and resources. These communities offer policymakers, policy analysts, and development practitioners tools for harvesting ideas, seeking responses to development policy issues, accessing information on best practices, and incorporating lessons and experience in managing specific economic policies and programs.

Among other possibilities, a typical interest network provides for:

> **"Communities are the primary resource for transfer of tacit knowledge to explicit knowledge."**
> **—Bob Turner**
> **KM strategist, Federal Aviation Administration**

- A network of centers, professionals, practitioners, and academics forming a community of practice that collectively reflects on development issues, poses questions, and proposes solutions
- Members of the community sharing information and knowledge based on their experiences, research, and interactions, from which it can develop best practices and policies as well as program guides of value to other stakeholders
- The community serving as a peer review mechanism for research and studies, and helping to raise the value of products and services

The community supports activities that may include the following:

- Sourcing and disseminating relevant best practices
- Documenting operational excellence, lessons, program design, and implementation among network members
- "Scanning globally" and commissioning studies that could help spur growth and development by generating knowledge, synthesizing information, and discovering knowledge gaps
- Organizing short, audience-specific, theme-driven seminars and workshops to share knowledge and information
- Synthesizing research findings for dissemination
- Supporting publications
- Maintaining lists of subject-matter specialists on specific issues and development areas

■ Maintaining a Web site, which offers a portal on its activities and encourages virtual exchanges of both hard and soft knowledge

Other activities interest networks may support include:

■ Seminars, workshops, conferences, and summits focused on issues related to the knowledge subject

■ Exchange and collaborative programs among national institutions in the form of sabbaticals, work-study assignments, and internships

■ Specialized data survey and collaborative research to guide planning and/or research

■ Special studies to document or publish materials of value to the development management process, to guide institutional reforms, and to strengthen social and related programs

■ High-level stakeholders' consultative meetings or meetings of national experts and/or professional associations

■ Skills transfer programs, including strengthening understanding and application of information and communications technology

> **"To further this feeling of belonging, we redesigned what we called our 'communities'—local groups of 100 to 150 people across career levels, focused on networking and skill-building—so that most individuals in a community share a common specialization."**
> **—Joe W. Forehand**
> **Chairman, Accenture**

THE ORGANIZATION ITSELF

The KMS involves the total organization. For the KMS to be effective, an organization must change to become a "knowing organization." All organizations and every individual within an organization need to continuously grow, learn, and stay current. But customers want to do business with organizations that know—and use—the latest best practices and approaches, not organizations that are still just learning. Knowing organizations are current and offer customers the best value because they've incorporated current best practices and are using knowledge to provide new and better products and services than their competitors.

> **"Now the definition of manager is someone who makes knowledge productive."**
> **—Peter Drucker**
> **Author and consultant**

The biggest obstacle is converting the people from a knowledge-hoarding culture to a knowledge-sharing culture. To make this transformation, an effective approach to organizational change needs to be developed—one that includes changing the rewards-and-recognition system. And everyone needs to become both teacher and student: Managers need to share their knowledge with employees, and employees need to reciprocate. Everyone has valuable experiences and ideas to share and add to the knowledge base. Knowledge sharing needs to be included as part of all employees' and managers' job descriptions and performance evaluations.

Profile 3.1 Mars Inc. Achieves Knowledge Management Breakthrough in a Strategic Alliance With Cass Information Systems

Background

Each year the NALS division of Mars Inc. moves more than eight billion pounds of raw materials, packaging, and finished goods throughout North America, providing 250,000 truckloads of transport.

The over-arching goal of the NALS is to develop comprehensive logistics and strategies that deliver the best possible level of customer service at a price that's below competition and better than market. NALS works to ensure responsive customer service by coordinating the physical distribution of both materials and knowledge, from supplier to factory to warehouse to customer. The NALS slogan is: "We transport."

Knowledge Management Strategy

The key to cooperative knowledge management is to find ways to link suppliers, transportation, and warehousing vendors as well as internal and external customers. To that end NALS created a strategic alliance with Cass Information Systems Inc., to report logistics cost information back to Mars business units quickly and accurately. This system links transportation and warehousing payment data with customer and supplier databases as well as the order entry system, providing a clear view across the entire supply pipeline. The resulting logistics and cost database supports financial planning and reporting, tactical decision making, and strategic initiatives, such as network modeling.

Success Story

Entering the 21st century, Mars' NALS is ready with technologies that provide real-time connectivity between suppliers, manufacturing logistics vendors, and customers. The Mars network of warehouses use bar coding scanning devices to speed inventory to customers. The traffic management system allows NALS to know the precise location and contents of all trucks. Warehouse managers also know when products are scheduled to arrive from inbound trucks and can coordinate customer-bound trucks to avoid or minimize the cost and time delay of warehousing.

Mars tracks a total of $1 million in goods and services each day, more than 500,000 individual transactions per year. Cass audits, processes, pays, and reports these transactions for Mars, acting as a third-party logistics agent. Ultimately, the transformation of data into information in a timely and accurate manner is the job of Cass' knowledge information systems.

NALS is responsible for collecting and gathering information and knowledge, analyzing its cost and service drivers, and taking proper actions. Mars believes that real value is created when information contained in the order entry system is matched and integrated to create a knowledge-based cost database measurement system. This system is used to measure performance, identify variances, and decide on appropriate action.

Mars' success with its strategic alliance with Cass begins and ends with good communication. Cass has an in-plant representative and uses e-mail to provide quick, paperless exchanges of

(Continues)

Profile 3.1 Mars Inc. Achieves Knowledge Management
Breakthrough in a Strategic Alliance With
Cass Information Systems *(continued)*

information. Also, senior management representatives from both Mars and Cass are readily available and involved on a regular basis. Both organizations look to reduce or eliminate paperwork and redundant activities. Both also impose system discipline by handling information only once; using correct first-time measurements, concepts, and thinking; and making sure that data and knowledge are accurate and consistent.

(Source: Strategy Associates Inc. Used with permission. For more information, contact Frank Voehl at *fvoehl@aol. com.*)

The Role of Top Management Within the KMS

In a small organization, employees at all levels can meet easily and frequently to trade stories and experience, and in doing so they create an informal yet efficient knowledge system. Since most high-level knowledge is people-centered, in larger organizations top management can help create a similar knowledge-sharing environment by promoting interdependency. It seems intuitive that a knowledge system would work best in an atmosphere of zero contempt, one characterized by complete trust, and sharing, but this isn't necessarily so. In academia, for example, there's intense competition and intellectual rivalry, but this doesn't prevent brilliant academics from producing great research.

> **"Already an estimated two-thirds of U.S. employees work in the service sectors, and 'knowledge' is becoming our most important 'product.' This calls for different organizations as well as different kinds of workers."**
> **—Peter Drucker**
> *Post-Capitalist Society*

The tasks of top management for the KMS include the need to:

- Establish and maintain knowledge policy and objectives.
- Ensure that the KMS is established, implemented, and maintained.
- Promote awareness of, and involvement in, knowledge policy and knowledge objectives.
- Ensure focus on knowledge requirements throughout the organization.
- Identify and provide resources.
- Periodically review the KMS.
- Improve the system.

Knowledge Policy and Objectives

A knowledge policy announces an organization's broad intentions about managing knowledge in its key competency areas. Knowledge policy is translated into specific objectives that focus employee efforts, and that help measure progress from year to year. Knowledge policy and objectives help the organization to identify resources and plans needed to achieve results. Achieving knowledge objectives year after year favorably affects an organization's operational and financial performance, helps increase staff morale, and contributes to a positive working environment. The following is an example of a typical knowledge policy statement.

"KM has to be strongly supported from the top down."
—Eric Lesser
Associate partner, IBM's Institute for Business Value

> "Leaders send a simple, clear message that sharing and innovation fostered by knowledge management is important to the organization. Management funds and sponsors high-profile projects, encouraging systematic innovation, and by making agility and innovation a personal priority, management creates buy-in to the process."
>
> —HJH

THE BURLINGTON NORTHERN RAILROAD STORY[2]

Background Information

In the mid-1990s the president of Burlington Northern (BN), Bill Greenwood, received a suggestion from a friend that would transform his thinking and that of his company as well.

"My friend suggested that I read a book by Robert Schaffer called *The Breakthrough Strategy*," said Greenwood." It was written by a consultant from Connecticut who went on to popularize the concept through a couple of articles in the *Harvard Business Review*. Well, my friend thought there may be some possible applications of the ideas at BN and it turns out he was correct. It turned out to be a million dollar idea."

Over the next few years, BN would begin to put together its knowledge management strategy around the four following components:

- Small-scale teams
- Urgent, measurable goals
- Real business issues involving multiple stakeholders
- Capabilities and confidence building that takes place using adaptive learning for breakthrough results

Small-Scale Teams

At BN, small-scale teams typically consist of five to ten people who are recruited from the area being targeted for improvement, such as equipment management or billing. To work effectively and achieve the needed improvement, the team must be cross-functional in nature. As Bill Greenwood describes it:

"If timely billing is a problem, then you must have accounting people, customer service people, and the people who do the billing in the field and who are directly involved with developing the solution to the problem. It is important that these people work not as departments, but as a problem-solving team working on a process."

Previously, employees at BN often started improvement activities without fully understanding the problem. People would become uncomfortable, wondering whether the correct problem was being addressed, or whether there wasn't more important work to be done. The bottom line was, the actual problem areas needed to be discovered. Problem areas become obvious when one compares the actual circumstances to the business objective, process requirements, and customer expectations.

Perception plays a key role in this process. On one hand, there's a strong human need for stimulation and change, and also resistance to change. In many ways humans are animals best adapted to gradual change. In industry as well as society, it's common for serious problems to be ignored for months and years while trivial matters receive great attention. Serious problems can remain with us for so long we adapt to them, while sudden change—even if trivial—disrupts the status quo, so we notice. Our animal comfort with routine is another reason employees don't acknowledge serious problems; people get busy doing their "normal jobs." Most people—and most organizations—don't make time for problem recognition.

Problem-solving activities at BN began with separating problems from symptoms, understanding the facts, organizing the data, and exploring data through analysis. One of the most common mistakes in problem solving is trying to solve a symptom. A key use of the knowledge management journey is to improve the problem-solving process by ensuring that organizations work on problems and not symptoms.

Urgent, Measurable Goals

At BN, a goal-setting process for knowledge creation was used. Similar to goal-setting for policy deployment, in this process team goals were aligned to specific business objectives.

BN planning focuses on three types of work goals: individual, team/work-unit, and corporate (organizational). All three are considered essential to successfully conducting business. At BN, setting and achieving measurable goals provides the motivation and direction necessary for growth and success in important breakthrough areas, as Bill Greenwood explains:

"Urgent measurable goals are ones where the team works on things that matter now! The team knows exactly what to achieve and how success will be measured. Communicating without a desired outcome is like traveling without a specific destination. You may or may not end up in a place you really enjoy. Outcomes help us end up at the goal destination we want."

Outcomes are the specific results an organization wants to achieve, expressed in words and terms describing the way an outcome will happen, the way people will feel when it does, and how others will respond. Goals and objectives are broader in scope than outcomes. Think of outcomes as goals that have been clarified and sharpened.

Achieving effective outcomes increases in importance within work teams. The goal-setting process encourages the team to identify and develop a sound understanding of customers' needs as well as the organization's business strategy. Teams that make goal setting a key part of their working processes encourage diversity of input, increased consensus, and stronger commitment among team members.

Goal-setting for breakthrough outcomes has proven successful at BN for the following reasons. The process:

- Improves teamwork through a shared sense of approach and purpose
- Heightens achieved performance by setting targets to be achieved
- Identifies resource constraints or limitations
- Distinguishes workload priority
- Is challenging, yet achievable

Project Example: Moorhead Malting Facility

The objective was to implement an electronic data interchange (EDI) KMS at the Moorhead Malting facility by December 1, 1993. The breakthrough was achieved in an eight-week period, producing dramatic results because the team was empowered to develop and implement solutions and the barriers were removed. According to Greenwood:

"A breakthrough team does not produce studies that get analyzed and reviewed and analyzed again, and someday may even get implemented," said Greenwood. "No, a breakthrough team develops and implements solutions and usually gets results in as little as a week and usually in eight weeks or less."

Business Issues Involving Multiple Stakeholders to Improve Capabilities and Confidence

The key point in this step, both at BN and in many other organizations, is for team members to collectively put themselves in the shoes of customers and develop simple surveys to determine appropriate areas of team focus. These may include:

- Quality
- Speed/timeliness
- Cost and functionality
- Availability and flexibility
- Responsiveness
- Durability
- Reliability

The main goal is to become a high-value organization, and becoming one depends upon the rate of improvement. Customer data and business statistics help speed up learning, the central purpose of information, and this in turn speeds up improvement. Without organizational change there's no improvement. However, change requires new knowledge, and new knowledge requires learning. Thus, rapid improvement is supported by rapid learning, and both are encouraged by issue-oriented, problem-solving techniques. According to Bill Greenwood:

"At BN, breakthrough teams deal with business issues that typically involve service to our customers. For example, providing forty-five additional covered hoppers per month so a specific customer could expand into new markets in the Pacific Northwest was a challenge for one of our teams. As a result, the team members came away from the project with increased business literacy and a more in-depth understanding of the customer's needs and wants. Team members also learn skills that can be applied to other parts of their job and to the way in which the railroad operates and continuously improves itself."

Project Example: ARCO

ARCO is a major customer of BN, and is served by the Cherry Point Refinery north of Seattle, Washington. BN handles movements of petroleum coke to Pacific Northwest aluminum smelters. To better handle this business, in 1993 BN assigned 155 of its covered hopper cars to supplement ARCO's fleet. The 155 cars were needed because of rail yard congestion and poor utilization of covered hoppers. A knowledge management team was formed and chartered to improve the situation.

Identifying issues and documenting the team charter is the critical first step in the problem-solving process. Ironically, it's also the least understood and most frequently omitted or short-circuited step. The nucleus of the charter involves establishing a performance promise that the team will consistently deliver to ensure success. According to Bob Lynch of QualTeam, flawless delivery on performance promises depends upon seamless internal execution. At BN, seamless execution is the result of strong links between internal customers and suppliers. The knowledge charter enables the team to consider its role in accomplishing an organization's greater purpose.

The knowledge charter can be viewed as a chain of objectives that begins with a team mission statement and is followed by the supporting purposes. The mission statement should be brief—between twenty-five and fifty words in length—and provide a description of the team's core purpose. The next section covers the team organization and reporting structure, followed by the team member responsibilities. This is followed by procedures for each of the team's supporting purposes, as well as issues that are beyond its scope. Completing the knowledge charter is a list of the team's goals.

The following are key items typically covered within the charter framework:

- Team mission and objectives
- Products, services, and information to be provided
- Synopsis of team processes, customers, and valid requirements
- Competitive benchmarks, if known
- Supplier requirements, if available
- Problem statement and related symptoms
- Charter boundaries, including items not included

The BN/ARCO knowledge management breakthrough team found that many of the cars were "safety stock" required to ensure that ARCO wouldn't run out of freight cars. Thus, the team embraced the opportunity to improve service to ARCO and also reduce the number of required cars.

"This looked like an ideal situation to test the knowledge creation breakthrough concept," Greenwood reports, "But we needed a new way of doing this. . . . [I]n the past each department (train operations, freight car management, and marketing) would each do their own thing. All these employees were working as hard as they could, but the traditional BN approach lacked the cross-functional and cross-organizational cooperation required to fix this situation with ARCO. In other words, no one person was responsible and accountable for the ARCO business."

But all that changed in 1993, when BN launched its "account leader initiative," with a one-point contact. Account leader Clint Watkins was now in charge of coordinating all ARCO business with BN, including freight car utilization. Watkins assembled six appropriate people for the ARCO breakthrough team.

"Three of the key people were: Doug Verity, the trainmaster at Bellingham, Washington; Gary Dunn, who was in charge of managing the covered hopper fleet; and Stu Gordon, the terminal superintendent in Everett, Washington," Greenwood explains. "Without the full participation of these people, the project would have failed, for the approach had to be cross-functional." The seven-person team met and reviewed all the pertinent information and then took the next key step in making the breakthrough approach work—creating razor-sharp goals.

In other words, goals need to be precise, clear, and timely. After identifying an area in need of improvement, goal setting for razor-sharp outcomes allows a team or an individual to create an incremental plan to increase their problem-solving and business effectiveness. Goal setting illuminates possible solutions, and helps measure successful endeavors. Razor-sharp goal setting improves performance by providing clear, tight targets to aim for. When teams adapt and meet relevant, razor-sharp goals, areas of concern improve systematically. (See figure 3.1.)

According to Bill Greenwood, the goal of the ARCO knowledge management break-through team was to "reduce excess inventory in pool assignment No. 5104 by 50 percent by June 1994," a precise, clear and timely goal. Next came the true challenge—implementation—which the team was also responsible for accomplishing.

"The team worked together with the ARCO people and reviewed in depth the shipping patterns, frequencies, and schedules. ARCO's customers who were the recipients also had their shipping patterns, frequencies, and schedules reviewed, thus extending their work throughout the entire value chain," Greenwood notes. "Finally, BN's handling practices in distributing covered hoppers and in working through terminals were examined as well."

Note that the knowledge management goal-setting system[3] relies on the use of action verbs to signify what will result from the completion of the goal. Use the following list to help identify action verbs.

The process Greenwood describes was a new way of doing things at BN, the direct result of introducing breakthrough goal setting that set the stage for the way the organization continues to do business today. The knowledge management breakthrough team's detailed plan resolved the situation to the benefit of both ARCO and BN. The team got buy-in to make reductions in the fleet, but to make fleet reductions work they needed one more thing—precision execution. Bill Greenwood illustrates this point with a story about a man changing a flat tire:

"It takes me about fifteen minutes to change a flat tire. Under normal conditions, this may seem fine. But let's say that I'm a driver at the Indy 500. Here, it takes a pit crew less than fifteen seconds to change a tire. What's the difference? First of all, at Indy, the customer is the driver of the racecar and a fifteen-minute changeover would be totally unacceptable. A few seconds can mean the difference between winning and losing.

"Second, at Indy there is a well-trained pit crew that acts as a team with each person knowing exactly what to do in a very precise way. Third, the team's focus is on the abso-lutely essential movements to change the tire, for there are no wasted moves in the pits at Indy. Fourth, every member of the team knows exactly what the goal is: to get that tire changed as quickly and safely as possible.

"Fifth, every member of the team has been trained to do his or her own job exactly right. And lastly, the team has practiced and practiced and practiced so that when it's race time, they perform each movement as precisely as they should. And with any luck, their customer—the driver—and the entire team will win the race."

Bill Greenwood's tire-changing example may seem extreme, but it clearly illustrates what a focused, high-performance team can do if they have precise execution. The racing pit crew may not have called the process "knowledge management breakthrough think-ing," but that's exactly the kind of thinking they used to figure out how to change a tire in less than fifteen seconds.

Figure 3.1 Knowledge Management Goal-Setting System

Accept	Control	Fix	Name	Research
Accomplish	Convert	Forecast	Negotiate	Resolve
Accumulate	Cooperate	formulate	Notify	Restrict
Achieve	Coordinate	Forward		Return
Acquire	Counsel	Furnish	Observe	Review
Activate	Create	Further	Obtain	
Adjust	Criticize		Optimize	Schedule
Administer	Critique	Gather	Order	Score
Adopt		Get	Organize	Secure
Advise	Decrease	Give	Orient	Select
Advocate	Defend	Guarantee	Originate	Sell
Aid	Define	Guide	Overhaul	Send
Align	Delegate	Grow		Serve
Allocate	Delimit		Participate	Show
Analyze	Deliver	Identify	Perform	Sketch
Appoint	Depict	Implement	Persuade	Solicit
Appraise	Describe	Improve	Pick-up	Solve
Approve	Design	Inform	Pilot	Sort
Arrange	Distribute	Initiate	Plan	Specify
Ascertain	Detach	Inquire	Prescribe	Staff
Assemble	Detect	Inspect	Present	State
Assess	Determine	Install	Prevent	Stop
Assist	Develop	Instruct	Process	Study
Audit	Devise	Insure	Procure	Submit
Authorize	Direct	Interpret	Program	Suggest
	Do	Interview	Project	Summarize
Balance	Draft	Inventory	Proofread	Supervise
Bargain	Draw	Investigate	Protect	Supply
Brief		Issue	Provide	Survey
Budget	Edit	Itemize	Pull	
Build	Eliminate		Purchase	Take
Buy	Encourage	Join		Teach
	Endorse	Judge	Rate	Test
Calculate	Enforce	Justify	Read	Train
Catalog	Ensure	Jeep	Recall	Transfer
Check	Erect		Receive	Transmit
Choose	Establish	Label	Recite	Tutor
Classify	Estimate	Lecture	Recommend	
Collect	Evaluate	List	Record	Utilize
Combine	Examine		Recount	
Communicate	Exchange	Mail	Recruit	Verbalize
Compile	Execute	Maintain	Regulate	Verify
Complete	Expedite	Make available	Reject	
Comply	Expand	Make happen	Remove	Weigh
Compute	Experiment	Manage	Render	Withdraw
Conduct	Explain	Manipulate	Repair	Word
Connect	Express	Measure	Replace	Write
Conserve		Mediate	Report	
Consider	Fabricate	Meet	Request	
Construct	Facilitate	Motivate	Require	
Consult	File		Requisition	

So how did the ARCO breakthrough team do? It did exceptionally well. The team's initial efforts reduced the fleet by sixty-five cars, or what amounted to 42 percent of the assigned freight cars. These cars were deployed to other business needs for ARCO and other customers in need of covered hoppers.

"Remember, the razor-sharp goal was 50 percent and the team achieved 42 percent, or almost 85 percent, which was considered breakthrough results. Also, this was the first time through the breakthrough process for this group. Why is this a big deal?" Greenwood asks. "Because these are the results of only one breakthrough team. By the end of 1994, we had more than 200 breakthrough teams, all making productivity and cycle time improvements on a customer-by-customer basis. When you add up the results of the 200+ teams, they are in the tens of millions of dollars."

Accomplishing all this required quite a bit of training, of course. In the first year alone, more than 400 BN people received formal training in the breakthrough process and how to effectively use razor-sharp goal setting.

Lessons Learned

BN learned that its team must include, from the start, all individuals and parts of the organization with a major stake in the project's success. This means that they must be part of setting razor-sharp goals and developing and implementing the plan. Second, razor-sharp goals must be in focus. Without that, the team will flounder. Third, the team needs a knowledge management work plan, which provides a clear understanding of the roles each team member plays—essential to the team's success. Finally, the team must be empowered to obtain necessary resources and to do what needs to be done.

"The need for knowledge management breakthrough thinking exists because nothing in this world stands still," says Bill Greenwood. "And it never will. Our customer requirements, our markets, and our technology keep evolving. And that's good, for it creates improvements to out products and services. This constant change makes us focus on the essential parts of providing our services; and on which parts add value and which ones don't; and on new ways to do things—breakthrough ways!

"The introduction of the knowledge management learning process at BN has been a very successful and rewarding experience. I also think that we have just scratched the surface of the potential that breakthrough thinking has in breakthrough thinking for the future generations."

KNOWLEDGE MANAGEMENT SYSTEM DOCUMENTS

Documents and documentation processes figure prominently in the application of a KMS. Documents support the accumulation of data and information. Codification of tacit knowledge produces documents.

KMS documents may include:

- A knowledge manual containing at least the knowledge policy and objectives, along with the assignment of responsibilities for the system and procedures, or a reference to these.
- Knowledge plans describing how the KMS applies to specific projects.
- Knowledge guidelines stating recommendations and requirements for knowledge management.

SUMMARY

"In the digital age, knowledge is our lifeblood. And documents are the DNA of knowledge."
—Rick Thoman
Former CEO, Xerox

We often overlook the importance of an organization's structure in supporting the implementation of a KMS. This is a very critical consideration, because an organization will undergo significant change in the shift from a knowledge-hoarding to a knowledge-sharing culture. A KMS isn't a software package that's easily installed then forgotten about. It's a network of people willing to share ideas and build upon their experiences. This communication process quickly breaks down if the communication cycle fails. A KMS isn't bites and code; it's people talking together—people who are proud of what they're doing and are willing to stop and help someone else along the way. There are few other programs within an organization that will require such a drastic culture change, and effective organizational change management processes.

All too often a KMS simply becomes a portal that people go to for information. But knowledge isn't being effectively managed if users aren't also putting their experience and ideas back into the system. When a KMS becomes "one-way" and outdated it will soon disappoint its users, who will then stop using it.

To make a KMS effective there needs to be a complete change in the ways in which performance plans are written and employees are evaluated. Major changes also need to be made in individual job descriptions. People need to be promoted not on the basis of how much they know, but how much they've shared what they know.

"Don't put the KMS in IT. Put human resources in charge of it."

—HJH

REFERENCES

1. Kent Green's effort has added millions of dollars in new business for SAIC.
2. This case study is based on material from *Macrologistics Management: A Catalyst for Organizational Change* by Martin Stein and Frank Voehl (CRC Press, 1997).
3. This goal-setting system is based upon the work of Maxcomm Inc. and Strategy Associates. It's been implemented in a number of client organizations and is presented here as one of the key components to knowledge management implementation. Different organizations profiled in this book call this approach by different names but the key components are the same in each.

CHAPTER IV

KNOWLEDGE MANAGEMENT INFORMATION TECHNOLOGY INFRASTRUCTURE

IT INFRASTRUCTURE'S ROLE IN THE KNOWLEDGE MANAGEMENT SYSTEM

Knowledge management technology is designed to make the most of the collected wisdom of an organization's employees. This technology supports management's desire that all employees openly share their thoughts, creative ideas, and accumulated experiences. This desire for open communication is demonstrated by management's willingness to invest heavily in necessary technologies.

> "Organizations could use techniques and methods that were developed as part of knowledge technology to analyze their knowledge sources. While using these techniques, they can perform knowledge analysis, which is a necessary step for the ability to manage knowledge and knowledge planning."
> —**Dr. Maurten Sierhuis**
> **Senior researcher,**
> **RIACS/NASA Ames**

Knowledge must always be treated as a driver for technology, not the other way around. The software is well defined and works well. There's a lot of competition in software knowledge management, and software companies are willing to work with organizations to explore effective knowledge management options. For this process to be worthwhile an organization needs a profiling mechanism for a push-and-pull knowledge management system (KMS) based upon knowledge delivery, a mechanism that balances costs and value for each additional enabling component. (See figure 4.1.)

The information technology (IT) infrastructure has two prerequisites for the effective transport, structure access, and collaborative management of electronic data. They are:

■ Messaging and collaboration
■ Complete intranet

The KMS enabling modules needed to support services such as content management, information delivery, data analysis, data tracking, and workflow processes make up the rest of the KMS infrastructure. They are:

■ Communities, teams, and experts
■ Portals and search
■ Content management
■ Real-time collaboration
■ Data analysis

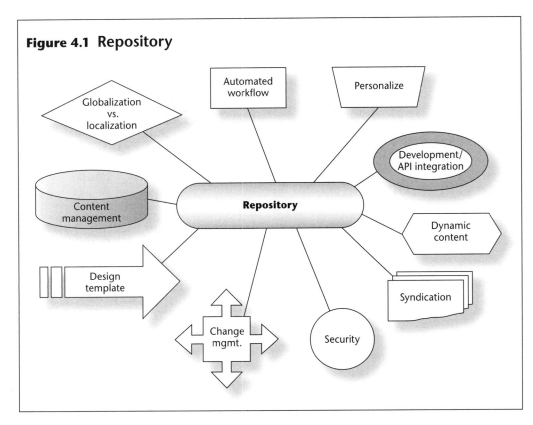

Figure 4.1 Repository

People are ready to work with technology and document their work. The KMS must be designed in a way that makes it easy to create, store, and retrieve work. The following is a list of twelve useful KMS software tools with their respective Web addresses:

- Angoss—Knowledge Seeker (*www.angoss.com*)
- Ascent Technology Inc. (*www.ascent.com*)
- Convera—Retrieval Ware: The Knowledge Discovery Solution (*www.convera.com/products/*)
- Egain—Content Adapter (*www.inference.com/products/integrate_content.asp*)
- Hyperwave—Hyperwave IS/6 (*www.hyperwave.com/e/products*)
- IBM—Rational Portfolio Manager (*http://www-306.ibm.com/software/awdtools/portfolio/index.html*)
- ISYS Search Software—ISYS: Desktop 7 (*www.isys-search.com.au/products/desktop*)
- Intranet DASHBOARAD (*www.intranetdashboard.com*)
- Knowledge Powered Solutions Ltd.—KM Software (*www.kpsol.com*)
- MIS—Deltaminer (*www.mis.de/ca/ke/ujn*)
- Open Text Corporation—Livelink ECM (*www.opentext.com/2/so./products.htm*)
- Tufts Academic Technology—Vue 2.0 (*www.vue.tccs.tufts.edu*)

KNOWLEDGE MANAGEMENT COLLABORATION AND GROUPWARE TOOLS

These groupware tools are mainly useful for non-real-time collaboration; they're listed below in alphabetical order.[1]

ACollab

[ACollab] is an access standards-compliant, multi-group, Web-based collaborative work environment. ACollab is available now as a standalone application that will run on its own and will be available as an ATutor add-on for an upcoming release. ACollab is ideal for groups working at a distance developing documentation, collaborating on research, or writing joint papers. *Reviewer's note:* A demo and download are available if you want to learn more.

> "Knowledge management (KM) is not a software product or a software category. KM doesn't even start with technology. It starts with business objectives and processes and a recognition of the need to share information. . . . [I]t is nothing more than managing information flow, getting the right information to the people who need it so that they can act on it quickly. . . . [I]t is a verb, not a static noun, a means, not an end. The end is to increase institutional intelligence, or corporate IQ."
>
> **—Bill Gates**
> *Business @ the Speed of Thought*

Annotea

Annotea is a LEAD (Live Early Adoption and Demonstration) project enhancing the World Wide Web Consortium (W3C) collaboration environment with shared annotations. Annotations are comments, notes, explanations, or other types of external remarks that can be attached to any Web document or a selected part of the document without actually needing to touch the document. When the users get the document, they can also load the annotations attached to it from a selected annotation server or several servers and see what their peer groups think. . . . The first client implementation of Annotea is W3C's Amaya editor/browser. *Reviewer's note:* You can download and install the Amaya editor/browser and the server to try it out.

AskMe Enterprise

The knowledge sharing problem requires a complete solution, one that captures employees' expertise, catalogues it, transfers it to those who need it when they need it, and stores that valuable knowledge for future use. AskMe's software products boast proprietary, patent-pending technologies that address the complexities of the knowledge sharing problem as well as each organization's unique requirements. *Reviewer's note:* Take a look at the demo for an example of how it could be used within an enterprise.

Axista.com

XCOLLA Collaborative Software for Project Management: intuitive and convenient Web-based project management software for team collaboration. Features include: secure Web-based access to real-time project data such as project deliverables, task monitors, project templates, Gantt charts, personal and team journals, meetings, events, and documents. *Reviewer's note:* Take the "Quick Tour" for more information about how it works.

Bloki

Bloki is a Web site on which you can create Web pages, publish a blog, and host online discussions, right in your browser, with no additional software required. Think of it as a word processor for the Web. All of the pages on *bloki.com* were built with Bloki. *Reviewer's note:* You can share your Bloki pages, blog, and forums with anyone you like—co-workers, friends, family, the whole world—or keep them private for your own personal or business use.

Calendars Net

Calendars Net is a free interactive Web calendar hosting service, where you and anyone you choose can post events visible and printable by whomever you choose, or everyone. You can post events that span more than one day (with text flowing across days or even weeks) or that recur every first and fourth Tuesday of each month, etc. You can copy the calendar data to your own computer and edit your calendar offline. *Reviewer's note:* calendar sharing.

coachingplatform

Based on the szpace design that was developed by Canada-based coachingplatform Inc., the coachingplatform collaboration software was created to support the needs of people, how they communicate, and how they work. It does not require the user to conform to technology. The name "coachingplatform" describes the concept. The combination of "coaching" and "platform" highlights coaching as a synonym for a focused empowerment process, and platform that stands for the context where this can actually happen. The coachingplatform product provides both. The coachingplatform software enables business activities in which collaboration is the key to creating solutions or services. The software is a dynamic, flexible system that enables the entire range of roles and actions required for online, asynchronous information sharing, teamwork and collaboration. *Reviewer's note:* Free trial subscription possible.

coMentor

coMentor is software that allows users to create multi-user learning environments on the Internet that are accessible without the need for any special client-side software. The system provides a collaborative virtual environment in which students can take part in real-time and asynchronous discussion, along with a set of learning tools to support debate and collaborative work. Available from Huddersfield University.

CommunityZero

CommunityZero is an interactive Web site that allows a group of people to communicate and exchange information over the Internet in their own private and secure area. Within each area, called an online community, participants are provided access to a suite of powerful tools that enable a group to effectively get organized, share knowledge, and communicate. *Reviewer's note:* Sign up for free.

Creative Manager Pro

Creative Manager Pro is the leading project management software for the creative design industry, produced for design firms, ad agencies, in-house creative/marcom departments, and creative service firms. *Reviewer's note:* Interactive demo and test drive opportunities.

DocuPortal.NET

DocuPortal is an innovative tool that focuses on collaboration; document-, content-, and asset management; and knowledge management. The tool is designed for personal and small- and medium-size business use. It's very easy to install and to use. *Reviewer's note:* DocuPortal.NET can potentially save more than 50 percent of the working time of your employees. Explore how easy it is to start with an effective collaboration and document management solution.

EPMAC Team Collaboration Portal

EPMAC is a Web-based enterprise solution for project management and team collaboration. Using EPMAC, organizations can easily conduct online project collaboration between distributed workforce (multiple office locations, telecommuters, offsite consultants, etc.) and geographically dispersed customers, partners, contractors, and suppliers. EPMAC is available as a hosted solution on a monthly subscription basis and can also be purchased as licensed software for standalone installation. *Reviewer's note:* Demo tour available on Web site.

eProject

[eProject is] the latest in project management and collaboration software, designed to make your projects more successful. The new version allows project teams around the world to develop a solid project plan, improve communication between team members, and provide progress updates to managers and stakeholders. *Reviewer's note:* Take the online product tour.

eRoom

[eRoom] provides a rapidly deployed and rapidly adopted Web-based collaborative workplace that enables distributed teams to work together to accelerate and improve development and delivery of products and services, optimize collaborative business processes, and improve innovation, problem-solving, and decision making. eRoom is flexible and configurable, and can be adapted to support a wide range of business processes. *Reviewer's note:* eRoom.net provides a subscription-based, hosted eRoom workplace solution in which both departmental teams and large organizations can take advantage of a completely out-sourced collaboration solution.

Flypaper

Flypaper collaboration sites centralize information and dynamically link documents, discussion, notification, calendars, and corporate applications. Now, people across a range of locations can share real-time data and speed business processes using a standard Web browser. *Reviewer's note:* combines collaborative features with content management features.

ForumOne

Forum One's Project Spaces Extranet lets users connect their critical stakeholders in a centrally managed set of virtual workspaces, designed specifically to ease the burden of team-based collaboration. *Reviewer's note:* Take a look at the feature tour.

Google Groups

Google Groups is a free service that helps groups communicate effectively using e-mail and the Web. Every group has a home page hosted by Google where members can start new discussions or reply to older topics. Every group also has its own e-mail address to help its members stay in touch with each other. Members can read and search all public Google Groups content, including more than 1 billion postings from the Usenet bulletin board service, dating back to 1981. Every group has its own Google-fast search, making it easy to find discussions locked away deep in your group's archive. *Reviewer's note:* Google Groups lets you easily create your own announcement lists, mailing lists and public discussions in minutes. Google Groups also makes it easier to read and participate in discussions. All the replies to an initial post are now gathered on one page. You can bookmark topics you're interested in, and have new replies to that topic delivered to your inbox.

Groove Virtual Office

Your office is where you keep your most important files, and where you meet and work with others on important tasks. These days, your office is wherever you and your wireless laptop happen to be: in a conference room, your home, an airplane, a hotel, or on-site with your customer. Groove Virtual Office allows teams of people to work together over a network as if they were in the same physical location. *Reviewer's note:* Download a free sixty-day trial version.

hotComm

hotComm provides powerful collaboration tools for group navigation to deliver guided tours around Web pages or shared files. hotComm supports shared applications where groups can access and manipulate content, including documents, spreadsheets, or Web pages together, simultaneously and securely. *Reviewer's note:* You can download hotComm Lite for free.

Infowit Creative Manager

Creative Manager is a Web-based project management software solution that allows clients, vendors, and agencies to communicate and collaborate on projects in real-time twenty-four hours a day. It includes estimating, integrated scheduling, time cards, tracking, client review and approvals, asset management, contact management and prospecting, procurement, purchasing, financials, and more. *Reviewer's note:* A collaborative project management tool that can be used for e-learning purposes.

intranets.com

Use this hosted solution to share documents in workgroup, manage projects and tasks, track group and individual calendars, communicate with customers and partners, collaborate through online discussions, and sync with Outlook and Palm. *Reviewer's note:* You can have a thirty-day free trial before you sign up.

Kavi

Kavi Workgroups is rapidly defining itself as the collaboration tool of choice for standards developing organizations and technical associations. Kavi Workgroups helps coordinate an organization's membership by providing secure workgroup areas for specification development and membership work activities. *Reviewer's note:* Managed hosting also available.

LimeWire

LimeWire is a software package that enables individuals to search for and share computer files with anyone on the Internet. A product of Lime Wire LLC, LimeWire is compatible with the Gnutella file-sharing protocol and can connect with anyone else running Gnutella-compatible software.

Magi Enterprise

Using the Magi Enterprise system, enterprises can implement ad-hoc virtual private networks for collaboration without disrupting existing applications and networks. The product does this by transforming unsecured, read-only Web networks into two-way transparent collaboration environments, through the use of such features as cross-firewall connections, advanced data extraction, an intuitive graphical interface, and universal name spaces generating "follow me URLs." *Reviewer's note:* Peer-to-peer technology.

MJI TeamWorks

MJI TeamWorks is a UK-based enterprise application that allows organizations to streamline project, resource, document, and knowledge management. One hundred percent Web-based. MJI TeamWorks can be deployed to both internal and external users, supporting collaboration in a distributed environment. *Reviewer's note:* MJI TeamWorks is a software solution that enables teams to work together more effectively.

OPMcreator

Share files, calendars, bulletin boards, 3-D CAD designs, project feedback, and much more. *Reviewer's note:* UK Web-based collaboration system with a free trial.

PopG

This browser-based collaboration service for virtual teams, which extends Groove through PopG for additional browser-based access, is a must-have for education and business. Interacting with people as well as working smarter, not harder and longer, are necessary in both places. Students must learn these skills, and organizations expect them. *Reviewer's note:* Useful for both business and education—you don't have to be using a computer that has Groove installed in order to access a Groove account.

ProjectPlace.com

Projectplace.com is a professional application service where project participants collaborate and get their work done. Projectplace.com lets users share documents and files, schedule meetings, do project scheduling with to-do items and time charts, hold online discussions, and much more. And best of all—it's absolutely free to try. *Reviewer's note:* Get started in two minutes.

Quorum Tools

Document conferencing in a box. Quorum Tools enables visual collaboration between any number of people regardless of location, in real time. As easy and as immediate to use as a telephone. No complications and no ongoing cost of use. Simple and effective. *Reviewer's note:* Much more than just an electronic whiteboard, but just as easy to use, Quorum provides a shared visual space that overcomes all these limitations. It delivers the benefits of visual thinking to all teams, local or distributed.

Same Page eStudio 6

eStudio's TaskTracker system for Web-based project management enhances your team's ability to keep track of tasks, resources, issues, and budgets. Use TaskTracker's supervisor features to provide clear analysis regarding task/issue status and to generate concise work log reports. The Web-based project management program can be operated by any member of a team, and it will help a company coordinate its efforts and run better than ever before. *Reviewer's note:* Try online project management tools free for thirty days.

Scrivlet

Scrivlet is a quick way to create and collaboratively edit notes on the Web. Use it for group shopping lists, arranging meetings, or just plain fun. *Reviewer's note:* Anyone who knows your note's URL can read, edit, or delete the material.

SmartGroups.com

SmartGroups.com is all about making life easier. It's a great new way of organizing different groups of people by using e-mail and the Internet. SmartGroups.com keeps people in touch and helps them to share information, manage events, and even make group decisions. Anyone can set up and run a SmartGroup. It's really quick, very easy, and it's free. *Reviewer's note:* SmartGroups.com combines Web-based group information with e-mail messaging, keeping group members updated about urgent or interesting group issues.

Team Workplace

IBM Lotus Team Workplace is the Web-based solution for creating team workspaces for collaboration. *Reviewer's note:* With Team Workplace, nontechnical professionals can instantly create an electronic shared workspace to support a task, project, or initiative.

TrioProject

Triotime proposes a project management solution, based on project management software (TrioProject) and training. TrioProject adapts to business needs, supporting project management method and procedures. For the steering committee, TrioProject has a project dashboard; for the project manager, TrioProject structures the project (project risk management, Gantt diagram, etc.); for the project team, TrioProject is a project groupware solution. *Reviewer's note:* Interactive demo available.

Yahoo! Groups

One e-mail address and Web site that allows you to . . . share photos and files; plan events; send a newsletter; stay in touch with friends and family; and discuss sports, health, current events, and more. *Reviewer's note:* This makes it easy for you to start your own e-mail group and manage all of your e-mail subscriptions using a simple Web interface—and it's free.

Profile 4.1 Cooking Up Knowledge Management at Pillsbury

Background

In May 1997 Pillsbury, which has brought us such household icons as the Jolly Green Giant and the Pillsbury Dough Boy and which owns the Häagen-Dazs ice cream brand, launched a knowledge management pilot project in its research-and-development division.

Founded in 1869 as a flour miller, Pillsbury is now a $6.2 billion-a-year market leader in many baked and frozen food categories. In 1989, the Minneapolis-based food company merged with UK conglomerate Grand Metropolitan, which later combined with Guinness (beer) to form Diageo. Diageo's four main businesses are Burger King, Pillsbury, Guinness, and United Distillers & Vintners.

Knowledge Management Strategy

Pillsbury's strategy was to bring new products to market more quickly by implementing knowledge management practices in the company's 550-person R&D organization.

Structure

Pillsbury's knowledge effort breaks down into four divisions: information management, continuous learning and performance support, technology knowledge center, and knowledge management strategy. These fall under two officers of the company, the CIO and CTO. While three sections report to the CTO, information management, which deploys information systems, reports to the CIO.

Success Story

Under Pillsbury's old system, it took seventeen signatures and nearly ninety days to run a label design through the entire organization. Each label had to get approval from marketing, food safety, nutritionists, consumer response, and many other internal divisions that contribute to label content and design. With the knowledge management program in place, it takes just nine days to approve a new label.

Another special knowledge management project was creating a virtual library, where employees can find research patents, recipe specifications, and engineering processes as well as business and technical documents. Other knowledge management activities are underway throughout Pillsbury. Parent company Diageo is watching closely to assess prospects for knowledge programs in its other business units.

(Source: Bruce Culberson, "Cooking Up KM at Pillsbury," *Knowledge Management* magazine, October 1998. Used with permission. For further information see the profile on the Ark Group, the magazine's publisher, in chapter I.)

KNOWLEDGE MANAGEMENT SOFTWARE

The successful rollout of knowledge management software requires knowledge and concepts, methods, processes, and techniques that support the ability of the software system to change, evolve, and survive in the marketplace. The process begins with the initial development and configuration of the system then proceeds through its installation, day-to-day operation, and maintenance. It may eventually include re-implementing the system to increase its maintainability or to make major changes in system requirements.

Knowledge and concepts support understanding how software systems evolve, studying and analyzing their maintenance costs, developing and using processes that are needed for effective and efficient maintenance, and creating strategies to deal with legacy systems. It's important to note that "in every technical workgroup, there is one go-to person, that guy or gal who just seems to know everything there is to know about the software. Often this person has to juggle between their formal work requirements and the constant interruptions from co-workers who 'need to know just one thing.' When that person is unavailable, group productivity suffers."[2]

Knowledge management software installation is concerned with methods and techniques for installing a software product and continuing its effective operation. This aspect provides for a system's smooth, orderly transition from the developer organization to the user organization, and includes the documentation and training necessary for proper system operation. In the paper "An Ontology-Based Knowledge Model for Software Experience Management," by Abdulmajid H. Mohame, Sai Peck Lee, and Siti Salwah Salim of the University of Malaya, it's noted that one of the crucial decisions to be made when building and rolling out a knowledge management solution is the characterization of the knowledge components to consider.

Mohame, Lee, and Salim agree that organizational knowledge can be categorized as either tacit or explicit. As discussed previously, tacit (soft) knowledge refers to knowledge that typically isn't explicitly captured—knowledge usually held in an individual's memory in the form of perceptions, beliefs, viewpoints, and know-how. Explicit (hard) knowledge refers to any knowledge that can be documented, archived, and codified. This includes plans, business documents, guidelines, process models, and other types of knowledge. An organization has little control over the usage and lifetime of tacit knowledge, although it could represent a threat to that organization's business interests. The emerging challenge is how to recognize, generate, share, and manage tacit knowledge.

The biggest barrier to knowledge sharing is an inability to share understanding of key concepts, which is in some cases partially solved by the use of an ontology-based knowledge management model.

Designers and implementers of software-oriented knowledge management tools will have a strong motivation to use some type of ontology-based knowledge model[3] to record and retrieve experience knowledge. The model's underlying knowledge infrastructure includes various types of integrated ontology, thereby representing experience knowledge as a semantic network through which conceptual search tools and engines can be employed.

Since knowledge management components are usually created or modified collaboratively, any knowledge generated as the outcome of such collaborative knowledge filtering needs to be captured as part of the history ontology. According to Mohame, Lee, and Salim this aspect is crucial in capturing tacit knowledge.

This model is simple, but powerful enough to model various types of knowledge management experience components in software, such as test suite, functional diagrams, code, tables, data models, development tools, and screenshots along with bug workaround, installation procedures, and knowledge management process descriptions.

And let's not forget about a final category for lessons learned, which aligns directly with the knowledge management component ontology.

KNOWLEDGE MANAGEMENT STRATEGIC TECHNOLOGY PLAN

Most organizations have an array of knowledge management IT systems. Frequently, they include enterprise resource planning (ERP), computer-aided design (CAD), geographic information systems (GIS), building automation systems (BAS), capital planning systems (CPS), computerized maintenance management systems (CMMS), and computer-aided facility management (CAFM). Yet few facility managers report that they achieve the anticipated increase in productivity. Systems are frequently underutilized.

The failure of knowledge management technologies is often related to poor planning and use rather than a system's inability to perform. Invariably, a specific knowledge management strategic technology plan is an essential precursor to installing knowledge technology that produces the desired results. Even when an installation is successful, if an organization doesn't plan properly it will have questions demanding attention and resolution. Following a defined process to develop a strategic technology plan can provide significant benefits for both new installations and existing systems. Whether acquiring a new technology system or simply repurposing an existing one, an appropriate technology plan should take a whole-system perspective. A primary need for a whole-system focus arises from the fact that most organizations that have installed knowledge management technology use only a small fraction of the capability that's been licensed and installed.

Often, managers complain that the KMS they've installed doesn't work. The reality is that software generally does what the vendor says it can do. A system's failure lies in problems such as using the wrong software, using the right software for unclear reasons, poor software configuration, poor training, a low level of user and manager commitment, or an inefficient and confounded database structure. Knowledge management technology has increased the role and visibility of CIOs, and has provided increased management efficiencies. This has created increased reliance on information and a boom of new technology and software vendors.

Among the key benefits of using and optimizing knowledge management technologies are:

- Improved communication
- Increased workforce efficiency
- Improved maintenance quality and labor tracking
- Organized knowledge management data
- Improved tracking of knowledge and intellectual capital
- Lowering an organization's total cost of knowledge (TCK)

The overall goal of a strategic technology plan is to reflect an organization as a single system. This involves integrating individual knowledge and corporate data. When creating a strategic technology plan, understand that all stakeholders have expectations about what will be involved in the installation and optimization phase. These stakeholders should understand the significance, complexity, and time required to configure the database and train all users.

THE KNOWLEDGE MANAGEMENT OPTIMIZATION ROLLOUT PROCESS

Recommended knowledge management technology optimization rollout process steps include:

Needs Evaluation

The concept of client-centered knowledge management is integral to this process. It's critical to view the process as a systems approach, one that focuses the outcome on the needs of stakeholders. The needs evaluation identifies the needs and expectations of executives, staff, and administrators. Interviews are typically a good way to gain needed insight.

Technology Audit

The technology audit includes a careful evaluation of hardware, software, and personnel. Assess IT infrastructure for capacity, scalability, and performance of Web- or client-based servers; terminal units; backup and disaster-recovery systems; cabling; or wireless network infrastructures and handheld devices. Software audits require focusing on the requirements and capabilities of existing systems as well as desired ones. Data integrity and the suitability of system configurations should also be addressed in this step. A strengths, weaknesses, opportunities, and threats (SWOT) analysis will help determine the best knowledge management deployment options.

KM Process Analyses

The next step requires thorough documentation of knowledge management workflow. Knowledge management process analyses can developed with deployment charts of all relevant processes, including service calls, preventive maintenance, third-party contractors, project management, knowledge management, inventory control, and asset-management. Determine the touch points of technology, where knowledge management systems support these processes. Finally, evaluate processes and leverage points to reduce delays, increase efficiency, minimize problems, enhance communication, and optimize performance.

Strategic Plan

Armed with a thorough understanding of needs, current resources, and work processes, organizations should commission a knowledge management technology advisory committee. The committee, consisting of the right mix of cross-discipline users, needs to "own" the knowledge management technology system, then develop and commit to a strategic plan. The plan includes descriptions, rules, and processes for:

- Developing and maintaining long-term knowledge management standards
- System administration (installing updates and upgrades, and troubleshooting)
- Data maintenance, reporting processes, and procedures for quality assurance and quality control
- Enhancing identification and prioritization
- Report development, validation, and rollout
- User rights, roles, and responsibilities
- User training programs
- Continuous improvements

Metrics and Reports

In this step, refine benchmarking and metrics, preferably using knowledge management technology to provide the measurement. Analyze effective processes, document them accurately, and report them in ways that make decisions clear. Also identify key performance indicators. These system drivers highlight the few success factors that, when performing properly, significantly increase the likelihood of knowledge management technology success.

Improvements

The final step includes systematically carrying out continuous improvements. Proceed one step at a time, focusing on small successes in key knowledge management areas and reporting improvements to maintain organizational support.

Useful KM Technology Plan Questions

Knowledge management strategic technology rollout plans answer the following critical questions to achieve success:

- Who needs to participate on the technology advisory team?
- Who needs to commit to the strategic plan's objectives?
- What are the roles of staff, vendors, and consultants in preparing a plan?
- What should be included in the plan?
- What are the predictable dos and don'ts?
- Are the right expectations included in the strategic plan?

RETRIEVE: AN EASY-TO-USE SYSTEM

Retrieve (*www.retrieve.com*, formerly known as Anzwerz.com) is a Web-based knowledge management system.[4] In many cases, knowledge management software tends to be expensive, complex, and neglected in day-to-day practice. It requires a "go-to person" to change his or her work habits, never an inviting prospect. Average users tend to view knowledge management software as a crutch. Ideal software should banish all myths and misconceptions about knowledge management with a user-friendly approach to gathering and disseminating information. The ideal KMS needs to be a Web-based system that enables a team—local or dispersed—to quickly and efficiently compile answers to questions asked by other team members, clients, or (if you implement it on the Internet) anybody online. The software needs to be designed to track and retrieve information for frequently asked questions, and should be based on a simple question-and-answer model. In other words, when a question is posted to the system, it's posted on a Web page that designated experts can see; a manager should also be able to route the question. When the question is answered, it will become part of the organization's database.

Functioning as a Web-based information publishing and retrieval system, Retrieve instantly provides answers to people seeking information. By matching natural language questions with information found in a knowledge base, the system quickly finds all relevant information—answering 80 to 90 percent of all questions—and facilitates an accurate response to remaining questions. Retrieve can function as a Web site, intranet, or Web engine. The Retrieve engine captures, organizes, publishes, and readily accesses information via a browser—greatly increasing an organization's productivity, efficiency, and customer service. The Retrieve engine enables nontechnical staff to easily revise, update, and add new documents, regardless of their format. An organization using Retrieve can control the amount and type of information staff, customers, and vendors can access.

At an implementation preview of Retrieve, the demonstrator showed how the software is implemented (as either an active server page or an enterprise application), and how the distributed nature of the query-and-retrieval process makes it easy to maintain and use. The system can also calculate how much money an organization saves by using the system. For example, the system manager can assign a dollar value to each time Retrieve answers a query instead of an employee. If it costs nine dollars in company overhead every time an expert has to stop other duties to respond to a question, Retrieve tracks those transactional savings over time.

Underlying Retrieve's performance is a somewhat sophisticated structured query language (SQL) database. Answers to queries can be provided in any digital file format commonly displayed in a Web browser. Through continued use, the database not only becomes a repository of questions and answers, but also creates historical records of communications and issues.

Retrieve may become important to an organization in the following ways:

- Alerting team members to project-related changes
- Settling disputes by reviewing the historical record
- Improving collaboration by supporting the natural question and answer process
- Becoming the central repository of knowledge management information

The price of Retrieve installation depends on the format (ASP or enterprise) and the size of the organization. The city of Henniker, New Hampshire, pays thirty dollars per month to use Retrieve software on its public Web site, to answer common questions from city residents. The actual fee for the ASP version is based on traffic, number of administrators, and other factors. Enterprise installation starts at $3,000, with a typical installation costing between $4,500 and $6,500. Compared to other knowledge management products with similar goals, Retrieve is priced at about 10 percent of the usual price—quite a discount.

According to users, Retrieve "eats its own dog food," a most important measure of a software's real value, as the following story indicates. One day Dave Arnold, CEO of Retrieve Technologies Inc., realized he and other experienced employees were spending time showing new employees how to shut off the building alarm system. So he took two minutes to record a video showing how to shut off the alarm, and posted the video to the Retrieve Technologies internal site. "We answered a common question, solved a real knowledge management issue, and we did it with no IT involvement," as Arnold puts it.

Companies searching for low-priced knowledge management solutions can use Retrieve as their ready-made internal intranet, complete with forms, statements of policy, and other useful templates. The ease with which the site can be maintained means it should avoid the fate of many internal corporate knowledge management Web sites—disuse and increased obsolescence. Retrieve is ready for the WiFi era, too, with the ability to reformat the presentation screen when accessed by a personal digital assistant (PDA). Retrieve appears to be a

Profile 4.2 AutoSupportDesk: A Joint Venture Between KTeK Solutions and Retrieve

Background

Launched in 2004 with the goal of bringing affordable computer-aided design (CAD) technical support to the masses, AutoSupportDesk.com, a platform designed by Retrieve Media, has been a success since its inception. KTek Solutions is comprised of a team of certified CAD consultants dispersed throughout the United States. The company is among the foremost authorities on all things CAD, and is one of the nation's leading CAD consultants and trainers.

Knowledge Management Strategy

KTek came to realize that although its technical support is highly specialized, over time the company was repeatedly answering the same questions. As each new support issue arose, the consultants recognized that similar questions were likely to be asked by many more people in the future. Was there a means to track questions then link repetitive questions with similar questions and appropriate answers? Was it possible to present answers in multimedia formats? These questions were the basis for the development of an affordable automated online support system that would provide people with high-quality responses to technical questions.

Traditional searches on Web sites are just that—searches. AutoSupportDesk.com is vastly different. Whenever a question is asked, the system instantly links the question to the correct answer. If an answer is not in the knowledge base, a person can submit the question directly then receive a personal mail response from a certified CAD consultant. That answer is then captured by the Retrieve engine, and automatically added to the knowledge base—so the next time someone asks the same question, Retrieve will know the answer and reply automatically.

Success Story

AutoSupportDesk.com is an affordable 24/7 support solution for Autodesk products. In addition to automated multimedia support, it provides five other support options, including personal e-mail, instant messaging, phone, and webinar. It uses the Retrieve search engine to capture, organize, publish, and deliver relevant information to those needing answers. Retrieve matches natural language questions with information found in a detailed knowledge base. Retrieve efficiently manages support solutions, notifying support professionals about incoming questions and managing timely responses by experts most knowledgeable in specific disciplines.

Knowledge management Web tools such as Retrieve can help transform a company's Web site into an active knowledge management information sharing system by delivering the following benefits:

- Simplifying delivery and access to needed information
- Enhancing and improving customer service by providing instant answers to questions
- Delivering searchable manuals and other communication online
- Measuring customer inquiries, to guide product development and improvements
- Increasing sales by turning site visitors into customers
- Producing sales leads by capturing contact information for future marketing

(Source: Strategy Associates Inc. Used with permission. For more information, contact Frank Voehl at *fvoehl@aol. com*.)

good-value software offering that would create instant productivity improvements wherever it's installed. Also, Retrieve is an interactive information query and retrieval system. Traditional searches on Web sites are just that—searches. The Retrieve knowledge retrieval system is soon populated with answers to all of the most common questions and other information that a company wishes to make available to its staff and customers.

The Retrieve system links natural language questions with answers found in an organization's knowledge base. But if an answer isn't found, the person asking the question is able to submit the question via e-mail. An administrator is automatically notified, and responds with a personal e-mail. That response is then captured by the Retrieve engine and becomes part of the company's knowledge system. The next time someone asks the same question, Retrieve will know the answer. Thereby an organization's Web site continues to get smarter every time.

Costs and Revenues

Of the total budget to install a KMS, usually 20 to 30 percent is spent on external IT services and software. IBM, Lotus, and Microsoft are the leading suppliers of knowledge management technology. Software will typically account for about 10 percent of the KMS budget. Typically it's spent on the following:

- Enterprise information portals
- Document management
- Groupware
- Workflow
- Data warehouse
- Search engines
- Web-based training
- Messaging

The Radicati Group, based in Palo Alto, California, estimated that knowledge management-related applications generated the following revenues in 2004:

- Portals ($2.5 billion)
- Search engines ($1.9 billion)
- Workflow tracking ($1.2 billion)
- Document management ($1.6 billion)
- Content management ($1.1 billion)
- Real-time collaboration ($650 million)
- Distance learning ($1.12 billion)

Figure 4.2 List of Software Developers

Software developers	Data capture, mining report analysis, business intelligence	Knowledge management infrastructure technologies	Knowledge management	Portals, Web services	Search engines, agents, wizards
80-20 Software		x	x		x
Anacubis	x	x	x		x
Captiva Software Corp.	x				
ClearForest	x				x
Convera	x	x	x	x	x
Copernic Technologies Inc.	x		x		x
Document Imaging Solutions Inc.	x	x			
DST Technologies Inc.			x		
eiStream Inc.	x		x		
Entopia Inc.	x	x	x	x	x
Exact Software North America			x	x	
Fast Search & Transfer (FAST)	x		x	x	x
Hummingbird Ltd.	x	x	x	x	
Hyland Software Inc.	x	x	x		
Identitech Inc.	x		x		
Image Processing Technologies Inc.	x		x		
Inmagic Inc.	x		x		
InSystems Corp.			x		
Integrify				x	
Inxight Software Inc.		x	x		x
Kamoon Inc.	x	x	x		
KMTechnologies Inc.		x	x	x	x
LEGATO Software	x	x	x		
Liberty IMS	x	x	x	x	x
Lockheed Martin Corp.	x	x	x		
Noetix Corp.	x				
Open Text Corp.		x	x	x	x
Primus Knowledge Solutions Inc.	x	x	x	x	x
RedDot Solutions			x		
ServiceWare Technologies Inc.	x	x	x	x	x
SiteScape Inc.			x		
Stellent Inc.		x	x	x	
Stratify Inc.	x	x	x		x
SupportSoft	x	x	x	x	x
TheBrain Technologies Corp.	x	x	x	x	x
Thomson Elite			x		
TimeVision Inc.	x		x		
TOWER Software	x	x	x		
TripleHop Technologies		x	x	x	x
Ultimus	x	x	x	x	x
Verity Inc.		x		x	x
ZyLAB North America LLC			x		

You need software that runs in the background process, classifying information into a taxonomy of concepts
by comparing the statistical patterns embedded within the
documents against concept models derived from artificial
intelligence and information theory (e.g., Semio Corp.,
Autonomy Inc., and Stratify Inc.).

Figure 4.2 shows a list of software developers and their
related solutions.

BUILDING BLOCKS FOR A SUCCESSFULLY IMPLEMENTED KNOWLEDGE MANAGEMENT SYSTEM

When considering the construction of a KMS, there are seven key building blocks: business intelligence, knowledge discovery and mapping, expertise location, collaboration,
knowledge transfer, semantic modeling, and knowledge management portals.[5]

The First Five Building Blocks Summarized

Business intelligence (BI) describes the processes that together enable improved decision
making. BI includes data mining and warehousing, online analytical processing (OLAP),
and other advanced technologies that can glean valuable insights from stored data. Knowledge discovery includes text-mining techniques that enable knowledge discovery from
text sources, and knowledge mapping is the technique of representing knowledge sources
(people and information) in a context defined by their relationships. Expertise location
includes finding, cataloging, and making available the best expertise available in the corporation when needed for business decision-making.

Collaboration enables people to share information, expertise, and insights, a process
that should amplify tacit knowledge and enhance innovation and motivation. Knowledge
transfer extends the reach of available knowledge and skills, to transfer resources to remote
locations and enable virtual teams to perform at high levels.

Building Block Six: Semantic Modeling

Semantic modeling technology provided a major breakthrough in knowledge management. Prior to semantic modeling, information capture and retrieval technologies and collaboration tools focused on content. Semantic modeling technology connects associated
context to content, greatly increasing the functionality of the KMS. Content may take the
form of ideas, documents, e-mails, and facts. Context adds meaning to content by recognizing and combining related content, to derive greater meaning. This relationship between
different content objects enables a user to draw conclusions with a high degree of accuracy,
knowledge of much greater value than the individual data points alone can provide.

Building Block Seven: Knowledge Management Portals

Everyone is familiar with portal services like Yahoo! Portals categorize information into knowledge silos, to serve a customer's special interests. They group information by interest groupings, such as stock prices, news, sports, and entertainment. This allows for easy browsing within these information groups. Major groups are often divided into subgroups, for ease of use. This same technology allows personalized portals to provide easy access to changing information that's of interest to a specific individual. Portals provide the primary interface between knowledge warehouses and knowledge stakeholders.

> **"You can call it a portal. We call it a place to share knowledge."**
> **—Anders Hemre**
> **Owner, interKnowledge Technologies**

KMS users want to go to one place to get the knowledge they need. They don't want to research multiple documents just to find a few key nuggets. They want the digested knowledge to be presented in a user-friendly format. A well-designed portal will do all of this if it has a good knowledge warehouse behind it.

By the end of 2005, 65 percent of the Global 2000 companies listed by Forbes were expected to have portals in place for their employees. There are four basic types of portals:

> **"Fifty percent of leading-edge technology-driven companies will incorporate an enterprise portal and most of those will include an enterprisewide entry point for employees to access and share information throughout the organization."**
> **—Gartner Group**

- *Corporate portals*. Usually support a large organization's core knowledge areas. They contain a lot of detailed information about specific limited subjects.
- *Published portals*. Designed to serve stakeholders with varied backgrounds and interests. They have little ability to be customized except for online search engines such as the ones used on the Web.
- *Personal portals*. Customized and designed for the individual that will be using it. The knowledge warehouse is filtered to present only what an individual's interested in.
- *Commercial portals*. Often referred to as "channels" because they put Web information into a standard format. They're subject-matter specific and appeal to people interested in specific information, like stock prices or news.

The Army Knowledge Online (AKO) portal serves 1.6 million soldiers, both active and retired. The present version of AKO was developed during the summer of 2001 and was designed to meet the need of Army personnel around the world. It includes elements such as:

> **"The Army Knowledge Online portal can be traced back to the Army's strategy to transform it into a network-centric, knowledge-based force and is a critical enabler of Army knowledge management."**
> **—Col. Timothy A. Fong**
> **Director, U.S. Army Chief Technology Office**

- Instant messaging
- Collaboration
- Whiteboarding

"Mold the IT system to fit the people that will use it. Don't ask the people to change to fit the system."

—HJH

"At the individual level, everyone who logs in can see information about his or her last medical exam, dental exam, test results, and vaccinations that are required. You can see right away whether or not you are deployable. If there are problems, you can see what you need to do to correct them."
—Col. Timothy A. Fong
Director, U.S. Army Chief
Technology Office

The AKO portal was developed using Appian Portal from Appian Corp. (*www.appiancorp.com*) as a hub for the Army's knowledge communities, collaboration, and e-mail. The portal provides a communication channel where late-breaking news items and policy statements are updated. It's also used to transmit logistics, personnel, and training information. It also serves as the center for all personalized medical records.

An effective employee portal integrates four relationships:

- *Employee to organization.* Human resource information and activities such as personnel data, vacation, and education.
- *Employee to work activity.* Tools and knowledge directly related to employee skills.
- *Employee to employee.* Establishing and supporting collaboration between employees. Knowledge sharing is a must for all organizations.
- *Employee to the outside world.* This part of the portal recognizes that employees have an outside life. It provides both internal and external knowledge related to nonorganizational activities such as news, travel, financial planning, education, and entertainment.

There are three common approaches to establishing a portal program. All three approaches will take between four to six months to prepare the first release:

- Organizationwide
- Business function
- Core capabilities and/or correspondence

The organizationwide approach usually starts out as a very shallow portal with general organizational content and becomes more robust over time. This approach is usually effective at reaching a large audience quickly, but it lacks depth and often disappoints employees before there's a chance to develop more meaningful content.

"To be truly effective, portals have to acknowledge that employees have a life away from work and that it's very important to them."
—Francine Haddock
Portal specialist, Accenture

The business-function approach sets up a pilot project in a specific area, such as sales, engineering, or procurement. This approach provides a concentrated knowledge package that's specifically oriented to work assignments. It has much more depth and is more valuable to users, but it reaches only a small part of an organization's population. Its content will also grow over time as content and functions are added.

The last, recommended approach is to develop a portal directed at an organization's core capabilities and competencies. This approach begins by focusing upon the most important knowledge points within the organization, and additional scope is added over time based upon the organization's priorities.

> **"In 2001, more than 50 percent of leading-edge, technology-driven companies will incorporate an enterprise portal, and most of those will include an enterprisewide entry point for employees to access and share information throughout the organization."**
> **—Gene Phifer**
> **Vice president and distinguished analyst, Gartner Group**

SUMMARY

The defining question seems to be: Where is the need for knowledge management most critical?[6] Ironically, critical knowledge is that which hasn't yet been identified, articulated, or tracked. It's called critical not necessarily because it's so important, but because it's an unknown, and exposure for organizational loss is also unknown. Excluding the management of financial data or business intelligence systems, knowledge management implies some degree of formal document management and related enablers for collaboration and workflow.

> **"No person or company should be content to stay where they are, no matter how successful they now seem to be."**
> **—Stephen R. Covey**
> ***The Seven Habits of Highly Effective People***

Each industry has some requirement to manage its knowledge in a formal manner. This is especially true for the industries of manufacturing, with its prints, specifications, standards, and best practices; finance, with its loan packets and portfolios; insurance, with claims and policies; government, with procedures, legislation, and policies; and professional services, with résumés, reports and proposals. In other industries—such as entertainment, professional services, government research, and retail service industries, with their specific skill bases—knowledge is embedded in peoples' heads. In still other industries, knowledge is embedded in suppliers or customers. Coupled with the creation and effective implementation of processes, policies, business software, and organizational structure, knowledge management implementation easier to justify because the investment in technology has usually already been made.[7]

Traditional operations management solutions are typically unable to provide the detail, responsiveness, and flexibility needed to support exploratory analysis and real-time process monitoring. These operational requirements are best treated in real-time management information systems that maintain more detail for shorter periods of time and are specifically designed for monitoring, exploration, and problem-solving functions.[8]

REFERENCES

1. Listings and reviewer's notes are provided by the e-Learning Centre, a UK-based organization that provides independent advice, consultancy, and professional development services on all aspects of e-learning to both large and small organizations, as well as to colleges and universities. For more information, see *www.e-learningcentre.co.uk/eclipse/vendors/collaboration.htm*.

2. Mohame, Abdulmajid H., Sai Peck Lee, and Siti Salwah Salim, University of Malaya. "An Ontology-Based Knowledge Model for Software Experience Management," *Journal of Knowledge Management Practice*, May 2004. See *www.tlainc.com/articl67.htm*.

3. Ibid.

4. Newton, Randall S. "Retrieve: Knowledge Management Software for the Rest of Us," published in the online newsletter AECnews.com, March 2005. Editor's Note: This is a revised version of an article originally published in *AECnews*, June 2004. Enough has changed with the company to warrant a revision. *http://aecnews.com/articles/999.aspx*.

5. Tkach, Daniel. "Advances in Knowledge Management," *Knowledge Management*, March 1999. Daniel Tkach is IBM's worldwide marketing manager for knowledge management solutions. He serves as technology director at the Institute for Knowledge Management.

6. Interviews with Rian M. Gorey (Arthur Andersen's director of knowledge services), Robin Nelson, and Gregory Gillett (KPMG's director of knowledge management practice), who have been writing about technology for national magazines since 1980. Nelson is the founding editor-in-chief of *Information Technology Advisor*, a newsletter for IT managers in midsize and entrepreneurial firms.

7. Schwartz, Peter. *The Art of the Long View: Planning for the Future in an Uncertain World* (New York: Doubleday, 1996). A founder of the Global Business Network, Schwartz uses real-world case studies to demonstrate how scenario planning is more useful than applying quantitative predictive models.

8. Pearson, Thomas. "Measurements and the Knowledge Revolution," *Quality Progress*, September 1999.

CHAPTER V

BEST PRACTICES IN KNOWLEDGE MANAGEMENT

"Know what's best and then improve upon it."
—HJH

In its initial stages, knowledge management has been applied most fully in industries that are process-intensive, research-driven, information-based, logistical, or subject to deregulation. From this base, knowledge practices will spread to many more sectors in the years to come. These include:

- *Telecommunications.* With an explosive mixture of technology and competition providing the infrastructure for the new economy, the business differentiator is knowledge.

- *A/E/C.* The architecture, engineering, and construction of large building projects require creating and exchanging knowledge among the parties involved.

> "Not too long ago, back in the 'dark ages' of the 1970s, a coffee machine and a water cooler was the only technology needed to facilitate in-house knowledge sharing."
> **—Frank Voehl**

- *Transportation.* Moving people and freight is the end result, but efficient transportation increasingly involves information. Logistics systems ensure profitable operations.

- *Media and entertainment.* Content industries sell information as product. Increasingly, digital media are replacing books, newspapers, and other traditional forms of media as core information segments are redefined.

- *Energy.* Competition in the gas and electric utilities markets will drive innovations. Petroleum discovery, extraction, and refining are knowledge-based processes.

- *Pharmaceuticals.* Development of new drug therapies is a knowledge-enabled process that involves biological science, product development, and regulatory approval.

- *Chemicals.* Regulatory compliance and production efficiencies weighed against risk assessment yield knowledge-based product innovation and market advantage.

- *Technology.* Computer hardware and software embody knowledge as functionality. Information industries rely heavily on management of intellectual property rights.

- *Financial and legal services.* From banking to insurance, securities, and law offices, new financial products and legal services are information-based. When knowledge is managed, it accelerates innovation.

Profile 5.1 Brodeur Porter Novelli: Demonstrating the Value of Shared Knowledge

Background

Brodeur Porter Novelli, a fairly young, growing team devoted to public relations and client service, has developed a sophisticated system to ensure that all employees have access to the company's collected intelligence. "We want to tap into each other's brains," says Jan Lawlor, senior vice president.

Knowledge Management Strategy and Structure

This KMS has been accomplished through a series of databases, including the company intranet, which is used for internal knowledge sharing and management, and The Knowledge Network, a customized internal system that shares information about employees, services, and skills.

These databases, networked with a Lotus Notes Domino backbone, put people in contact with each other for true collaboration, according to Jennifer Wysocki, marketing communications manager at Brodeur Porter Novelli. "If you needed an expert on HTML programming who is fluent in French and has experience developing extranets, you could execute a search, and the Knowledge Network will tell you who meets that search criteria," she says.

Success Story

When the company rolled out its KMS in December 1996, it was quickly adopted in part because upper management was involved from the start, according to Wysocki. "Management, in turn, rallied the troops, getting their buy-in early on. We empowered the people to drive this initiative, having teams identify client and employee needs, along with the best systems and practices to meet both. And then we made it measurable so we could track responses and usage to refine the system."

Employees tap into The Knowledge Network system through the company intranet, Connect, so response and usage can be measured much like hits on Web sites. By monitoring such feedback, management is able to address lower-usage areas using focus groups, small team meetings, and informal surveys.

"Once we identify some causes for low usage, we can make adjustments, put it back on Connect, and let people know what's changed. Then we're back to measuring usage again. It's an ongoing cycle, but if knowledge management is going to work it's necessary," Wysocki says. "Generally, the end users see value in the process and haven't needed any additional incentives."

(Source: Michelle Delio, "Keys to Collaboration," *Knowledge Management* magazine, October 1998. Used with permission. For further information see the profile on the Ark Group, the magazine's publisher, in chapter I.)

- *Consumer products.* Packaged goods are developed, marketed, and delivered to consumers via information systems. Retailers are on the front lines of customer service.
- *Health care.* Changes in the U.S. health care system are enabled by knowledge from insurance companies, hospital administration, and individual health workers.

BENCHMARKING KNOWLEDGE MANAGEMENT SYSTEMS

The purpose of doing a knowledge management benchmark study is to define the best practices for harnessing the accumulated intellectual accomplishments of an organization's employees and managers. Benchmark studies related to the systems of knowledge management suggest that best practices include:

- Setting up portals as the major interface with network users. Cap Gemini Ernst & Young (CGEY) has one of the most advanced portal systems, with the portal customized to the individual user.
- Using data warehouses for collecting all inputs.
- Collecting public domain data for databases.
- Using communities of practice to collect and exchange information.
- Avoiding monetary awards to encourage contributions to the (KMS). Many organizations tried monetary awards, but stopped because they didn't work.
- Rewriting job descriptions to include knowledge management, and changing employees appraisal systems to make knowledge management a major category.
- Adding a chief knowledge officer (CKO) as needed. Of all the organizations visited, only IBM and CGEY had hired a CKO. The CKOs were required in both cases due to the numbers of people worldwide who needed to be motivated to contribute information into the database, and who needed training on how to use the KMS. In these cases the CKO was central to changing the organization's international culture and keeping the KMS active in hundreds of simultaneous projects.
- Assigning a facilitator to each community of practice. Knowledge management is a major assignment and takes a lot of time and experience.
- Assigning a content expert to each major knowledge category, to select essential data for the knowledge database. Only screened data should be included.
- Top management continuously demonstrating strong support for the KMS, in order to change the organization's culture.
- Encouraging personal contact for communities of practice, through e-mail and scheduled face-to-face meetings. Knowledge management won't succeed if only the Web site is relied upon for information.

ORGANIZATIONAL CHANGE MANAGEMENT FOR KNOWLEDGE MANAGEMENT SYSTEMS

There have been numerous KMS failures, or efforts that at best haven't reached their full potential, because organizations relied on technology to drive them without considering essential culture changes. This is a sure way to waste both time and money. The source of knowledge is people, and if you can't convince them that they'll benefit more from sharing their knowledge than hoarding it, then even the most elaborate and costly KMS will fail. If knowledge flows out of a KMS but little new, updated data and information are deposited, the system will quickly become obsolete and an organizational handicap rather than a competitive advantage.

> **"Knowledge management without respect, integrity, and trust is chaos and failure."**
> **—Curtis R. Carlson**
> **CEO, SRI International**

The organizational change management (OCM) methodology discussed in book III of this series, *Change Management Excellence,* presents current best practices related to making this cultural transformation. When required to drastically change behavioral patterns throughout an organization, as a KMS needs, your KMS team must include individuals with specials skills and training in behavioral modification. For this reason a cultural change agent skilled in OCM should be one of the first members selected for a KMS team.

> **"We have to learn more things and learn them faster. And we have to master our knowledge, not just acquire it."**
> **—Bob Galvin**
> **Former CEO and current chairman of the board, Motorola**

The primary objective of a KMS is to transform an organization from a knowledge-hoarding to a knowledge-sharing culture. The purpose of a KMS is not to establish knowledge portals, establish communities of practice, or to bring online all of the best research papers, books, and periodicals. Yes, these are effective tools for selecting and transporting knowledge, but the heart of an effective KMS is an organization's culture. Putting software in place is an easy job; getting people to use it and provide reliable data and information is the real challenge—90 percent of the work—and the primary reason for KMS failures.

Such a major culture shift won't happen by itself. It requires a carefully considered approach, one that will break down people's natural resistance to change and build up their resiliency, making employees more adaptable to the continuously changing organizational environment.

People like to feel that they are in control of their environments. Most people are most comfortable and confident when their expectations of control, stability, and predictability are satisfied. The comfort of the *status quo* comes from these expectations. An individual may not be happy with the status quo, but in most cases that individual has learned to accept it and has developed methods that allow him or her to exist in that environment. For example, most people dislike the daily deluge of e-mails—the status quo—and to survive it, they establish some system to analyze e-mails, to distinguish those that are essential to our operation from those that aren't. *Change* is when this system suddenly shifts, and expectations are disrupted. In other words, *change* is defined as a disruption of expectations. Another example: If an employee comes to work one morning and discovers that his or her desk is gone, that is *change*. How would someone feel under those circumstances—upset? Angry? Would that person wonder if the management team had forgotten to mention something important, particularly if a group of consultants had been wandering through the office looking for ways to improve organizational efficiency?

When change occurs, the four Cs are disrupted:

- *Competence.* You question if you'll be competent to function in the future role.
- *Comfort.* You're uncomfortable with the situation because you don't have a complete understanding of what's going to happen.
- *Confidence.* You're not confident about what your future role will be.
- *Control.* You've lost control over your future destiny.

Disruption of the four Cs produces bad results throughout the organization. It brings about:

- Low stability
- High stress
- Decreasing productivity
- Anxiety
- Fear
- Increased conflict

> "Only 5 percent of the organizations in the West truly excel. Their secret isn't what they do, but how they do it. They're the ones that manage the change process."
>
> —HJH

A critical component of an integrated KMS is a structured and disciplined process for managing and implementing change. The adoption of a KMS philosophy will create organizational change that will have a major impact upon the organization members' current beliefs, behavior, knowledge, and expectations. To make this challenge even more demanding, changes brought about by implementing a KMS will affect people who are probably already overwhelmed with accelerating change in their professional and private lives. Therefore, all organization members must realize that organizational change can and must be managed. Change must be seen as a manageable process made up of three major stages: the current, transitional, and future states.

Profile 5.2 The World Bank KMS Clearinghouse

Background

The World Bank is leveraging global knowledge sharing through its KMS to attain its goal of becoming a clearinghouse for expertise on sustainable development. The mission of the World Bank is to alleviate poverty and improve living standards in the poor countries of the world. For more information on the World Bank's KMS, go to *www.worldbank.org/ks/*.

Knowledge Management Strategy

Knowledge management is key to helping the World Bank accomplish its mission. In the past, when a country's leader asked for help a team would be selected to conduct a study. Now when a request is made, such as when Pakistan requested new technology for a deteriorating highway system, a task manager contacts a "community practice" expert to ask for advice on applying technologies and global experience. This information is then shared and stored in a knowledge database for future use. The World Bank's KMS includes 110 communities of practice around the world that are in the process of connecting with each other.

Success Story

The World Bank's KMS is a systematic approach to capturing and organizing the wealth of knowledge and experience gained by their stakeholders (clients, partners, staff, etc.). The program is called Knowledge Sharing (KS). The World Bank has created a collaborative, multi-directional, international, continuous, and active knowledge sharing and learning process designed to:

- Support the bank's knowledge community. More than 100 different thematic groups share practices and results.
- Support advisory services. The KMS provides important information that is used by the bank's twenty advisory services to process thousands of inquiries yearly.
- Support a worldwide development forum. Online discussions bring together thousands of practitioners from nongovernmental organizations, universities, research institutes, and development agencies to share knowledge and learning.
- Facilitate communities of practice. The KMS supports new communities of practice in key development areas.
- Serve as knowledge portals and advisory service. The many KMS portals serve as repositories of knowledge about programs, events, tools, and activities. Each portal is supported by KS advisors who respond quickly to inquiries.
- Support the knowledge intern program. The World Bank places more than 100 knowledge interns in various throughout the bank each year, to assist in the bank's knowledge sharing.
- Support advocacy, outreach, and partnerships. These activities seek to improve the bank's knowledge sharing.

(Source: Strategy Associates Inc. Used with permission. For more information, contact Frank Voehl at *fvoehl@aol. com*.)

For a KMS to bring about sustainable business improvement, it's imperative that managers at all levels of an organization have the ability and willingness to guide people through the tough issues associated with implementing major change. This involves convincing people to leave behind the comfort of their current state and to move through the turbulence of a transitional state to arrive at what may be an uncertain future state. These three stages are defined as follows:

- *Current state.* The status quo or the established pattern of expectation; the normal routine an organization follows before the implementation of a KMS.
- *Transitional state.* The point in the change process where people break away from the status quo. They no longer behave as they did in the past, yet they still haven't thoroughly established a new way of operating. The transitional state begins when a KMS solution disrupts an individual's expectations and that person begins to change the way she or he works.
- *Future state.* The point at which change initiatives are implemented and integrated with new behavioral patterns required by change. The organization is converted from a knowledge-hoarding to a knowledge-sharing organization.

The following are key ideas for implementing change management methodologies required to support a KMS.

- Establish a "burning platform" by defining the business imperative that necessitates the change to the status quo.
- Define the cost of the status quo.
- Develop clear vision statements.
- Build cascading sponsorships.
- Define key change management roles.
- Develop change agents.
- Understand people's emotional responses.
- Understand the impact that past projects have on the change process.
- Support cultural alignment.
- Define desired behavioral patterns and measurements.
- Understand the impact of internal and external organizational events.
- Design and define implementation architecture.
- Eliminate black holes. In change management, these are defined as sustaining sponsors who, when provided with information, don't pass it on as a meaningful communication with their target audience.
- Analyze the landscape.

ORGANIZATIONAL CHANGE MANAGEMENT STRATEGIES

The organizational change management challenges and KMS strategies of three organizations—Cap Gemini Ernst & Young (CGEY), Long Island College Hospital, and Florida Power & Light—offer particularly useful insights. In addition to the discussion below, see also profiles 5.3 and 5.4

CGEY and Communities of Practice Score Cards

CGEY's knowledge management process consists of four activities wrapped around communities of practice:

- Capture
- Submit
- Review
- Reuse

**"I use not only the brain I have, but all I can borrow."
—Woodrow Wilson**

CGEY maintains a scorecard for each community of practice to measure its KMS usage and how frequently it participates in knowledge updates. This measurement helps determine if each community of practice is still a value-added organizational entity, or if it has outlived its usefulness. Each content manager for a community of practice is required to communicate with everyone in that community at least once each month. This is frequently done by sending out an e-mail to notify community members of new Web site features or changes. Quarterly, there's a major Web site update.

CGEY has also faced difficulty in getting people to contribute knowledge. To aid this process, the company has established a point system wherein individuals who contribute to CGEY's knowledge base accumulate points based upon the importance and frequency of their contributions. These points are used in the employee appraisal system; knowledge is one of the mega-processes on which people are evaluated. (The company has found that monetary rewards aren't effective in stimulating participation.) A minimum number of points must be accumulated by each employee each year, or that individual doesn't receive an annual bonus. CGEY has adopted a push system to encourage the accumulation of tacit knowledge. In addition the company sponsors a "tip of the day" program, and also provides extensive training to consultants on the importance of the KMS in saving time and improving work quality. There are a total of eight special CGEY training programs related to knowledge management.

Profile 5.3 The Cap Gemini Ernst & Young Knowledge System

Background

Cap Gemini Ernst & Young (CGEY) is the nation's fastest-growing professional services firm, with more than 30,000 employees and nearly 100 locations worldwide.

CGEY's KMS got its start in 1997 as a pilot project at Ernst & Young (EY) that incorporated the company's first CKO and many knowledge programs, including EY/InfoLink and EY/KnowledgeWeb. Using features such as scalability, Lotus Notes connectivity, and advanced search technologies from Verity, EY/KnowledgeWeb went from pilot program to full U.S. implementation in eight weeks.

In 2000 Ernst & Young merged with Cap Gemini—a major challenge for the KMS, because relevant knowledge was housed in many separate silos. The next year was spent blending these silos together into organized knowledge ports. The CGEY KMS provided a repository for the new firm's collective knowledge as well as that of outside sources such as industry analysts and reports.

Knowledge Management Strategy and Structure

CGEY's present knowledge system makes extensive use of communities of practice Web sites. Communities of practice are divided into regions and into services provided. An individual region may have a community of practice for each major service, and these service-related communities may also be combined into a total worldwide community of practice.

CGEY's communities of practice, both formal and informal, range in size between 20 and 20,000 people. Formal knowledge communities are organized and led by knowledge managers. Informal ones develop because individuals wish to exchange information that is not assigned to any official community of practice (e.g., all the activities going on in Ford Motor that CGEY is engaged in or interested in) or because people with common interests want to get together in a "playground" to discuss topics as if they were meeting by the coffee machine (an excellent way to collect tacit knowledge).

The knowledge system's My Portal is a customizable portal for individual consultants to link them directly to the knowledge they seek without going through a search process. This is an excellent feature, allowing each consultant to obtain the latest and best information related to the subject matter he or she is interested in.

Another key part of the company's KMS is its Center for Business Knowledge (CBK) research group, located in Boston. (This is CGEY's "secret weapon," says John Peetz, a high-level CKO.) This group continuously scans developments related to CGEY's main knowledge areas and methodologies, and inputs this data into the KMS.

Success Story

It is interesting to note that CGEY employees visit the CGEY/KnowledgeWeb some 20,000 times daily, making the company's KMS resoundingly successful. In the beginning, though, there was some employee reluctance. How did CGEY overcome these barriers?

"We were blessed with a collaborative culture to begin with," Peetz says, "so changing this mindset was less difficult for us. We incorporated sharing into the compensation system, trained people to use what was shared, encouraged people to visit the KWeb, wherein they found value, and did all the usual communicating to explain the vision."

(continues)

Profile 5.3 The Cap Gemini Ernst & Young Knowledge System
(continued)

Peetz credits top management support for CGEY's successful implementation of its knowledge management plan. "We have an extremely supportive management group. They talk and walk the game every day. Knowledge management and the CBK are firmly embedded in the company's business strategy. But ultimately, people contribute because they get value out the back end. There's a critical mass principle operating here."

Another strong reason that CGEY employees share what they know is that the company values their participation. "Ultimately, being recognized as an expert is a critical career goal for most of our people. And the best way in today's environment to become known as an expert is to publish," Peetz points out. "If someone needs a toy manufacturer supply chain specialist, the best way to locate one is to find our best material in that area and find out who created it. If you don't contribute, you don't become known."

(Source: Michelle Delio, "Keys to Collaboration," *Knowledge Management* magazine, October 1998. Used with permission. For more information, see the profile on the Ark Group, the magazine's publisher, in chapter I.)

The CGEY Web Site and Portal Strategy

"K! New" is the Web site CGEY provides for its employees. In fact, the company has standardized all of its Web sites so that they all look alike and contain the same basic information. The Web site is broken down into the following:

- People
- Events and communication
- Standards and policy
- Learning resources
- Articles and research
- Sales and marketing
- References and engagements
- Deliverables

The portals for each of the communities of practice identified in profile 5.3, which are related to methodology, have a standard format as follows:

- Welcome
- Knowledge
- Links
- Newsstand
- Discussion
- Events
- People

"T Rooms" are team rooms, a Web-based knowledge solution. These team sites rely on Microsoft SharePoint, a fully customized approach that allows teams to share information. The process for capturing best team practices is as follows:

- Determine knowledge to be captured and processed
- Identify the scope of this knowledge
- Package this knowledge in a useable form
- Deliverables
- Knowledge to be developed
- Lessons learned
- Agree on action for use and submission

"K! New" has a set submission form that's simple to use. This form includes a short abstract and a series of classification categories. It also links to a major report.

The system's knowledge manager is responsible for:

- Data capture
- Data submission
- Data review
- Publishing the best of the data

Of all the organizations benchmarked, CGEY and Long Island College Hospital were among the very best, in part due to the longevity of their knowledge management systems, which have endured despite turnover among executives and key management personnel. This resilience has led to recognition for best practices, because these organizations are sterling examples of process-dependent versus person-dependent operations.

The following profile of Florida Power & Light provides a closer look at another KMS success story, though one that turned out to have many bittersweet moments.

FPL CASE STUDY: THE GUIDING LIGHT THAT FLICKERED[2]

Above the Florida Power & Light (FPL) office doors in 1989, and on every desk and remote location, was the twenty-word challenge that was to change the course of quality history in the United States and beyond: "We will be the preferred provider of safe, reliable, and cost-effective products and services that satisfy the electricity-related needs of all customer segments—and recognized as such!" This was a vision for the ages but would not even last a decade. The quality policy that won the Deming Prize and the Edison Award turned on its masters, became a bureaucracy, and became the first major downsizing effort of the 1990s.

However, in spite of these setbacks, FPL successfully used its KMS to effectively integrate, in a vertical manner, its generation, transmission, and sale of electricity for use by

Profile 5.4 Long Island College Hospital Off the Critical List

Background

When Don Snell took over as CEO of the Long Island College Hospital (LICH) in 1996, the patients weren't the only ones who were sick. The New York state teaching hospital, with some 516 beds, 2,700 employees, and 200 residents and medical students, was hemorrhaging some $1.5 million a month. With only about $5 million in reserves it was nearing bankruptcy. Yet there was hardly a laptop in sight.

The health care industry has been amassing a wealth of information on patients, their treatment histories, and costs for years. But only recently have hospitals started to mine that data to restore profitability and determine how to deliver the most cost-efficient and effective care in the process. "All reporting and accounting was done pretty much by hand," Snell recalls. To make matters worse, New York state was just about to deregulate its schedule of fixed fees for services and the hospital had no way of figuring out what to charge to make a profit. "We had a desperate need for an information system," Snell says, "yet we couldn't afford some of the megasystems, which can cost in the millions."

Knowledge Management Strategy and Structure

To get the hospital back on its feet, Snell presented a plan to slash $25 million from operating expenses. He purchased a $30,000 decision-support system. That system was HealthShare One from HealthShare Technology Inc., a small privately held software company in Acton, Massachusetts, and the KMS gets at least some of the credit for the resulting financial turnaround. "The chief medical officer has quantified potential savings of $1.5 million in two departments alone," Snell says.

When HealthShare Technology constructs Databases, which form the core of the decision-support system, the company gathers discharge data reported by hospitals to agencies in the majority of states. Information on some 800,000 patients comes from Massachusetts alone. Aside from the patient's name, which is kept confidential, each record includes almost every other detail from age and gender to the name of the patient's physician and payer. There's information on illnesses and their severity, treatment, tests performed, length of stay, and the amounts hospitals charge for each factor. To complete the competitive picture, HealthShare marries that data with actual costs of that care from reports each hospital must prepare for the federal government to receive Medicare reimbursement.

Success Story

The information provided by HealthShare One, which is based on ACI US Inc.'s 4th Dimension, is so detailed that Snell used it to determine his own hospital's internal costs, negotiate fees with health care providers, and to review the practices of the hospital's physicians.

"You have your costs and revenue per DRG [Diagnosis Related Group, a standard health care diagnosis classification system], per procedure, per physician, and per patient if you want it," he says. Now, a new version of the software, called HealthShare Two, will "allow LICH to generate a more detailed level of product line cost analysis and will be used in negotiations with managed care companies."

For Snell, HealthShare One proved critical in contract negotiations with a commercially managed care organization. Snell determined the hospital would actually lose $200 a day on an offer to pay a flat per diem fee for treating patients. "Within half an hour we knew what it was costing every single one of our competitors and that we had the second lowest cost on the market, so we could walk away from the contract," he says. Eventually the hospital was able to renegotiate the contract with a reasonable profit margin.

The hospital has also used the software to cut costs by figuring out what fees it should pay a group of physicians for the use of their ultrasound kidney stone crushing machine and what to charge patients for the procedure. "We negotiated a reasonable fee that gave them a profit margin and kept ours as well. In the past they were able to take advantage of our organization because we couldn't do the analysis," Snell says.

But the most important contribution to cost cutting by HealthShare One and Two is likely to be long range, as the hospital figures out the best and most cost-effective ways of treating patients. To this end, the hospital has prepared a profile of each of its physicians' practices to determine which were doing the best job at keeping costs down.

Figuring out these "best practices" and getting physicians to build them into standard protocols is one of the major benefits of this type of software, says Doug O'Boyle, the director of health care information strategies practice at the Meta Group in Reston, Virginia. "This is where the big performance gains in health care will be. All hospitals will need software like this."

Special Projects

HealthShare Technology is a small company with a big idea. Company president Richard Siegrist realized back in 1992 that the medical profession was sitting on an untapped gold mine of publicly available information that ought to be the envy of data mining proponents everywhere. Imagine an industry where you can not only track your competitor's market share and the prices they charge, but also know the detailed history of each customer, the quality of the products your competitors offer and how much it costs to produce them. "Hospitals have had access to this type of information for about fifteen years," says Siegrist. "But it is not until the last four or five years they have started to make use of it." Instead of fancy data flythroughs or statistical analyses, HealthShare Technology has added a set of features that executives can use to automatically prepare a printed report comparing any hospital unit to that of its competitors. The report makes recommendations on ways to reduce costs and illustrates them with charts and tables.

Though small, HealthShare Technology has gathered an impressive list of customers. These include New York's Beth Israel and Sisters of Charity health care systems, the Partners Healthcare System in Massachusetts, and two multi-state HMOs: Oxford Healthplan and Healthsource.

(Source: Jiri Weiss, "Rx for Hospital Finance," *Knowledge Management* magazine, October 1998. Used with permission. For more information, see the profile on the Ark Group, the magazine's publisher, in chapter I.)

individual customers, businesses, and industries. State-of-the-art information systems and highly automated physical distribution, coupled with a well-integrated policy and quality deployment systems, became the cornerstone for advancing FPL's successful bid for the Deming Prize in 1989. Knowledge management also played a key role in completing its nuclear power plants in the 1980s and its downsizing efforts in the 1990s.

The well-integrated knowledge management information system (IS), in which FPL invested almost $100 million during the Deming Prize era, helped provide critical data for regulatory agencies and its corporate measurement system for both strategic and daily control. Cross-functional management and breakthrough teamwork helped the utility save hundreds of millions of dollars for its customers, while improving service and reducing cycle time on key activities.

Due to Florida's subtropical climate, FPL experiences heavy demand loads during the months of June through September, when air-conditioning usage is high. The company's annual system peak also occurs for very short periods during the winter months on cold days when customers use electric heating. This saturation of air-conditioning, electric heat, and other appliances resulted in FPL having one of the largest rates of electricity consumption per residential customer, thus affecting the management of the load planning process.

During the early 1990s, the FPL quality improvement system received a black-eye across corporate America when then-Chairman Jim Broadhead began downsizing, but since then the company has successfully rebounded, both in public image and stock price.

Brief Corporate Description

The FPL Group is a holding company, the principal subsidiary of which is Florida Power & Light Company (FPL), one of the largest investor-owned utilities in the nation and the largest utility in the state of Florida. FPL is the fastest growing electric utility in the nation in terms of customer accounts. The company also has the highest annual customer turnover rate. Growth and turnover rates affect construction activity, and the number of service personnel and knowledge management support required to provide service.

The FPL service territory covers approximately 28,000 square miles, about half of Florida, and reaches some six to seven million people. At the time of the Deming Prize challenge, FPL operated 13 plants, 400 substations, and more than 50,000 miles of overhead and underground transmission and distribution lines. Annual revenues were almost $6 billion and total plant in-service worth was approximately $12 billion.

FPL's Knowledge Management System

An electric utility company has the legal obligation to serve all present and future customers by providing electricity at any time and in any amount required within its designated service territory. The obligation to serve, and the need to generate and deliver electric power at the instant the power is demanded, is a distinguishing feature of utilities ,and provides a perfect application for knowledge management principles. Knowledge management helped FPL maintain very high standards of reliability in its generation and delivery systems. Additionally, to meet customers' future needs, utilities must develop long-term supply plans, because it takes many years of preparation to produce additional sources of electric power generation capacity.

In the United States, electric utilities are highly regulated. FPL's retail rates are regulated by the Florida Public Service Commission (FPSC), and its wholesale rates are regulated by the Federal Energy Regulatory Commission (FERC). Nuclear operations are regulated by the Nuclear Regulatory Commission (NRC), and environmental areas are regulated by local, state, and federal regulatory bodies. FPL's knowledge management strategy played a key role in dealing with all regulations in a consistent manner.

Business Situation Prior to FPL's Quality Improvement Program and Knowledge Management System

From 1946 to 1974, FPL experienced rapid (double-digit) growth, making it difficult to keep up with the need to plan, finance, construct, and operate an electric system in fast-growing South Florida. Throughout this period of rapid expansion FPL maintained stable prices for its customers. Then came the oil crisis of 1974, with its period of high inflation. In 1978 the government passed the National Energy Act, which resulted in competition for utilities and promoted electricity conservation.

Due to these challenging conditions, the trust the company had developed with its customers suffered. During the 1970s FPL was forced to increase utility rates repeatedly because of increasing costs, slower sales growth, and stricter federal and state regulations. The company had also become bureaucratic and inflexible. In 1981 Marshall McDonald, FPL's chairman of the board, realized that the company had been concerned with keeping defects under control rather than improving quality. McDonald addressed the problem head on:

"As FPL grew, we had become more bureaucratic and cumbersome. We were often inflexible in our operations and often treated all of our customers the same regardless of their individual needs," McDonald recalls. "At the same time, we could foresee no significant technological innovations to reduce the escalating power supply. A change in management philosophy was needed to achieve customer satisfaction and reduce costs through greater management effectiveness."

Change was occurring faster than FPL could adapt, according to McDonald, and the company recognized that "corporate goals needed to be established and achieved using new knowledge management techniques. In order to achieve our new corporate vision, goal setting was introduced to change the corporate culture as part of the introduction of our QIP [quality improvement program]."

McDonald introduced quality improvement teams to FPL in 1981, based upon the combined teachings of W. Edwards Deming, Philip Crosby, and Joseph M. Juran. The objective of these teams was to provide a structured environment for employees to work together in a new way. MacDonald's vision was to move the organization toward the following four goal-setting areas:

- Improving the quality of products and services
- Developing the skills of employees

- Promoting communication and teamwork both within and between suppliers
- Enhancing the quality of work life

Management knew this was a step in the right direction, but such teams alone would not bring about the change needed for the company to survive. McDonald tried to convince other executives that a knowledge-based quality improvement process was needed, but all the experts that FPL talked to were in manufacturing, while FPL was primarily a service company. In 1983, while in Japan, McDonald met the president of Kansai Electric Power Co., a Deming Prize winner. The president told him about Kansai's total quality and knowledge management efforts. Company officials began to visit Kansai regularly, and in 1983, with Kansai's help, FPL began its own companywide quality control knowledge management effort, known as the QIP, or quality improvement program.

"FPL had to change our way of thinking from supply-oriented to customer-oriented; from a power generation company to a service company," McDonald emphasizes. "We needed new knowledge creation strategies to provide a means of addressing the key issues surrounding the satisfaction of customer needs and expectations. We began our renewed quality efforts in 1981 with a limited and narrow approach called quality improvement [QI] teams, similar to Japan's Quality Circles. We soon realized, however, that QI teams alone would not achieve the results needed to change the company."

Enter Policy Deployment

Policy deployment was the driving force—or the engine—behind the full development of FPL's QIP knowledge management program. In 1985, FPL Chairman John Hudiburg announced that the company would broaden the QIP program to include policy deployment.

"After thoroughly investigating TQC [total quality control] and knowledge management methods, I am convinced that these approaches, coupled with a policy deployment approach, are the best management systems ever conceived," Hudiburg explains. "The QIP philosophy and related systems would be deployed throughout FPL and would be the method used to accomplish the corporate vision. Our primary motivation in introducing an expanded QIP was to establish a [knowledge] management system and corporate culture to assure customer satisfaction. A fundamental change would be needed to listen to the voice of the customer and to identify their needs and expectations. As a result, a number of policy deployment short-term plans are being initiated to address priority issues."

Policy deployment became the cornerstone of FPL's knowledge management system. This is a management process designed to achieve breakthroughs on major corporate problems, one that focuses on customer needs by deploying resources on a few high-priority issues. It's a method that uses corporate vision to determine priority issues that will make that vision a reality. For FPL, key issues involved improving reliability, customer satisfaction, and employee safety while also keeping costs under control. Each department then became responsible for developing plans to help improve these areas. Once plans were determined, their progress status was checked regularly to make sure they were on schedule. Each department was limited to working on no more than three items that had the most influence on their department's performance, but work on these items was expected to be done on time and in great detail.

At FPL, policy deployment targets breakthrough achievements by concentrating company resources and efforts on a few priority areas. According to Hudiburg, the early focus was to:

- Increase performance levels.
- Improve communication of company and department direction.
- Improve coordination within the company and the value chain.
- Attain broad participation in the development and attainment of corporate goals.

Prior to 1985, the company used management by objectives (MBO) as the principle method for achieving corporate objectives. Although MBO focused on the company point of view, it didn't adequately consider the customers' viewpoint. Also, it didn't provide a systematic process for ensuring that corporate objectives were met. Policy deployment was introduced to provide a process for achieving corporate objectives and deploying knowledge effectively. However, the company attacked too many problems and solved only a few. Also, early improvement attempts weren't focused on customer needs. Therefore, it was necessary for the company to take corrective action for the next cycle and in each successive cycle thereafter. In 1988, cross-functional teams were introduced to help executives coordinate FPL's major corporate activities.

Many improvements that were made helped clarify how corporate knowledge management activities tied to overall quality management, which was enhanced with each successive policy deployment cycle. The following are the four key characteristics that Hudiburg and McDonald extolled about the FPL management system:

- *Focus on customer needs.* By using the quality function deployment tool, policies are identified and developed based upon quality elements. These quality elements are established through a combination of the customer's voice and the utility industry's obligation to serve.
- *Management reviews.* Improvement activities are reviewed by the office of the chairman, the president, and responsible executives and managers, to check for progress in achieving company policies. Action is taken as necessary to promote QIP. (FPL has three levels of knowledge management reviews. Level I reviews are conducted by the president and executive vice presidents, by reviewing the business plan with an emphasis on cross-functional and short-term plans. Level II reviews are conducted by appropriate vice presidents, and are designed for managers to present their progress on associated business

plans. Level III reviews are conducted by department heads with their managers and supervisors, to focus on how well the QIP has been implemented within their departments, with a particular emphasis on priority problems, daily control systems, and process management activities.)

- *Cross-functional management.* Responsibility for achieving improvements is assigned to executives, although activities cross organizational boundaries.
- *Integration of policy deployment and budget.* Through the processes of management consensus and catchball (competitive yet cooperative participatory decision making), resources are allocated to support annual improvement activities.

Deploying QIP Knowledge Management and Information Systems Helps FPL Win the Deming Prize

Although policy deployment was implemented in 1985 to provide a system for improving customer satisfaction, that approach didn't provide a system for standardizing initial improvements and replicating these throughout the value chain (including suppliers). This next phase, called process daily work control, or quality in daily work, provided a tool for FPL's managers to control their work processes throughout the entire knowledge management chain, from customers back to the supplier chain.

Process daily work control had the following characteristics, as outlined by John Hudiburg: "First of all, it focuses on [a] manager's and supervisor's key accountabilities. The idea is to develop control systems for all top priority jobs in order to standardize, replicate and improve all aspects of the daily operations of bringing electricity to our customers. Thus the focus is on the customers needs. The key outcome is also to identify areas for the development of computer systems that free many line employees from repetitive tasks."

FPL's computer systems have provided the necessary tools to resolve some of the difficulties in implementing logistical control systems by giving FPL the ability to:

- Tailor services to meet individual customer needs.
- Offer quick access for problem solving at FPL's many remote areas.
- Stratify, analyze, and graphically display data.
- Replicate processes and standards across multiple work locations.
- Collect, store, retrieve, and analyze data consistently throughout the company.
- Provide training for repetitive activities.
- Maximize the economic logistical operation of the power supply system.

FPL's Information Systems and Services Organization

In 1989, the year FPL won the Deming Prize, FPL's Information Systems and Services Organization consisted of about 600 knowledge workers, 288 of these in systems and programming and 314 in computer operations. Nearly $100 million had been spent to bring the entire operating system to a level of peak performance in support of the following information systems priority areas:

- Systems and programming, consisting of:
  - ☐ Two-hundred-and-nineteen application development and support employees who developed new systems and performed maintenance and enhancements
  - ☐ Thirty-seven information planning employees who ran the development center, did data processing training and QA, performed user liaison and data security, and helped with planning and administration
  - ☐ Thirty-two user-access personnel who ran the information center, provided personal computer and local area network support, and offered end-user computing support

- Computer operations, consisting of:
  - ☐ Seventy computer center employees who ran the operating systems, the help desk, and the network control center
  - ☐ Fifty-eight technical systems employees who handled systems programming and database administration
  - ☐ One-hundred-and-forty-seven data preparation employees who performed data entry, output control and balancing, and payment processing
  - ☐ Thirty-nine telecommunications employees who handled data communication activities, voice communications, and fiber optics services.

- Operating environment hardware and software, consisting of:
  - ☐ Three 3090/600 processors—one for MVS batch and development, one for MVS on-line systems and one for VM end-user computing
  - ☐ Fourteen thousand terminals and printers
  - ☐ More than 3,000 personal computers
  - ☐ Software including corporate-based MVS, CICS, IMS/DB, DB2, COBOL, and end-user computing using VM/XA, FOCUS, TELL-A-GRAF, AS, SAS.

Application Programs to Support Daily Control and Knowledge Management

The application environment consisted of fifty online applications, portfolios functionally divided as follows:

- *Customer and marketing.* Customer billing, customer information system, and electronic meter reading
- *Distribution and construction.* Management of trouble calls, construction, facilities graphics, and division maintenance
- *Engineering and generation.* Generating equipment, nuclear control, and information management
- *Financial and personnel.* Financial accounting, purchasing, inventory control, accounts payable, and human resource management

As the Deming Prize challenge unfolded, the overall objectives of management, especially in the area of knowledge management, were fourfold: change to customer-oriented thinking, create resilience to change, seek breakthroughs in achieving cost reduction through the deployment of KMS efficiency, and counter bureaucratic attitudes throughout the supply chain.

As previously mentioned, quality in daily work is the expression that FPL eventually used for the concept of improving business systems' quality control of daily work processes. As such, it involves standardizing and redesigning work routines, removing waste from them, promoting the concept of internal customers, and enabling better practice to be replicated from one location to another. Quality in daily work means measurement-driven, knowledge-based control systems consisting of flowcharts, process and quality indicators, procedure standards, and computer systems. By repeatedly examining and analyzing work, employees in every area contributed to simplifying their work and improving the knowledge-based value chain.

The goals of the daily control system activities were to apply the plan-do-check-act (PDCA) philosophy to processes and work activities to meet the needs and expectations of customers by:

- Maintaining gains already achieved through improvement projects
- Achieving consistency in operations as well as results
- Clarifying individual contributions toward achieving customer satisfaction
- Improving daily operations throughout the entire value chain

One illustration of how knowledge management was incorporated into operations involved developing a computer system for processing customer trouble calls. In the new system, the computer first checks to find out if a customer has been disconnected for non-payment, then begins to locate places and devices that may be malfunctioning, and finally routes the call through a dispatcher to a troubleshooter. A repairman heading to the scene may have a diagnosis before arrival. The information is stored in the system's database to be used for future improvement planning.

Computer systems were a unique feature of FPL KMS standardization. Standard work steps were either eliminated or automated. Employees all along the value chain could check the results and take the appropriate actions. With the aid of computers, they also analyzed data trends. Management used the KMS to analyze trends over longer time periods. By implementing daily control systems, the understanding of customer needs improved significantly, with the following results, as reported by Hudiburg:

"The customer perspective has been integrated throughout corporatewide activities. Management is now involved in reviewing the application of daily control systems to control and improve work processes. Also, SPC [statistical process control] and knowledge management techniques were applied to stabilize and validate work processes for the purpose of increasing customer satisfaction."

Taking Knowledge Management Control to the Utmost in Nuclear Operations

FPL's nuclear plants use the fission of uranium to produce electricity. These fission products are radioactive, and as they decay they produce high-energy radiation. Excessive exposure to this type of radiation can be harmful to employees and the public. Knowledge management plays a key role in improving safety, and it's the prime input into the nuclear safety department. "The ability of our nuclear plants at Turkey Point and St. Lucie to produce power depends upon the strictest conformance to NRC regulations, according to Hudiburg. "If FPL or the Nuclear Regulatory Commission (NRC) identifies a condition considered adverse to safety, the unit will be shut down until the condition is remedied. The NRC may suspend or revoke our license to operate, as they have five other utility units at the present time."

Knowledge-Based Suggestion System for Improved Methods

To help acknowledge individual contributions throughout the entire value chain, FPL revamped a centralized suggestion system it had been using for many years. Only about 600 suggestions had been submitted annually, and it often took six months for suggestions to be read and evaluated. A new, decentralized knowledge management suggestion system was proposed, with simplified procedures to improve response time. Employees would participate in the implementation of their own suggestions. In 1987, about 1,000 knowledge ideas were submitted; by the end of 1989 this had increased to 25,000 ideas, and many of these ideas involved day-to-day knowledge management-type activities. The results were dramatic. Communication and teamwork improved greatly, and bargaining unit team participation and involvement reached an all-time high of 43 percent—up from 10 percent in 1983.

FPL Knowledge Management Conclusions

Training played an important role in FPL's knowledge management transformation. The company found that training enhanced enthusiasm and participation. Supervisors were expected to train their employees and to play a more active role as coaches and cheerleaders. As first-line employees became more skilled in diagnosing and solving problems, they used data rather than intuition to solve problems that had previously been handled by management. All employees developed a much broader view of the company, and more flexibility in dealing with customers.

The KMS also changed. Customer satisfaction, rather than cost control, became the focus of attention. Management reviews checked monthly on improvement progress. Goals were now long term, but progress checks were frequent. Managers reviewed progress with better statistical insight, recognizing that variation would exist but seeking to rid the system of common causes. Cross-functional teams carried out large-scale improvement projects. Finally, budget and quality improvement aims goals were integrated.

Since 1995, FPL has maintained its policy deployment focus related to these knowledge management activities:

- Improving availability of customer and supplier information
- Improving availability of trouble call management system
- Improving response time of online systems at trouble call offices
- Reducing unavailability of online communications systems, including electronic data exchange links
- Implementing structured system development projects for new computer systems, using quality function deployment (QFD) and policy deployment tools
- Improving information center customer satisfaction by reducing the time needed to resolve customer and vendor calls
- Improving online systems response time at regional phone centers
- Improving inventory turns each year
- Reducing unplanned power outages at nuclear plants through improved knowledge management

The influence of knowledge management tools and techniques at FPL in the years leading to the Deming Prize years can be seen as follows:

- The average length of customer service interruptions dropped from about seventy-five minutes in 1983 to about forty-seven minutes in 1989.
- The percentage of online systems network unavailability was reduced by 75 percent from a high of 0.7 percent in January of 1985 to a low of 0.1 percent in 1990 and thereafter.
- Prime-time application outage frequency was reduced to an average of 0.1 percent.
- The percentage of customer call-backs not returned within one hour dropped from 70 percent to 29 percent and has remained on target.
- The number of complaints per 1,000 customers fell to one-third of the 1983 level.
- Safety improved substantially.
- The price of electricity has stabilized.

And at the core of these improvements was FLP's KMS.

Still, the pitfalls of FPL's quality improvement program were significant, and eventually led to its fall from grace, though for the most part each KMS has remained unchanged from the Deming Prize years. The main drawback was bureaucracy, in that every management system, left to its own devices, tends toward complexity. FPL's was no exception. At FPL quality improvement tasks came to be seen as being in opposition to real work. Often training was incomplete, and managers were left out. Staff groups were slow to accept the system's rigor and discipline, and complained that it slowed them down. In many cases, teams selected problems that were too large for any reasonable solution. The process management approach became difficult to apply, except in repetitive areas, until the tools of quality function deployment and Taguchi methods design were brought in.

In spite of the system's shortcomings, the impact of knowledge management upon FPL's information systems and functions was enormous. For the first time, customer needs were effectively translated into problems that were prioritized and solved. Every department measured its impact upon corporate goals, and this new focus resulted in customer satisfaction. Results were consistently measured, and process and quality measurement standards were developed for most jobs, resulting in increased employee obligation to improve the workplace. Management experienced an enhanced awareness of the impact of each group in the value chain, as well as finding itself more involved throughout the company. Subjective decision making was replaced by a renewed focus on process improvement, knowledge standardization, and improved data use. Everyone was also rewarded for the knowledge-enhancing benefits of his or her ideas.

SIMPLE LANGUAGE

Today, most business writing can't be easily read or understood. After a cursory glance it's usually routed to the nearest file cabinet or trash can. Although our fast-paced world makes receiving accurate and timely information more necessary than ever, the quality of most business writing—pompous, wordy, indirect, vague, and unnecessarily complex—undercuts this need. All too often management evaluates the merit of reports based upon their heft, rather than their knowledge content. The KMS team needs to evaluate documents used in the knowledge accumulation and distribution process to ensure they're written for the user. In some cases, new documents will be needed. In either case, what's needed are documents that communicate needed information in an easy-to-use format. Simple language will help accomplish this task. A KMS team's entire effort may be lost without effective communication. Unfortunately, most companies pay little attention to clarity of communication.

A major problem facing business today is that engineers and academics often write procedures and specifications—writing to impress colleagues more than inform system users. They demonstrate to the world their brilliance and importance by peppering documents with complex technical language. For hours, colleagues pore over the finished works to understand the meanings behind the words, learning and growing as they gain understanding. Yet those who don't have the time or energy to divine esoteric meanings may either toss that document into the wastebasket or send it to their secretary to interpret and implement. Sometimes users of these documents are functionally illiterate, or the document is written in the reader's second language. In all these cases, these knowledge documents won't be read or will be misinterpreted.

Two equally important factors must be considered when a document or letter is being prepared:

- What the author needs to communicate
- With whom the author needs to communicate

Most authors have a reasonably good understanding of what they want to communicate, because they have taken time to research and gain knowledge about the subject. Unfortunately, they may not take time to consider or clearly define their audience. The first rule of good writing is: "Know your subject." The second rule is: "Know your audience." The third rule is: "Make it easy to read." Most authors of knowledge-rich procedures and specifications use only the first rule.

These key factors will help KMS team members ensure that company documents adhere to these three rules of good writing and effectively communicate with their intended readers:

- Determine the reading and comprehension level of your audience (the people with whom you are trying to communicate). Work should be written so all readers can easily comprehend the message. If one reader has an eighth-grade comprehension level, prepare documents and other materials for the seventh grade. Just because you know your readers all graduated from high school, don't assume they can read and understand at the twelfth-grade level. In fact, many college graduates' reading and comprehension levels are below the tenth grade. Also keep in mind that for documents written in a reader's second language, reading and comprehension levels are often much lower than that person's general education level. When a document is written in a second language, target the language level for three grades below general education level and use the dictionary's first preferred meaning only.
- Find out how familiar the audience is with abbreviations and terms. Unless jargon and specialized terms are critical to the work assignment, don't use them. If they are necessary, clearly define meanings.
- For all procedures with descriptions and directions more than four pages long, start with a flowchart containing annotations that lead the reader to detailed information within the procedure.
- Use acronyms with care. It's often better to repeat the phrase and take a little more space than to use a shortened version. Don't force the reader to learn a new acronym unless it will be used frequently throughout the document. Never use an abbreviation or acronym unless it's clearly defined in the document.

The Fog Factor

Robert Gunning, a communications expert who has conducted clinics on clear writing for hundreds of U.S. corporations, refers to unnecessary complexity as "the fog." Recognizing that the two most important factors affecting readability are sentence length and word familiarity, he developed a scientific method, called the Gunning Fog Index, to measure the clarity of a written piece. His premise is simple: Long sentences and big words, particularly when combined, can bore, confuse, or, worst of all, alienate the reader.

Consider a typical business letter, this example presented in Robert Gunning's and Richard A. Kallan's book, *How To Take the Fog Out of Business Writing* (Dartnell Corp., 1994):

> "In accordance with suggestions embodied in your memorandum of June 5, issuance of a supplement to the April report was undertaken. Two (2) copies of said supplement are enclosed herewith for your information and records. We beg to thank you gratefully for this thoughtful suggestion and hope that you give forthcoming reports the same sort of careful consideration."

As Gunning and Kallan point out, "Deciphering the meaning of such foggy writing requires time and energy, reduces efficiency and profits, and leads to misunderstandings and mistakes. Unfamiliar words and an unwieldy sentence structure distract the reader from the essential element of a business communication—the ideas."

In the previous example of a business letter, the same ideas could be expressed more effectively by writing: "On June 5, you suggested we issue a supplement to the April report. Here are two copies of it for you. Thanks for your thoughtful suggestions. Keep them coming."

Business people often mistakenly assume their writing style must be ponderous to be authoritative. Consequently, their written communications may come across as impersonal, unclear, and occasionally even menacing. Far from sounding impressive, they succeed only in making their correspondence difficult to read and understand.

Anyone can learn to write better by using a two-step process. First, measure the complexity of your prose using the Fog Index; then follow the basic guidelines of good writing discussed later in this report.

To calculate the Fog Index:

- Select a writing sample. The sample should be at least 100 words; the larger the sample, the more reliable the results. To analyze the readability of a long manuscript, select a number of samples at random throughout the piece.
- Calculate the average sentence length. Determine the average number of words per sentence by counting the number of words in the sample, then dividing it by the total number of sentences. Treat independent clauses as separate sentences.

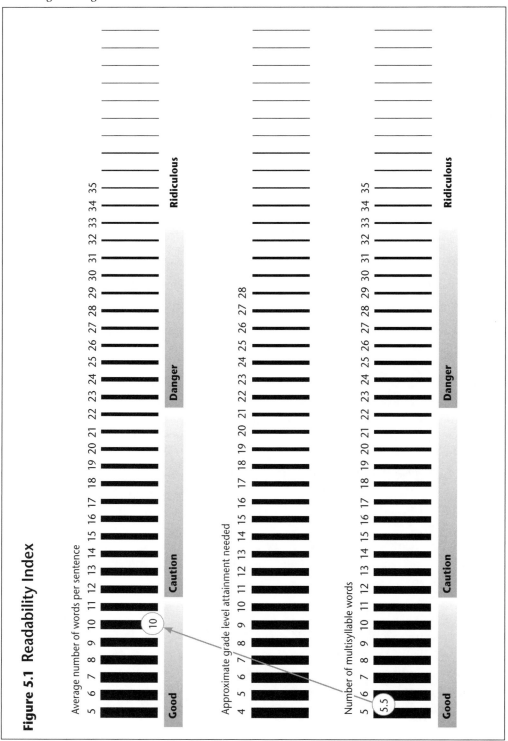

Figure 5.1 Readability Index

- Determine the percentage of multi-syllable words. Count the number of words containing three or more syllables, excluding:
  - ☐ Capitalized words
  - ☐ Combinations of short, easy words (e.g., bookkeeper, stockbroker, businessman)
  - ☐ Verb forms made into three syllables by adding suffixes such as "-ed" or "-es" (e.g., created, trespasses, repeated). Do include those ending in "-ing" or "-ly" (e.g., increasingly).

- Divide this count by the total number of words. This gives you the percentage of difficult words.
- Add the average sentence length and the percentage of complex works
- Multiply the result by 0.4

The Fog Index formula is as follows: average number of words per sentence + percentage of words of three or more syllables) x 0.4.

To ease the arithmetic, *The American Peoples Encyclopedia* (Columbia University Press, 2003) published a graph to visually measure the complexity of a piece of writing. (See figure 5.1.) Simply place an X on the right column, indicating the average number of words per sentence in your sample. Then place another X on the left column, indicating the percentage of multisyllable words. Draw a line connecting the Xs. The point where this line crosses the center column of the graph is the readability index.[2]

In figure 5.1 the average number of words per sentence is 11.2. The percentage of multisyllable words is 7.3, and the readability index is 8.3.

Index numbers roughly correspond to reading comprehension levels of children and adults in various grades. The lower the index, the easier the piece is to comprehend. For instance, an 8 indicates that to read your sample with ease, the person should have at least an eighth-grade level of ability. A 15 requires achievement at the college level, and so on. For general Fog Index reading levels, see figure 5.2.

The Bible, Shakespeare, and Mark Twain all have a Fog Index of about 6. *Time*, *Newsweek*, and the *Wall Street Journal* all have a Fog Index of about 11.

Figure 5.2 Fog Index Reading Levels

	College Graduates	High School Graduates
Good	10 or less	8 or less
Caution	10.1 to 16	8.1 to 12
Danger	16.1 to 22	12.1 to 14
Ridiculous	Above 22	Above 14

Don't confuse reading level with intelligence level. You don't have to write at the college level to challenge your readers. In fact, anything above a 10 rating would challenge the average college student. Most best-selling novels rate between 8 and 10. *Reader's Digest* rates a 10. *Time* magazine rates an 11. *The Atlantic* rates a 12. Most business memos, letters, and reports are much more difficult to interpret.

A high rating alone doesn't mean that the writing can't be understood. It suggests that your readers will have to work harder to make sense of what you're saying. Sustained reading of complex material is tiring, so why not make it easier?

Let's go back and analyze the last two paragraphs to see at what level they were written.

- There are 110 words in the two paragraphs.
- The average number of words per sentence is ten words (110 words divided by eleven sentences).
- There are six words with three or more syllables that don't comply with the exclusion rules.
- By dividing six (multisyllable words) by 110 (the total number of words in the two paragraphs), we find that 5.5 percent of the words are multisyllabic.
- Go back to figure 5.1 and draw a line from 5.5 percent on the left-hand scale (multisyllable words) to ten on the right-hand scale (average number of words per sentence). You'll note that this line intersects the center line (approximate grade-attainment level needed) between six and seven. Based on these calculations, the two paragraphs being evaluated were written for people who read at an seventh-grade level.

There are a number of software programs that will calculate readability. Readability Plus is a favorable one because it includes formulas for most of the different approaches to calculating a readability index. Some of these different formulas are:

- Spache
- Fry
- FORCAST
- FOG
- SMOG
- Powers-Somner-Kearl
- Dale-Chall
- Flesch Grade Level
- Flesch Reading Ease

Anyone with the latest version of Microsoft Word can check a passage's readability using Flesch-Kincaid Reading Level. Just go to the "tool" menu, click "options," and then click "spelling and grammar." Then select "show readability statistics" and you're on your way. Unfortunately, this method doesn't measure the logical progression of ideas, nor can it determine if you've used the right words. A low readability rating is no guarantee of good writing, but a high score indicates bad writing. The KMS needs to be written for the people who need to use the system's knowledge.

Good business writing, like any other skill, requires practice. To improve, try to spend twenty minutes each week analyzing and revising your memos, letters, and reports. Above all, try to write the same way you speak.

Consider these tips from Robert Gunning's and Richard A. Kallan's book, *How To Take the Fog Out of Business Writing* (Dartnell Corp., 1994):

- Strive for simplicity and brevity. Don't rely on long words when short ones may be just as effective. For example, replace "endeavor" with "try," "objective" with "aim," "commence" with "begin," and "aggregate" with "total."

- Don't rely on passive verbs. Use the active voice. Write "we discussed" instead of "we had a discussion about."

- Avoid pomposity. Rather than write: "The number of persons to attend any one of the various functions planned for June 10 cannot, of course, be reliably estimated until shortly before that date. It is therefore desirable that detailed measures be initiated, on the assumption that there will be capacity attendance at all functions and that there may be overflows at some." Simply say: "We have no way of knowing until shortly before June 10 how many people will attend that day's functions. We should plan, therefore, for capacity or even overflow crowds."

- Delete unnecessary words. Words and phrases like "herewith," "this is to inform you that," "the necessity of," and "in our effort to" add bulk, not understanding.

- Keep sentences short and simple. Don't overburden them with several thoughts at once. Punctuate them appropriately to clarify meaning, and divide the material into digestible bites.

- Be precise. Don't burden the reader with unnecessary information, or leave out important facts. Include relevant names, dates, and details.

- Avoid hedging. Words like "seems," "perhaps," "possibly," and "might" sound weak and uncertain. The fewer qualifiers you use, the more confident you sound.

In short, impress the knowledge worker with the value and intelligence of the ideas in your KMS, not with the weight of your words or convolutions of sentences. You may be surprised at their positive response.

> "A document written at the tenth-grade level can be read by a college graduate in 30 percent less time with 33 percent better comprehension."
>
> —HJH

It doesn't have to be long to be good. Just think about the documents included in figure 5.3.

Forms

Generally, people don't give enough thought to forms while developing them. Much needless effort is expended, and many errors are created, because forms are poorly designed. Good form design requires a great deal of thought. The form should be self-explanatory, with information recorded only once. All abbreviations must be defined on the form. The data recording area should be large enough to accommodate normal-sized writing—a square about 3/16" per letter or number is sufficient, but 1/4" is even better. Consider whether the data will be recorded by hand or by computer. If both can be used, design the form for hand

Figure 5.3 List of Documents and Length

Document	Number of words
Lord's Prayer	57
Ten Commandments	71
Gettysburg Address	266
Declaration of Independence	300
U.S. Government Contractor Management System Evaluation Program	38,000

Profile 5.5 Avery Dennison Gains With Intellectual Property

Background

Avery Dennison (AD) is one of those invisibly everywhere companies. The $3 billion school and office supplies firm leads various product categories with brands (Marks-A-Lot and Hi-Liter) that are among the most recognized in the industry.

Even more invisible to the consumer are AD's intellectual property assets. The company's patents for many consumer products—notebooks, three-ring binders, organizing systems, glues, fasteners, business forms, tickets, tags, imprinting equipment, components, and other items—form one of AD's main revenue channels, which gives the company a key competitive advantage over top competitors including 3M, Esselte, and Fortune Brands.

Knowledge Management Strategy and Structure

"Hidden" wealth in intellectual assets provides companies with billions of dollars in licensing revenues from underutilized patents, and similar amounts from infringements on patents related to key product lines. The number of patents issued in the United States increased 150 percent since 1980, and patent-related revenues likewise have increased—from $3 billion to almost $100 billion in the same period. Yet with this explosion in activity, companies have had a difficult time managing patent assets and applications.

Avery Dennison's research-and-development division, based in Pasadena, California, has overcome this difficulty and other restrictions of the traditional hard-copy patent review process by applying Intellectual Property Asset Management (IPAM) software from Aurigin Systems of Mountain View, California. In turn, IPAM incorporates data visualization technology from Inxight Software, a Xerox PARC spinoff based in Palo Alto, California. The combination is already yielding big benefits.

entry, as that takes the most space. Forms designed to be double-spaced on a computer leave enough room for hand-entered data as well. Always require hand-entered data to be printed. Break up the data recording area with short horizontal lines to help the user record information in the proper place. This is particularly important for recording numerical data such as Social Security or telephone numbers.

Design the form from the standpoint of the customer—the individual who'll be recording the data. Then, consider the user—the person who'll be using the data—because the job is only half done when the information is recorded. You should never ask for information that isn't required for a specific use. Sometimes data on a form is directly used in another activity. (Hand-entered information on a sales order may be used by a stock person to pull articles to fulfill a customer order, for example.) More often, data are fed into a computer to generate reports, update stocking requirements, pay bills, and update mailing lists. Always be sure that the form presents data in a logical sequence to the person who will be filling out the form. In most cases, the person who fills out the form is much less familiar with it than the person who'll process the form.

Success Story

As manager of intellectual property at AD, it is Lori Morrison's responsibility, as she describes it, "to transform human knowledge into economic wealth." With IPAM, "I can see how to improve the quality of my patent. I can see what my competitor is doing and compare or contrast with our in-house patents." Using a 3-D presentation feature, the program not only enables Morrison to visually separate patents by type and division, but also to track the corporation's top inventors through patent visualizations, to improve inventor incentive programs. Morrison says turnaround time for individual patent evaluation has been reduced from weeks to a few hours. "This is a patent attorney's dream," she said.

The visualization component of Aurigin's IPAM software is built using Inxight's 3-D Hyperbolic Tree technology. It displays data in a branching design that lets users view and navigate up to 100 times more information on screen than might be viewable in a traditional file-and-folder or spreadsheet interface. This enables users to visualize and understand complex relationships between the company patents and competitors' patents.

AD has not yet quantified IPAM's effect on company revenues. But Dow Chemical has estimated that it expects to boost licensing royalties from $20 million today to $125 million by 2000, an increase partially due to the assistance of the decision-support tools from Aurigin. Dow also plans to cut $40 million in tax maintenance over 10 years by identifying unused patents that it can let expire.

Avery Dennison may keep a low profile, but those kinds of dollar swings are very visible on the corporate balance sheet. And that's a lot of impact from knowledge management technologies.

(Source: Sandra Kay Helsel, "Patent Medicine," *Knowledge Management* magazine, October 1998. Used with permission. For more information, see the profile on the Ark Group, the magazine's publisher, in chapter I.)

Does a good form make a difference? When British government agencies focused their attention on form design, errors plummeted and productivity soared. For example:

- British Customs processes approximately 50,000 lost bags per year. Before the lost baggage claim form was redesigned, it had an error rate of 55 percent. Now it's 3 percent.
- The British Department of Defense redesigned its travel expense form. The new form cut errors by 50 percent, the time required to fill it out by 10 percent, and processing time by 15 percent.
- By redesigning the application form for legal aid, the British Department of Social Security saved more than 2 million hours per year in processing time.

Completed forms provide an important source of data. Often, a matrix of interrelated forms is needed to support business processes. Take time to look at the way forms are used and how they interrelate, then carefully apply simple language and form-simplifica-

---

Profile 5.6 PeopleSoft: Providing Open Access to Collected Information

Background

PeopleSoft, now part of Oracle, builds client/server applications that redefine traditional approaches, putting power in the hands of users while adapting to the ever-changing nature of business.

"The PeopleSoft culture was designed around sharing information and tacit knowledge," says Tracy Leighton, manager of the PeopleSoft Knowledge Development Team. Leighton credits Lotus Notes groupware with moving the company toward a self-service knowledge management system before the collaborative process was begun in earnest. "Once we got the intranet knowledge solution (called Eureka!—The PeopleSoft Knowledge Base) online, we soon had requests from departments that wanted to add their knowledge for all to share."

Knowledge Management Strategy, Structure, and Success Story

The company's knowledge base was started with third-party content from Inference, a customer-relationship management software provider. Inference enabled new PeopleSoft users to customize content for their specific issues and solutions.

PeopleSoft's policy is to give all employees access to collected knowledge databases. "Information becomes knowledge only when it's useful to someone," says Marcia Connor of PeopleSoft's Corporate Education Services. "We can't second-guess where and when the information becomes useful. Just because I don't see information as useful to any given individual doesn't mean that it isn't or won't become useful to them."

"To limit access to information is diametrically opposed to the PeopleSoft core value of how we treat ourselves and our customers," she adds. "We provide all the tools for every person so that they can do their job the best way they know how."

(Source: Strategy Associates Inc. Used with permission. For more information, contact Frank Voehl at *fvoel@aol.com*.)

tion techniques. The time spent will have a big payback in increased efficiency and effectiveness.

SUMMARY

"Harnessing the intelligence and spirit of people at all levels of the company to continually build and share knowledge is a top priority for companies to succeed."
—Peter Drucker
Author and consultant

The information in the following four paragraphs is taken from Michelle Delio's article "Keys to Collaboration," published in *Knowledge Management* magazine (October 1998)[3]:

> Technology access is such a basic strategy that virtually every organization, from manufacturers to government agencies to hospitals with a successful knowledge management program, adheres to it. The strategies of the various organizations profiled all feature the common denominator of technology. PeopleSoft employees, for instance, get a portable computer loaded with Lotus Notes and other software that allows them easy access to corporate data from wherever they happen to be working. Employees from all departments also utilize a corporate intranet.

> Pillsbury uses a virtual library to warehouse key data sources and patents. At Ernst & Young, every professional is provided with a laptop and access to the vast resources of the firm's KnowledgeWeb from anywhere in the world. According to CKO John Peetz, "The only way for an extensive knowledge management process to function at optimum performance is to possess the technology that facilitates that process." Accordingly, Avery Dennison has tapped into the $100 billion annual patent market with innovative 3-D data warehousing and expects its licensing revenues to increase to over $125 million annually by the end of the year 2000.

> Long Island College Hospital has tapped into a $19 billion information sharing industry to gain competitive advantage and share vital information. As previously profiled, Buckman Laboratories also outfits employees with mobile technology. "Knowledge workers don't turn off their brains when they leave the office," said knowledge specialist Rumizen. "Their creativity, desire to share knowledge, and dedication to the job are not bound to regular working hours and the prescribed workplace. We give them the opportunity to work when and where they choose."

> Dave Sriberg, vice president of information technology at Brodeur Porter Novelli, agreed: "When building applications to expand knowledge-sharing capabilities, you must look at how the people work, and then give them the tools to do their work more easily." Mike Sockol, director of interactive services at the same firm, concurred: "You need to create a

utility that is intuitive, sensitive, and addictive. It needs to be easy to use, even for technophobes. It should address the needs of its users by providing an improved alternative to existing systems. And it should become so valuable that the user cannot imagine working without it."

REFERENCES

1. This section of Chapter V relied on multiple sources, including the FPL Summary Description of Operations; the Union of Japanese Scientists and Engineers (JUSE) counselors interviews and summary reports; Deming: The Way We Know Him by Frank Voehl (St. Lucie Press, 1993); Deming Management at Work by Mary Walton (GP Putnam and Sons, 1990); interviews with Marshall MacDonald and John Hudiburg; various articles from the Miami Herald (1988–1992); Winning with Quality: the FPL Story by John Hudiburg (Quality Resources, 1991); Japanese Management Systems by Howard Gitlow (CRC, 2000); and numerous notes and interview summaries conducted during and after the Deming Prize challenge (1988–1991).
2. Harrington, H. James. "Streamlining Business Processes," Ernst & Young Technical Report TR 90.006HJH.
3. Delio, Michelle. "Keys to Collaboration," *Knowledge Management*, October 1998. Used by permission.

CHAPTER VI

IMPLEMENTING A KNOWLEDGE MANAGEMENT SYSTEM

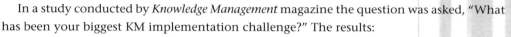

"Planning is fun. Implementing is just hard work,
but it's where the payoff is."

—HJH

In a study conducted by *Knowledge Management* magazine the question was asked, "What has been your biggest KM implementation challenge?" The results:

- 70 percent: Ensuring cooperation across business units
- 16 percent: Assembling the team
- 11 percent: Getting information system buy in
- 2 percent: Staying on budget

From personal experience, most businesspeople would also rate changing an organization's culture as the number-one challenge.

> "Our first (KMS) initiative ignored the people element and paid limited attention to business readiness activities. We also lacked project sponsorship and effective communication—all the familiar potholes."
> —**Sarah Dean**
> **Information system strategist, United Airlines**

STARTING AND IMPLEMENTING A KNOWLEDGE MANAGEMENT SYSTEM

Knowledge management can help any business in four major areas: planning, customer service, training, and project collaboration. A knowledge management program should begin with the simple notion that to succeed it must be multifaceted. Looking at only one or two aspects can quickly lead to the self-defeating opinion that it simply won't work. This type of limited thinking leads to questions and conclusions that stall knowledge management initiatives: Why manage knowledge if you can't measure it? What's the use of measuring it if management doesn't value it? Why would people go to the trouble of sharing what they know?

Implementing successful knowledge management solutions calls for an integrated approach and a multi-point action plan.[1] This requires an implementation approach that's essentially iterative, phased-based, and more widely inclusive than many traditional solution efforts.[2] Successful knowledge management solutions should be implemented using a model and process in an integrated approach. The Harrington Institute has identified an approach, which is loosely based upon Walter Shewhart's cycle of continuous improvement model, that uses six key sets of implementation activities which, when tied together with the proper infrastructure, can provide the foundation for successful knowledge management solutions.[3]

This KMS implementation methodology considers seven fundamentals:

- *Performance and decision modeling.* To define a knowledge strategy, one needs to clearly define the fundamental drivers of organizational performance and create a specific cause-and-effect relationship that links these drivers to company strategy. This helps an organization to link performance with effective process design and business rules decision making.
- *Knowledge enablers and delivery mechanisms.* The key factors that support the overall knowledge management process and enable high performance are:
  - □ *Information.* The organized data required for the activity
  - □ *Knowledge bases.* Information organized in an actionable context
  - □ *Skill modules.* The capability to act on the knowledge
  - □ *Collaboration.* The ability to obtain help from others and to provide it
  - □ *Action records.* What's been done in the past
  - □ *Outcome data.* The ability to relate past actions to results
  - □ *Shared insights.* New ideas and recommendations that lead to even better results

- *Solution design and rapid prototyping.* Once an organization has a clear understanding of what drives performance and the necessary knowledge to enable that performance, solution design and rapid prototyping lay the groundwork for ultimate success. The goal is to iteratively build a prototype that integrates various knowledge enablers into a performance support solution that's tied to the strategic performance model. A good solution design will clearly illustrate how performance will be improved.
- *Business benefits modeling.* Given a clear view of an organization's performance goals and how knowledge enablers are tied to performance, a business benefits framework for the knowledge management solution can be created. Business benefits for knowledge management solutions can be quantified in a structured manner to link the four perspectives of the Balanced Scorecard: financial well-being, customer satisfaction, internal effectiveness, and employee creativity and well-being.
- *Content management.* All successful knowledge management solutions must create a process to continuously turn insights into knowledge useful to others in the organization. Implementing this process requires multiple roles and responsibilities:
  - □ Infrastructure support supplying the necessary network-based tools and technologies to capture insights, edit structure, and broadcast to the larger user community.

☐ Knowledge managers establishing standards and templates for cross-organizational consistency and quality.

☐ Contributors providing content creation and editing capabilities using standards from knowledge managers.

☐ Content owners possessing the in-depth domain expertise to ensure that knowledge is relevant, and to manage a team of contributors.

☐ Librarians managing the knowledge library, ensure quality links between knowledge domains, and maintain the publishing support mechanisms.

Content management may seem to require significant additional effort, yet most organizations already have adequate resources to handle these roles and responsibilities. What's typically missing is the alignment required to integrate these activities to support the organization's strategic performance goals.

■ *Change management.* Knowledge management solutions often require significant change in personal and group culture—and in perception—to achieve their full benefits. Change management challenges are often daunting, yet the opportunity for success is significant. Implementing the knowledge management solution is often a change management program itself.

■ *Tying it all together.* Using knowledge to drive competitive advantage is what knowledge management's all about. The costs to compete are going up, while the ability to maintain customers is in decline. The new world of networked business relationships means that companies can no longer compete on scale, market share, costs, or other traditional metrics; instead, companies must compete on what they know.

SIX PHASES OF IMPLEMENTING A KNOWLEDGE MANAGEMENT SYSTEM

Although in a learning organization everyone needs access to knowledge, most knowledge management systems are designed around the core competencies of the organization. We recommend a six-phase approach to implementing a KMS. (See figure 6.1.) The six phases are made up of sixty-three activities.

1. Requirements definition (eight activities)
2. Infrastructure evaluation (sixteen activities)
3. KMS design and development (thirteen activities)
4. Pilot (fifteen activities)
5. Deployment (ten activities)
6. Continuous improvement (one activity)

Figure 6.1 Knowledge Management Road Map

Phase 1 Requirements definitions	Phase 2 Infrastructure evaluation	Phase 3 KM system design and development	Phase 4 Pilot activities	Phase 5 Deployment	Phase 6 Continuous improvement
Activities	Activities	Activities	Activities	Activities	Activities
1. Develop a KM vision statement. 2. Define KM categories (K-spots). 3. define KMS users. 4. Identify input sources. 5. Identify. 6. Prepare the change management plan. 7. Prepare project plan. 8. Organize the KM team.	1. Survey existing sources. 2. Identify KM communication systems. 3. Identify analysis tools. 4. Identify tacit data & exchange. 5. Change risk analysis. 6. Define K clusters. 7. Define IT gaps. 8. Conduct SWOT. 9. Prepare knowledge maps. 10. Update the OCM plan. 11. Set priorities. 12. Define ground rules. 13. Conduct user survey. 14. Perform a preliminary business needs analysis. 15. Align KM and business strategy. 16. Update project plan.	1. Conduct a benchmark study. 2. Identify integrated functional requirements. 3. Select platform. 4. Define intelligence layers. 5. Define search components. 6. Define silos. 7. Develop the KMS. 8. Audit K assets. 9. Define KMS interfaces. 10. Define tacit to explicit transfer. 11. Develop KM organization. 12. Create the KMS blueprint. 13. Develop the KMS rewards- and -recognition program.	1. Define layer capacity. 2. Install Internet. 3. Define platform independencies. 4. Establish security controls. 5. Install filtering layers. 6. Integrate middleware. 7. Connect legacy layers. 8. Integrate and test total system. 9. Develop training package. 10. Implement the change management plan. 11. Train the affected personnel. 12. Establish the data, information, and knowledge warehouses. 13. Start the pilot. 14. Monitor the pilot. 15. Make required improvements.	1. Define roll out stages. 2. Define incentives. 3. Deploy measurements. 4. Appoint subject matter experts. 5. Set up portals. 6. Conduct promotional campaign. 7. Organize communities of practice. 8. Train the affected personnel. 9. Balance change management and technical factors. 10. Implement the communication plan.	1. Evaluate performance, measure ROI, continuously improve.

It would take a great deal of space to detail each activity, so here's a brief overview of each phase and key activities:

Phase 1—Requirements Definition

Activities that take place during phase 1, requirements definition, are:

1.1. Develop a vision statement that defines how the knowledge system will be operating within the organization three to five years in the future.

1.2. Define the categories that will make up the KMS. These are sometimes called "K-spots." K-spots represent the knowledge niches on which a company must focus its knowledge management efforts. Based on audits of the strategic capability framework, an organization identifies promising processes that will gain the most through knowledge management.

1.3. Define the users of the KMS.

1.4. Identify key sources of data, information, and knowledge.

1.5. Identify the short- and long-term measurements for each knowledge category.

1.6. Prepare the organizational change management (OCM) plan.

1.7. Prepare a project plan.

- Define the scope of the project.
- Define the project deliverables.
- Compare the present culture to the culture of a knowledge organization and develop a change management plan.
- Develop the project work breakdown structure.
- Define the project schedule.
- Define who will do what.
- Develop a value proposition.
- Management accepts the project plan.

1.8. Organize the knowledge management development team.

Phase 2—Infrastructure Evaluation

Activities that take place during phase 2, infrastructure evaluation, are:

2.1. Survey existing data and information sources to define what's available in each of the knowledge categories.

> "Information absorbs the attention of the recipient. Therefore, an overabundance of information creates a deficit of attention."
> —Jeff Hire
> Insulation contractor business manager, Owens Corning Fiberglass

> "It is important to understand how knowledge is formed and how people and organizations learn to use knowledge wisely."
> —Hubert Saint-Onge
> "Tacit Knowledge: The Key to Strategic Alignment of Intellectual Capital,"
> *Strategy & Leadership*

> "For knowledge sharing to become a reality you have to create a climate of trust in your organization."
> —Robert Buckman
> Chairman, Buckman Laboratories

2.2. Identify the present ways data and information are communicated (e.g., Internet, conferences, meetings, books, desktops, networks, or intranets) and included this knowledge into the KMS.

2.3. Identify how data are stored and analyzed (e.g., data warehouses or DDS tools).

2.4. Identify present ways of exchanging tacit data.

2.5. Conduct a change risk assessment.

2.6. Define the knowledge clusters.

2.7. Define inadequacies and gaps in the present information technology (IT) system.

2.8. Conduct a strengths, weaknesses, opportunities, and threats (SWOT) analysis.

2.9. Prepare knowledge maps.

"When planning for an enterprisewide knowledge management system, companies should begin by mapping the system's relation to its strategic objectives and business processes."
—Gartner Group

Definition: *Knowledge mapping* involves finding where information is located in an organization, but the term is used at times to describe concerns with how to structure knowledge. Indeed, maps can range from simple directories of names, titles, and department affiliation to elaborate online search engines with hypertext links to databases of human expertise, research material, and abstracts of published information. Knowledge mapping is also called *knowledge taxonomy*. It's the process that provides an organization with a picture of the specific knowledge it requires to support its business processes.

2.10. Update the OCM plan.

2.11. Set priorities based upon knowledge data that exists today so that the KMS can provide fast results and then expand.

2.12. Define the ground rules that will be used to design the KMS.

2.13. Conduct a user survey.

2.14. Perform a preliminary business needs analysis to evaluate relevant knowledge server choices.

2.15. Align knowledge management and business strategy.

- Understand how to shift knowledge management in an enterprise from today to the strategic plan.
- Perform a knowledge-based SWOT analysis to create knowledge maps.
- Articulate, diagnose, and validate a clear link between strategy and knowledge management.
- Translate the link between strategy and knowledge management to KMS design characteristics.
- Determine the right diagnostic questions to ask, package knowledge, and reduce move.

- Define initiatives to "sell" the knowledge-management project internally.
- Balance exploitation versus exploration, just-in-time versus keep-it-coming delivery, and codification versus personalization using the KMS.
- Define what the KMS critical success factors are.
- Incorporate Amrit Tiwana's twenty-four critical success factors in the KMS design. They are:[4]

    1. There is no silver bullet for knowledge management. In spite of what consultants eyeing your checkbook might say, all research suggests that there is no *one right way* to do it.

    2. Successful knowledge management projects begin with a working definition of knowledge that is accepted equivocally throughout the company.

    3. A process focus is required, not a technology focus.

    4. Successful projects begin with the acceptance that there are no perfect measures or metrics for knowledge work. However, some metrics, even if vague, are needed to gauge the effectiveness of knowledge management.

    5. Selling knowledge management to both managers and end users requires demonstration of at least some short-term impact.

    6. Effective knowledge management must count in tacit knowledge right from the outset, even if the primary focus is on codification. Codification with no personalization is bound to fail.

    7. Shared knowledge requires the creation of a shared context.

    8. A successful knowledge management project must begin with knowledge that already exists, deliver initial results, and then continue to expand. Without such orientation, your knowledge management project risks being stifled in its early days.

    9. Accommodation for reasoning and support for assumption surfacing must be an integral part of knowledge management.

    10. Knowledge management projects that succeed have an eye on the future and not the past or present. In contrast, information management handles the present, and data archives document the past.

    11. Knowledge management systems must minimize unnecessary routing re-transmissions—a common source of noise and distortion.

    12. What your employees need are incentives, not faster computers. Technology provides many enablers except the biggest one of all: an incentive to share knowledge.

    13. A knowledge management system must allow everyone to both contribute and access knowledge. However, critical knowledge that represents confidential, competitive and innovative process knowledge or private records must be protected.

14. Effective systems for knowledge management respect confidentiality of users by allowing them to choose not to identify themselves. Although anonymity goes contrary to the idea of linking contributions to their originators, this balance is necessary.

15. Most successful knowledge management systems allow users to access, read, and contribute from anywhere and at any time. Remote connectivity therefore becomes necessary.

16. If the system is used extensively, its technical design should be such that its users can see updates and additions in real time without having to manually refresh content. This is a trivial technical problem that is often overlooked—with disastrous results.

17. As explicated content and tacit knowledge pointers within a knowledge management system grow, resource maps must be provided to help users navigate through them.

18. Best practice databases are essential, but they are not the primary component of an effective knowledge management system.

19. Ongoing management support is needed for both the knowledge strategy and the knowledge management system.

20. Effective knowledge management systems must support collaborative work and internal consulting. Knowledge management must also focus on product and service development processes.

21. Knowledge management systems need to be informal and communicatively rich. Effective knowledge management systems are easy to use. Extensive features that make the systems cumbersome to use or less intuitive can discourage its use.

22. Packaging knowledge is a goal that must be supported by knowledge management systems right from the outset. Remember that less (volume) is more when it comes to knowledge and its effective management.

23. Knowledge management technology should provide a logical extension for business units, and its choice should create a win-win situation primarily for its users, not your company's technologists.

24. Different users prefer different delivery mechanisms. This distinction implies that users of a knowledge management system should be able to choose whether they will pull content or it will be pushed to them. Similarly, users must not be bombarded by all-inclusive content.

2.16. Update the project plan and the change management plan.

Phase 3—KMS Design and Development

The KMS design must have what is called "knowledge velocity." Knowledge velocity overcomes the sluggishness that exists in most communication systems today. It streamlines the critical patches that transform data in applied activities to produce fast, measurable results. This quickly leads to improved business performance.

The IT system will normally be built in the following seven layers:

■ Interface

■ Access and authentication

■ Collaborative filtering and intelligence

■ Application

■ Transport

■ Middleware and legacy integration

■ Repository

> **"If people have to change the way they communicate to feed information into a KM system, they won't do it."**
> **—Mike Lynch**
> **Founder and CEO,**
> **Autonomy Corporation**[5]

Activities that take place during phase 3, KMS design and development, are:

3.1. Conduct a knowledge management benchmark study.

■ Benchmark best of class.

☐ Define what will be benchmarked.

☐ Collect data on how the process is performing today.

☐ Collect and analyze external published information.

☐ Identify benchmarking partners.

☐ Conduct interviews and surveys.

☐ Conduct site visits.

☐ Summarize the data collected on site and define which practices can be adapted or adopted to your process.

3.2. Identify the integrated functional requirements that include but aren't limited to:

■ Metadata

■ Content repository

■ Search requirements

■ Security directions

■ Application support

■ Taxonomy

■ Cashing and delivery

■ Personalization requirements

3.3. Select the collaborative platform and content to the edges versus centralized content storage.

3.4. Define collaborative intelligence layers (e.g., expert reasoning system, active agents, neural networks, artificial intelligence, data warehouses, genetic algorithms, rule basis, and care-based reasoning).

3.5. Define the components that will be used for searching, indexing, and retrieval. This is the part of the process that's best understood and supported by technology. Knowledge location and retrieval are supported by many combinations of search engines, intelligence agents, crawlers, filters, and Boolean searches. It's important to note that location and retrieval technology can use databases stored in many different locations.

3.6. Define the knowledge silos.

When it comes to classifying knowledge and information, there are a number of options that you should consider. Some of them are:

■ Alphabetical
■ Alphanumeric
■ Dewey decimal codes
■ Public library classifications
■ Predicast revised event codes
■ Universal decimal classification
■ Library of Congress classification
■ Association for Computing Machinery computing classification

Look at them all before selecting one to use. It's a costly mistake to select the wrong classification system then later have to change.

3.7. Develop the KMS.

■ Define the capabilities of each layer of KMS architecture in the context of your organization.
■ Optimize knowledge objects and the future abstraction layer.
■ Balance push-based and pull-based knowledge delivery.
■ Identify the right mix of components to search, index, and retrieve knowledge from anywhere, by any device.
■ Create platform independence, leverage the Internet and intranet, enable universal authorship, and optimize video.
■ Develop the access and authentication layer. Secure data, control access, and distribute control.
■ Develop the collaborative filtering and intelligence layer.
■ Develop the application layer and ensure that it's compatible with both the intelligence and transport layer.
■ Leverage the transport layer.
■ Develop the middleware and legacy integration layers.

- Integrate and enhance the repository layer.
- Create knowledge tags and attributes such as domain, form, type, product/service, line, and location.
- Shift to agent-computing orientation.

3.8. Audit existing knowledge assets and process.
- Understand the purpose of a knowledge audit.
- Use Roger E. Bohn's eight stages of knowledge growth. They are:
  - ☐ Complete ignorance
  - ☐ Awareness
  - ☐ Measurement
  - ☐ Control of the mean
  - ☐ Process capability
  - ☐ Process characterization
  - ☐ Know why
  - ☐ Complete knowledge[5]

- Identify, evaluate, and rate critical process knowledge.
- Select an audit method.
- Congregate a preliminary knowledge audit team.
- Audit and analyze your organization's existing knowledge.
- Identify your organization's K-spot.
- Choose a strategic position for your KMS.

3.9. Define generic systems interface.
3.10. Define how tacit knowledge is transformed into explicit knowledge.
3.11. Develop the knowledge management organization, and structure and prepare job descriptions to facilitate knowledge sharing.
- Identify sources of requisite expertise.
- Identify critical points of failure: requirement, control, management, buy-in, and end-user buy-in.
- Structure the knowledge management team organizationally, strategically, and technologically.
- Manage stakeholder expectations.
- Resolve team-sizing issues.
- Prepare job descriptions.

> **"Storytelling is the best way we have for conveying tacit (soft) knowledge. Stories profoundly capture things that cannot be captured in any other way."**
> **—Richard Stone**
> **Founder, Storywork Institute**

3.12. Create the KMS blueprint.
- Develop the knowledge management architecture.
- Understand and select the architecture components.
- Design for a high level of interoperability.
- Optimize for performance and scalability.
- Understand repository life-cycle management.
- Understand and incorporate requisite user interface considerations.
- Position and scope the KMS.
- Make the build-or-try decision and understand the trade-offs.
- Future-proof the KMS.

3.13. Develop the KMS rewards-and-recognition system. Don't underestimate the importance of this step. It will make or break your KMS. Few people give their knowledge freely to potential competitors unless they receive something back.

Phase 4—KMS Pilot

> **"Lessons learned from pilot projects can nourish your enterprisewide implementation."**
> —**Joe Mullich**
> **"Growing a Knowledge Solution,"** *Knowledge Management* **magazine**

Due to the complexity of the KMS, it's always better to pilot it before it's fully released. Select a part of the KMS within the organization to pilot, such as a department, function, or one of the system silos. It's wise to limit the pilot to within the system. Typical knowledge management pilots run for approximately three months. Selecting the correct pilot and the individuals who will be involved in the pilot is an extremely critical part of the total process. Select individuals who are receptive to new ideas and who understand the importance of sharing intellectual assets.

> **"Try to put well in practice what you already know. In doing so, you will, in good time, discover the hidden things you now inquire about."**
> —**Rembrandt**

Although the pilot will be applied to a small part of the total KMS, system designers must consider the total KMS as they define requirements and install pilot software, equipment, and procedures.

Activities that take place during phase 4, pilot of the KMS, are:

4.1. Define the capacity of each layer.
4.2. Install Internet if one doesn't already exist.
4.3. Define platform interdependencies.

> **"The first and most important result that should come from a pilot is a small success story that you can communicate to the rest of the company."**[6]
> —**Dave A. Anderson**
> **KM specialist, Robbins-Gioia**

4.4. Establish security, access, and distribution controls.
4.5. Install filtering and intelligence layers.
4.6. Integrate middleware.
4.7. Connect legacy layers and external systems.
4.8. Integrate and test the total system.

Figure 6.2 The KMS Training Cycle

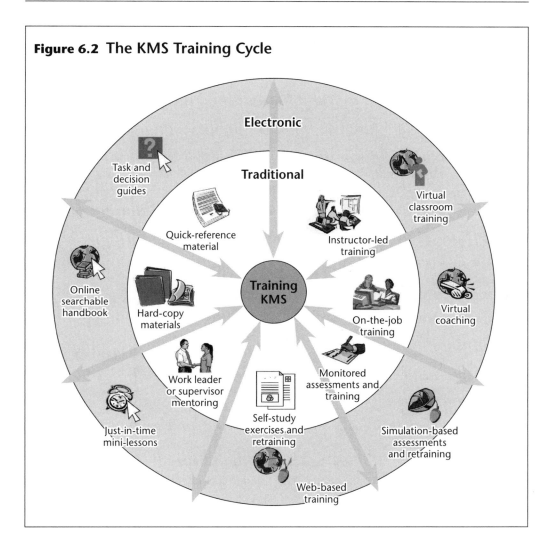

4.9. Develop training packages for the users and the knowledge management team.

Don't limit organizational training to the traditional classroom setting. This type of training, for the most part, reflects outdated thinking. Better options are available today. In most cases the just-in-time training required by a KMS needs to be provided one person at a time. The KMS training circle in figure 6.2 depicts the preferred approach.

4.10. Implement the change management plan.

4.11. Train the affected personnel.

"If you trust the people you're working with, you don't waste time worrying about their hidden agendas. Change happens faster and progress happens faster."
—**David Berdish**
Organizational learning manager, Ford Motor Co.

4.12. Establish the data, information, and knowledge warehouses.

4.13. Start the pilot.

4.14. Monitor the pilot.

4.15. Make required improvements.

Phase 5—Deployment

This is a critical phase. People resist sharing their knowledge. Organizational change management activities that parallel phases one through four should break down most resistance, but lasting change takes time and persistence. At this point knowledge clusters, communities of practice, and technical advisory team networks play an important part. Effective just-in-time training is also essential, preferably with a stage rollout—first internally and then externally to the organization.

Activities that take place during phase 5, Deployment, are:

5.1. Define the rollout stages.

5.2. Define incentives for using and contributing to the KMS. Use a result-driven incremental approach.

5.3. Deploy the knowledge management measurement system.

5.4. Appoint subject matter experts for each knowledge silo.

5.5. Set up KM portals.

5.6. Conduct a promotional campaign.

5.7. Organize knowledge clusters, communities of practice, and technical advisory team networks.

5.8. Train the affected personnel.

5.9. Balance change management and technical expertise with managerial, operational, interactional, social, and technical (MOIST) factors.

5.10. Implement a comprehensive communication plan.

Phase 6—Continuous Improvement

Knowledge is reusable, but it's also perishable. If it's not continuously updated, the knowledge warehouse soon becomes obsolete. (Figure 6.3 illustrates the information life cycle.) Core competencies change and new ones emerge, this requiring restructuring of the knowledge management teams and silos. New sources of generic information are continuously developing, requiring expansion of the information warehouse. By definition, knowledge is only good for a finite period of time and then it becomes obsolete. Without nourishing and replenishing the knowledge warehouse, the

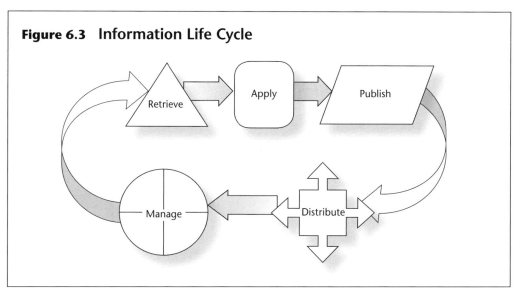

Figure 6.3 **Information Life Cycle**

system is worthless. Continuous improvement and updating is essential for the survival of a KMS.

Take caution when re-reading the process-based knowledge map (PKM) in figure 6.4; it provides more information on how to implement IT technologies than how to change the organization from a knowledge-hoarding culture to a knowledge-sharing culture. As stated earlier, installing technology for the KMS is easy. The hard part is getting people to use

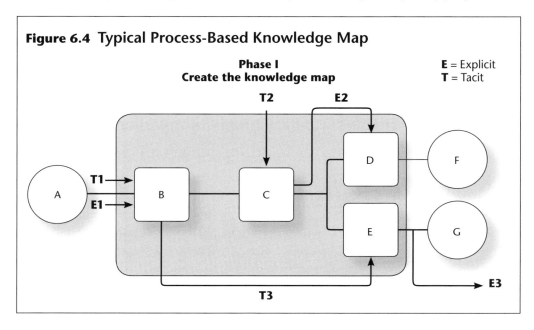

Figure 6.4 Typical Process-Based Knowledge Map

it. But by thorough use of IT to automate workflow, cultural barriers are reduced and the system becomes less dependent on employees. A KMS isn't just an IT strategy or methodology, it's a well-balanced mixture of technology, culture change, new rewards systems, and business plans.

PROCESS-BASED KNOWLEDGE MAP

Definition: *Process-based knowledge map* (PKM) is a diagram that visually displays knowledge within the context of a business process. It shows how knowledge should be used within the process and the sources of knowledge.

A PKM is very helpful in defining how knowledge flows through the process and in identifying knowledge black holes. The map includes all types of knowledge that drive the process or result from process activities. The map will show both explicit (hard) and tacit (soft) knowledge.

Typical knowledge inputs are hard (explicit) knowledge, like mission and scope statements. Typical knowledge outputs are soft (tacit) knowledge, such as lessons learned, or hard knowledge, such as change requests or phase gate reports. The PKM is used to:

- Identify knowledge gap and priorities.
- Define knowledge sources and knowledge seekers (communities of practice).
- Define knowledge audits.
- Redesign or reengineer the process.
- Benchmark other organizations.
- Improve knowledge flow.
- Develop competency improvement programs.
- Define intellectual assets.
- Input to the strategic business plan.

The major advantage of the PKM is that it provides a clear and tangible picture of the knowledge structure which otherwise is fuzzy and abstract.

Time to Implement

Organizations must be aware that a KMS isn't easy to implement. It takes long-term commitment and requires significant investments, not only in technology integration but in redesigning business processes and organizational change. KMS implementation typically takes between one and two years, sometimes as long as five years. It's important to start slowly, to first understand what users want from the system. Then select small pilots to learn from and to show measurable results.

Based on a survey conducted by *Knowledge Management*[7] and International Data Corp. (IDC), the major challenges that organizations will have to face in implementing a KMS are:

- Employees not having time for knowledge management
- Current culture doesn't encourage sharing
- Lack of understanding of knowledge management and its benefits
- Inability to measure financial benefits of knowledge management
- Lack of skill in knowledge management techniques
- Organizational processes aren't designed for knowledge management
- Lack of funding for knowledge management
- Lack of appropriate technology
- Lack of commitment from senior management

It doesn't come easy, but the results will more than offset the effort.

KNOWLEDGE MANAGEMENT SYSTEM BUDGET

The average budget to implement a KMS is about $3.2 million. This cost can range from $100,000 to more than $5 million, depending on the complexity of the system, number of users, and number of knowledge silos. Typically, the breakdown for IT service spending to develop a KMS is:

- Implementation (30 percent)
- Consulting/planning (28 percent)
- Training (13 percent)
- Operations (15 percent)
- Maintenance (14 percent)

> **"The human mind, once stretched by a new idea, never regains its original dimensions."**
> **—Oliver Wendell Holmes, Sr. American physician and poet**

KNOWLEDGE MANAGEMENT SYSTEM ENABLERS

To establish a successful knowledge culture and KMS, the organization needs to develop the following:

- High level of trust
- Excellent problem-solving approaches
- Effective teamwork between and across all levels and functions of the organization
- Harmony and cohesion between the organization's mission, vision, and business plans
- Reward system that rewards people for sharing knowledge

- Belief that an organization practicing prevention is much more successful than one just solving problems as they occur
- Team-based collaborative workforce
- Strong process focus
- Good understanding of all stakeholders' requirements
- Willingness to accept ideas from outside the organization
- Good understanding of their competition
- Ability to make decisions at the lowest levels
- Knowledge champions that keep the KMS a high organizational priority
- Knowledge assets measurement system
- Inclusion of knowledge management in everyone's performance plan and evaluation

SUMMARY

When you read this chapter, you may think that most of the work and cost in implementing a KMS is software and hardware-related activities. The truth of the matter is that this is only the tangible (hard) part of the implementation process. The most difficult and costly part is intangible (soft)—preparing people to accept the change and adapt to a new, more interactive communication system. The value of a KMS isn't the sophistication of the database and its portals, but how effectively knowledge is used to meet an organization's needs. It's extremely important that the KMS implementation team focuses most of its effort on understanding how users are presently acquiring the knowledge they need, and what additional knowledge they require to increase their value to the organization. Although the purpose of a KMS is to provide assignment-related knowledge, other types of information is often included for portal users (e.g., stocks that an individual may be following and their present value).

A good rule of thumb is to spend four times more effort developing the soft side of the KMS than the hard side.

"Ideas are worthless. Ideas transferred into
results are priceless."

—HJH

REFERENCES

1. This seven-point model is based upon the work of Renaissance Worldwide. Many of its solutions have been featured in *Knowledge Management,* and are cited as a practical model to solve many problems that knowledge management practitioners face when implementing their systems. Renaissance Worldwide can be contacted at *www.rens.com* or (781) 259-8833.

2. Ibid.

3. The implementation structure described is loosely based upon the work of Renaissance Worldwide. The company has described an approach by which knowledge management can fundamentally restructure an organization's competitive position. Understanding what drives performance and how that links to strategy is the first step. Identifying the knowledge that enables high performance and rapidly creating innovative solutions to deliver that knowledge directly into the hands of the people that make decisions are imperative. Creating the content management capabilities and cultural environment that foster knowledge sharing and enable continuous improvement is the key to maintaining competitive advantage.

4. Tiwana, Amrit. *The Knowledge Management Toolkit: Orchestrating IT, Strategy, and Knowledge Platforms* (New York: Prentice Hall, second edition, 2002).

5. Dyer, Greg, and Brian McDonough. "The State of KM," *Knowledge Management*, April 2001.

6. Bohn, Roger E. "Measuring and Managing Technological Knowledge," *Sloan Management Review*, Vol. 36, Fall 1994.

7. Dyer, Greg, and Brian McDonough. "The State of KM," *Knowledge Management*, April 2001.

CHAPTER VII

KNOWLEDGE MANAGEMENT VALUES

The following are key points to remember about knowledge workers:[1]

- New hires require two-and-a-half months to be fully effective.
- A knowledge management system (KMS) will reduce that time frame by 30 percent.
- At a loaded cost of $200,000 per year, that's $12,500 savings per new hire.
- The cost to keep the knowledge worker current is going up 20 percent per year.
- The cost to provide knowledge workers with knowledge in 2000 was $5,900 each.
- The Fortune 500 knowledge deficit was $12 billion in 1999 and $32 billion in 2003.

> **"The only irreplaceable capital an organization possesses is the knowledge and ability of its people. The productivity of that capital depends on how effectively people share their competence with those who can use it."**
> **—Andrew Carnegie**
> **U.S. industrialist and philanthropist**

Willem Roelandts, president, CEO, and chairman of the board of Xilinx, calculates that losing a trained engineer costs a quarter of a million dollars in lost intellectual property alone. Douglas Hensler, dean of the Craig School of Business, suggests that when an employee is getting ready to leave, the organization should give him or her $50,000 to write down everything he or she knows.

VALUATING KNOWLEDGE CAPITAL

> **"84 firms (in the U.S.) each has KC (Knowledge Capital) of more than $20 billion and as a group accounted for a total of $5,331 billion; 3,287 firms each has KC of less than $20 billion and accounted for $3,078 billion total."**
> **—Paul A. Strassmann**
> **Author and information-systems advisor**

The valuation of knowledge capital makes it possible, at least in theory, to assess the worth of people who've acquired and possess an organization's accumulated knowledge. These individuals leave the workplace every day or night, possibly never return, storing in their heads all the know-how acquired while receiving their days' pay. According to knowledge management guru Paul A. Strassmann, their brains are repositories of knowledge accumulated over untold hours of listening and talking while not delivering any goods or services to paying customers. In other words, both the minds and files managed by employees carry a share of the company's knowledge capital—thus every employee is a custodian of the firm's most important assets.

Profile 7.1 Acorda Therapeutics Rehabilitates Sharing Incentives

Background

Acorda Therapeutics develops recuperative and rehabilitative products for spinal cord injury and other central nervous system conditions. The company's "team or die" approach for its core group of research scientists includes direct financial incentives.

KM Strategy

Ron Cohen, president and CEO of Acorda Therapeutics, says its scientists were selected based on two key criteria. Each had to be at the top of fields deemed critical to the company's mission, and each had to be willing to contribute within a team structure.

"We emphasized teamwork in conversations with every scientist, and proposed to them that they might achieve worthy goals by working together and sharing information with their peers," Cohen says. They illustrated the concept with historically successful examples, such as the Huntington's Gene Project of the 1980s and the Manhattan Project. "Finally, we employed a carrot-and-stick technique, telling scientists that teamwork was the most important operating principle of the company, and if they participated, they would benefit by being part of a team of superb scientists working on cutting-edge projects. They would also vest stock in the company over time."

Along with the incentives, Acorda's approach included a healthy dose of disincentives, explains Cohen. "Lack of teamwork would result in immediate dismissal from the company's projects and forfeiture of all benefits. We asked every person we invited to be part of the organization to agree explicitly to these terms."

Success Story

In-house scientific consensus soon emerged that the only way to ensure truly open cross-communications within the company was to guarantee each member the security of his or her ideas, data, and knowledge until such time as the team member chose to make these more publicly available outside of the company. So far, this system seems to be working well.

Cohen compares his company's knowledge-sharing culture with his experience as an oarsman in college rowing in an eight-man shell with coxswain. "I prefer this to individual sculling," he says. "The victorious sculler receives individual glory; the eight receive glory as a varsity boat. But when you row in an eight, you feel as though you possess the strength of the whole team. That feeling cannot be replicated in a single scull. And even a mediocre eight will always beat an Olympic-quality sculler."

"Overall, I believe that many people want to feel that they are part of a mission that is bigger than themselves, that gives meaning to their lives, and that they could not possibly accomplish outside of a team structure. As long as they trust that everyone else in the enterprise is playing by the same rules, they will share knowledge."

(Source: Michelle Delio, "Keys to Collaboration," *Knowledge Management* magazine, October 1998. Used with permission. For more information, see the profile on the Ark Group, the magazine's publisher, in chapter I.)

Though these assets never visibly show up on any of the organization's financial reports, this is what's meant by calculating the value of knowledge.[2]

By contrast, custodianship of financial assets is a well-defined discipline that depends on procedures and regulations to precisely account for resources. In many organizations an elaborate framework involving accountants, auditors, reporting standards, and governance oversight has been developed to do that. Yet as discussed in this book, the financial assets of corporations represent a small share of total assets. An organization's most important asset by far is its knowledge capital, yet custodianship, accounting, and reporting standards for knowledge capital don't formally exist.

As explored in *Fortune* ("We're Worth Our Weight in Pentium Chips," March 20, 2000), Paul A. Strassmann likes the idea that "manufactured goods increasingly are congealed brainpower," and that per-pound cost calculations might help measure the worth of knowledge capital embodied in products. Yet these value approximations also begin to demonstrate that knowledge value can reveal itself only in the price someone is willing to pay for it—just like other commodities and products.

How to explain the enormous disparities in the per-pound prices of various products? The initial approach, first developed by Strassmann and advanced by others, studied differences in labor costs: "USX Steel had a high ratio of labor to revenues, but General Motors (GM) did not, and Intel's was even less. The GM case is particularly revealing. By far the largest cost for GM is the cost of component purchases, which amounted to some 54 percent of revenues; the cost of labor for assembly is small in relation to the price of a car." If operating costs don't explain cost differences, what about capital costs?

"The structure of capital assets clearly differentiates USX Steel from GM and Intel," Strassmann points out. "The amounts of financial capital employed by these firms vary dramatically. Intel requires $23.4 billion of financial capital to deliver its semiconductors. GM needs $15.7 billion of financial capital to deliver millions of cars. Yet USX Steel needs only $2.3 billion of financial capital to produce tons of materials that weigh more than all of the machinery employed by both Intel and GM."

Ultimately, Strassmann says, large differences in per-pound prices are explained not by financial capital but knowledge capital. (To compute knowledge capital, divide economic value added by the interest rate paid to acquire knowledge capital.) "Intel's $107.1 billion in knowledge capital exceeds its financial capital and accounts for 76 percent of the total knowledge capital for all three firms. GM's knowledge capital, $33.4 billion, accounts for 23 percent. USX Steel possesses only $2.1 billion of knowledge capital, which is less than its financial capital."

Such capital comparisons shed light on other aspects of the information-age economy, beyond product price. What about the ease of market entry and the competitive viability of firms that rely on a high ratio of knowledge to financial capital? Could it be more desirable to be an Intel, with 1998 revenues of $23.3 billion, than a GM, which in 1998 had $161 billion in revenues?

"One way of answering this question is from the shareholder's standpoint," Strassmann says. "GM's return on shareholder equity (ROE) has consistently declined, from 82 percent in 1994 to 17 percent in 1998. In contrast, Intel's ROE has climbed steadily, from 30 percent in 1994 to 41 percent in 1997. GM's falling profitability explains why, in keeping with the trend to associate the prospect of huge gains with things e-related, it is diversifying into information services. It has issued press statements announcing that 'the world's largest automaker is turning itself into the world's largest e-commerce company... moving into online mortgages, communications services, and information delivery.'"

Such pronouncements make good public relations, according to Strassmann, but the underlying conclusion may be misguided—and misleading. "For the time being, a dominant firm (such as Intel) that controls a large amount of knowledge capital is likely to be more profitable than a dominant firm (such as USX-Steel or GM) that depends primarily on financial capital. But such a simplistic view about the 'new economy' could mislead companies into making foolish investments. Sustaining competitive advantage through ownership of knowledge capital is a precarious proposition, much more vulnerable than the ownership of financial assets."[3]

KNOWLEDGE VALUATION ON THE CORPORATE RADAR SCREEN[4]

CFOs and other financial executives are remarkably reluctant to put numbers on something many business people consider to be intangible. However, Strassmann argues, with the rising importance of knowledge assets the time has come to place knowledge management on the agendas of CEOs/CFOs, executive managers, financial analysts, and, ultimately, shareholders. To that end, there must first be a way to independently verify the worth of an organization's knowledge assets or knowledge capital.

Knowledge capital can be calculated, because it's the most important unique contributing influence to explain how a firm earns its profits and preserves what is arguably its most important asset. Allocating the respective contributions of knowledge capital and financial capital to profits can be done only if financial capital is a commodity—one readily available at a price reflecting the interest rate that a firm pays to borrow. However, a company prospers not because of financial capital—which almost any organization can obtain for a price—but due to the effective use of knowledge capital. Therefore, annual returns realized on knowledge capital can be isolated after paying a "rental fee" for financial capital then subtracting that amount from profits.

What remains is what economists call an "economic profit," what some consultants call the "economic value-added." Strassmann has labeled it "knowledge value-added" because this amount accounts for missing elements that represent everything not shown on a conventional balance sheet. By filtering out the contributions of financial capital to reported profits, what remains can be attributed to what knowledge capital has actually delivered. In other words, knowledge value-added is the annual yield a firm realizes from managing knowledge capital. Once the yield from a capital asset is known, calculating the value of its principal is almost straightforward. All you have to do, argues Strassmann, is divide the value of knowledge value-added by the costs of that capital and you can get the verifiable, independently reproducible total worth of a firm's knowledge capital—a sum that can be compared against other organizations regardless of industry, size, or market share.

This method's dicey problem can be inaccurately determining capital cost in estimating knowledge value-added. To resolve this academics have spun elaborate theories, including the most popular approach taught to MBA students, the "capital asset pricing model." Strassmann argues that this theory is not only indefensible but also does not fit reality. The best valuations of capital cost are offered by the marketplace, as reflected in the interest costs a firm actually pays for its long-term debt.

Calculating Knowledge Capital

Much talk about the knowledge-based "new economy" is speculation unsupported by economic data. What drew attention at the turn of the 21st century were staggering profits created by bidding up Internet stocks. Yet the established rules of financial viability—such as making profits—have proven themselves over and over again. Excesses based on speculation may capture the imagination from time to time, so the valuation of assets requires a measured perspective.

To paint a reasonable picture of knowledge capital valuation, the Strassmann study collected financial data on 7,288 leading U.S. corporations whose stocks are listed publicly. At the turn of the century, these firms employed more than 36.2 million people. Their financial assets were about $20 trillion, or more than 64 percent of all corporate assets in the United States, certainly a credible sample.

Here are some of the study's findings:

- The financial assets of these 7,288 firms totaled more $19.8 trillion. Yet most of this valuation is offset by liabilities and debt equaling $16.1 trillion, which leaves a net worth of $3.7 trillion. A similar number—$3.4 trillion—represents the net value of property and equipment of these corporations.

- The total stock market valuations of these firms were about $11.6 trillion. This figure suggests that investors believed that knowledge assets were worth $7.9 trillion, or 214 percent of the net financial assets of $3.7 trillion.

- Using these calculations as the basis of valuation, the study concluded that knowledge capital for these corporations totaled $6.4 trillion. So the stock market has over-valued the corporations by $1.5 trillion, or 13 percent, if we use profits to judge a firm's worth. Several high-technology firms account for a disproportionately large share of this premium.

■ Unfortunately, the $1.5 trillion valuation premium may be seen, in Strassmann's words, as a "euphoric aberration," because the sum of the individual knowledge capital values included a large number of firms that delivered negative economic value. Considering the effects of these negative contributions, premium valuations reflect the optimism of shareholders willing to gamble on continued stock appreciation even when confronted with a long string of current losses.

As this important study indicated, wealth based on knowledge capital remains highly concentrated. It is limited in scope and can be observed only for a small number of firms. The knowledge capital for large segments of the workforce remains unaccounted for, in areas such as government services, defense, not-for-profit firms, and consumer services, not to mention part-time employees. The good news is that the knowledge economy is still evolving.

Baruch Lev, professor of accounting and finance at New York University, has proposed a new and innovative insight into the valuation of knowledge and ideas. Lev introduces a simple ratio for determining the valuation of a firm's knowledge capital. He defines it as ". . . the normalized earning minus earnings from tangible and financial assets divided by knowledge capital discount rate." The significance of Lev's article is great. In contrast to earlier attempts, most of these more akin to judging beauty contests, Lev offers a reproducible and independently verifiable calculation. Even more important is that Lev's concept of "com-

---

Profile 7.2 Covisint in the Driver's Seat

Background

The automobile industry has been maligned for reasons ranging from market dominance to poor financial performance. However, there are many reasons to look kindly on the industry and its members. The automobile industry ranks as one of the largest employers in the world, for one thing, with millions of people worldwide linked to the industry. Secondly, the industry acts as a barometer for the greater economy. And finally, the industry is a hotbed for knowledge management innovation, bringing together people and ideas to forge new, more efficient, and safer products.

Covisint is the automotive industry's B2B (business-to-business) purchasing consortium and online exchange, organized in February of 2000 by the Big Three automakers and more recently operated by a consortium of eleven automakers and some 5,000 suppliers. The exchange's stated purpose is "to create visibility within a company's supply chain [by] transforming the linear chain into an efficient networked model." Its Web site declares that Covisint "is not about incremental improvement [but] is a fundamental redesign of the enterprise."

Initial Knowledge Management Strategy

The original strategy of this automakers' alliance was that Covisint would take over a large share of procurement processes. The company would make cooperation between carmakers and suppliers faster, easier, and more efficient, lowering development costs for carmakers with its network of suppliers.

Covisint firms reap over half of all of the available industry profits while keeping their cost of information low relative to their cost of goods. This means increased purchasing power for Covisint. Such efficiency will enable it to impose terms on its suppliers, in an emphatic way that economically weaker competitors cannot. Covisint is not only efficient in its use of information resources—this efficiency expressed in the ratio of profits to information costs—but also has the potential to keep enhancing this advantage by having more profits to expend in competing for sources of supply.

Secondly, although other auto manufacturers spend more money than Covisint companies on information—which includes all spending on knowledge management—their ability to extract pricing concessions from their suppliers, who account for about half of their cost of goods, will diminish as Covisint's power grows. This will increase the pressure on them to join the exchange. As a consequence they will reduce their spending on knowledge management. The profits of the auto manufacturers not participating in Covisint are already squeezed to very low levels, and the efficiencies of B2B procurement will lower the prices of automobiles for consumers. The only option available to those manufacturers will be to keep cutting their information costs. The payoff for knowledge accumulation will appear in the transaction prices at which B2B supplies are purchased. Therefore, the auto manufacturers will have less incentive to spend money on knowledge management that concerns the production pipeline, which is where they spend most of their knowledge management dollars now.

Knowledge Management Strategy Shifts

In spite of its seeming success, Covisint has dropped online catalogues from its Web site and downgraded its reverse auction service. The organization, which led the drive for public B2B exchanges, is now focused on becoming a knowledge management communications provider, according to *ComputerWeekly*. In June of 2005, Covisint launched its XML-based Covisint messaging product, which aims to replace electronic data interchange and manual processes which automotive industry companies use to communicate. Jeff Liedel, Covisint's vice president of new product development, says the messaging service will reduce "the complexity of managing multiple formats that have been dictated by customers, and the multitude of protocols and connection points required to conduct business." Covisint has also expanded into communications management for the health care industry.

The news relating to Covisint's downgrading of its reverse auction service may confirm some analysts' views that online B2B exchanges have failed to fulfill their early promise. DaimlerChrysler executives have said the company has had savings by using Covisint, but Kevin Proust, automotive analyst at research firm GartnerG2, says Covisint products, such as auctions and catalogues, had only been used on a small scale.

Thilo Koslowski, lead automotive analyst at GartnerG2, says, "The whole premise of public exchanges was wrong. Companies are not going to want to give away their technology knowledge—a key competitive advantage. To go from competition to collaboration in one go was never going to happen. Private hubs make much more sense. Covisint could perhaps act as a connector for all these individual e-hubs."

(Source: Paul A. Strassmann, "How E-Business Affects Knowledge Capital," *Knowledge Management* magazine, November 2000. Used with permission. For more information, see the profile on the Ark Group, the magazine's publisher, in chapter I.)

prehensive value," defined as the sum of financial capital (e.g., book value) and knowledge capital, provides a way to determine the worth of corporate knowledge and ideas.

The following table is an extract from Lev's calculations, as shown in *CFO* magazine:

Figure 7.1 Lev's Calculations

Valuations in $ Millions

	Book Value	Market Valuation	Lev-Calculated Knowledge Capital	Market Valuation of Knowledge Capital	Market/ Calculated Knowledge Capital
Merck	12,614	139,910	48,038	127,296	265%
Bristol-Meyers Squibb	7,219	106,994	30,470	99,775	327%
Johnson & Johnson	12,359	92,884	29,695	80,585	271%
Pfizer	7,933	136,846	23,890	128,913	540%
American Home Products	8,175	63,392	22,822	55,217	242%
Forest Labs	614	2,653	553	2,039	369%
Barr Lab	156	909	376	753	200%
Perrigo	426	821	254	395	156%
Agouron Pharmaceuticals	236	1,049	152	813	535%

The stock market, however, didn't care much about the calculated estimates. For instance, Merck—with calculated knowledge capital of about $48 billion and book value of $12.6 billion—had a market valuation of about $140 billion. Thus the market valuation of knowledge capital was total market valuation minus book value, more than $127 billion. That's a 265 percent overvaluation, according to Strassmann. Similarly, the market valuations of knowledge capital for most of the 47 firms listed in the *CFO* article are much greater than what Lev suggested in his article.

Intrinsic Worth of Employees

In our knowledge-based economy, there are many kinds of capital: Organizational, intellectual, knowledge, human, structural, customer, and innovation capital are all recognized concepts. However, at least one source of capital in an organization's intangible assets has not been clearly identified: personal knowledge capital. Strassmann's work to quantify knowledge capital historically assumes that a knowledge-based asset is the residual worth remaining after a business deducts expected returns on financial capital. But this approach doesn't address the intrinsic worth of employees. After all, even employees of a firm with no knowledge capital whatsoever possess knowledge capital of their own, an asset that they can market to other employers. To recognize the worth of individuals, in addition to the worth of corporations, means acknowledging two manifestations of knowledge capital, which happens to fit the Strassmann model quite well.

Personal knowledge capital (PKC) is directly related to the total compensation a knowledge worker can obtain in the marketplace. We can calculate the relationship between an individual's PKC and salary on the assumption that employers "rent" a person's PKC. This approach discards classical theories about wages and sees individuals themselves as capitalists. The worth of someone's PKC is their annual salary divided by an interest rate that reflects the implied cost of capital. The "knowledge interest rate" will vary with the overall economy. Yearly salaries, then, are analogous to the worth of an annual bond coupon. Once you know the price of the coupon, you can find the nominal worth of the bond. For example, if labor markets are tight and a new employee represents a risky investment, the "coupon rate" for purchasing knowledge would be equivalent to a bond rated B or C. Thus, at 15 percent the PKC of an employee earning $40,000 per year would be $266,666 ($40,000 divided by .15). If the labor market is short on talent and employees need time to develop corporate know-how, however, the coupon rate for acquiring knowledge would be equivalent to a bond rated AA or A. In that case, at 6.5 percent the same employee's PKC would be worth $615,384 ($40,000 divided by .065).

In contrast, corporate knowledge capital (CKC) is reflected in the worth of corporate earnings to shareholders. We can value CKC by subtracting the worth of the company's PKC.

The concepts of PKC and CKC are not merely theoretical. They lead to insights into the economic role of corporate knowledge. To illustrate this use, Strassmann collected financial results for 726 U.S. banks. "The results show no relation between a bank's average employee salaries and its corporate profits. If salaries reflect employees' market worth, the scatter graph tells us that the corporate values of knowledge capital cannot reflect that worth. For instance, the graph shows a number of banks paying employees an average salary of $50,000. Yet the profits per employee for these banks range from negative $70,000 per employee to positive $130,000 per employee. Such disparities demonstrate that corporate results and employee worth (as measured by compensation) are unrelated.

In many banks, PKC exceeds CKC, which suggests that either the bank cannot afford to "rent" (pay the salaries of) its employees or the employees will find it more rewarding to move to another bank that generates a surplus. In such surroundings, employees often will end up depreciating their PKC and ultimately lowering their market worth. The converse argument is also true. In banks where PKC worth $100,000 is supporting CKC of $100 million, employees ought to use every opportunity to enrich themselves by acquiring more knowledge. This condition would call for adopting policies that would result in knowledge appreciation.

But the most important finding is that there is absolutely no correlation between how banks value the worth of their employees' knowledge and how well those banks perform in the marketplace. Similar comparisons for other industries all display identical characteristics. Whenever executives propose to invest in knowledge management to enhance the worth of their workforce, first they ought to examine their positive or negative valuations of PKC and CKC. According to Strassmann, when employees are overvalued, meaning that the CKC/PKC ratio is low, it would make sense for a bank to leverage employees' intrinsic capabilities by making employee knowledge enhancement a top priority. If the opposite is the case, employee retention becomes as important.

When the Numbers Don't Add Up

Because it isn't easy to quantify, knowledge management is vulnerable to a high level of uncertainty among executives. Therefore, distortions in the metrics applied to knowledge management could significantly influence its acceptance. That's why knowledge management metrics are a continuing focus of magazines such as *Knowledge Management*. One danger is the tendency to equate knowledge management with information technology. Reducing the complex, ongoing process of managing knowledge to simply buying computers presents an inherent risk of alienating business leaders when they don't get the purported benefits of knowledge management by just plugging in their new machines.

The most frequently mentioned example of this disparity is the so-called "productivity paradox," which states that computers are everywhere except in the productivity statistics. Hundreds of articles and several books have been written about this paradox, yet most academics have concluded that the paradox is an illusion—because we cannot measure the benefits that computerization actually delivers. Consultants and IT managers who seek bigger budgets for computerization often resort to 'twisting the numbers.' Numbers are "twisted" when one mixes real numbers with measures that either are not verifiable, or are numerically precise but not relevant.

It is difficult to expose number twisting, because the principal culprits don't reveal how they arrive at their projections. For instance, prognosticators of the Y2K disaster never supported their widely quoted forecasts that the change of the millennium would cost organizations anywhere from $600 billion to $1.5 trillion. (The true measurable cost ended up being about $150 billion.) In another example, five prominent market forecasters predicted prospects for electronic commerce. Their estimates for annual e-commerce spending in 2000 ranged from $185 billion to $3.1 trillion; their annual projections for 2000–2004 ranged from $1.26 trillion to $9.9 trillion. The differences are so great because these well-paid knowledge management experts twist the numbers while interpreting inaccurate statistics about e-commerce.

Market analysts may fudge numbers to inflate their own reputations, but it's a lot harder for government agencies to do that, because they are required to disclose the rationales for their analyses, along with their data sources. Even if number twisting still occurs, in most cases it can be easily discovered. For example: Recent statistics published by the U.S. Department of Commerce about the contributions of information to growth in the U.S. economy offered Strassmann an excellent opportunity to examine published metrics critically. In 1998 the commerce department reported that computer-based information industries had driven more than one-fourth of America's total real economic growth. A 1999 follow-up report stated that the IT sector had fueled 35 percent of the nation's real economic growth. Timed to coincide with an electoral campaign that presented the Clinton-Gore administration as strong supporter of high technology, a revised report in 2000 stated that information industries contributed nearly a third of the real growth of the U.S. economy.

Looking into these numbers, we find that the claim that information accounts for such an enormous contribution is supported by twisting the relevant numbers in a couple of ways. First, the government broadens the definition of the "information revolution" as far as possible, including radio and television broadcasting, office machines such as photocopiers and faxes, laboratory analysis equipment, manufacturing testing instruments, household audio and video equipment, wired telecommunications carriers, paging equipment, cellular communications, and just about all electronics. Second, the government assesses information technology numbers by applying inflationary or deflationary "adjustments" to the actual numbers involved.

The result reduces the output of all other sectors of the economy, and increases the contribution of information-based industries. Such boosting presumes that lower prices of personal computers and the increased densities of magnetic storage media somehow translate into economic effectiveness. (This manipulation is shown in "inflation adjustments.") No one would dispute that an enormous amount of money has been spent in the past ten years on various initiatives connected with computers, including the sums wasted on Y2K fixes. Yet the willingness of corporations to throw money at all kinds of Internet projects resembles, in many ways, an arms race. In various calculations—based on cash, not on twisted numbers—the contributions of IT-producing industries to U.S. economic growth turn out to be a still respectable but more credible 9 percent.

PROJECTING KNOWLEDGE MANAGEMENT VALUES

Projecting the value of knowledge management to an organization is as varied as the data it mines and harvests. There's no set way for determining the value a knowledge management project will have, as organizational structures, needs, and goals are varied.

Determining values start at the onset of a knowledge management project, as data and data silos are identified and analyzed. The importance of that data, and how it will be used, must be determined. Key questions must be answered, such as:

- Where are data stored and how are they used?
- How does the data affect an organization's business or product lines?
- Does the data give an organization a competitive advantage?
- What's the cause and effect of not having the data?
- What's the cost of data mining?

- What's the cost of implementation?
- Does an organization have the infrastructure needed to support data mining and harvesting?
- Can the data be kept current?

Knowledge management projects and processes must go beyond identifying knowledge silos and data requirements; they must also map out the intricacies of data relationships and the data's use, electronic capture and storage, human automated and manual interfaces, and the effect of change.

"It's a recognition of the importance of focusing on business benefits of knowledge management."
—Alex Bennet
Deputy CIO of enterprise integration, U.S. Navy

Valuing technology investments confound many organizations. Administrators rightly question rising technology budgets, but often lack the tools to effectively evaluate hardware and software decisions. Without a solid understanding of the return on investment, many firms hold back on investing in knowledge management—thus not taking advantage of technologies designed to improve efficiency.

Fueling concern is the fact that few knowledge management initiatives succeed unless organizations invest substantial resources in manually collecting and organizing research material.

What methods are available to measure, and, more importantly, recover the costs of these investments? How can an organization and its customers feel comfortable that the costs of technology are justified and that knowledge management systems offer good value?

The U.S. Department of the Navy has issued the "DON IM/IT Metrics Guide for Knowledge Management Initiatives," a guide for identifying metrics for knowledge management pilots and ongoing projects.

In a survey conducted by The Conference Board, a network of business executives that creates and disseminates knowledge on management issues, organizations were asked how they measured the effectiveness of their KMS. These are their findings:

- 70%—Customer satisfaction and value
- 52%—Cost reduction and savings
- 47%—Employee attitude, morale, and involvement
- 35%—Better time to market
- 22%—Sales effectiveness
- 18%—New product sales

Cost Recovery

The cost of software, based on a prorated or fixed-usage charge to an organization's customers, is an effective way to recoup KMS cost. This method is used by many organizations to charge customers for online research.

Internal Expense

Many recent studies demonstrate that the introduction of technology has yet to reduce the expense of filing systems. Forrester Research, for example, estimates that more than 80 percent of a corporation's business-critical information is locked in unstructured formats. Lucent Technologies found that the volume of unstructured information in large organizations doubles every two months. More important, other studies illustrated the inefficiencies of electronic document storage and retrieval systems.

Records Management Quarterly reports that only 20 percent of network storage is active data, while the remaining 80 percent is inactive.

Tony McKinley, principal of Intelligent Imaging, claims that 85 percent of documents filed are never retrieved, while 50 percent or more are duplicates.[5]

A study by the multinational firm BAE Systems discovered that 80 percent of employees waste an average of 30 minutes per day retrieving information, while 60 percent are spending an hour or more each day duplicating the work of others.

Effective KMS tools can help organizations reduce internal costs of maintaining electronic filing systems and reduce the administrative expense of locating documents. There's a great deal to be saved by managing electronic files more effectively.

When *Customer Relationship Management* magazine asked its readers, "What area would you like to improve within your service resolution process," they answered:

- 23%—Integration of disparate knowledge repositories
- 21%—Authoring and knowledge capture
- 20%—Access knowledge from outside customer service (i.e., marketing, engineering, or QA)
- 18%—Reducing the number of systems that agents use on desktops
- 15%—Structured collaboration

Increasing Profit

Effective knowledge sharing can substantially increase productivity. In addition, knowledge transfer enhances the quality and value of the output. While productivity improvement is important, the big advantage that KMS brings to the

> **"In the IT world, the average job lasts 18 months. If you keep an IT professional for longer, you're very fortunate."[6]**
>
> **—Erica Perry
> President, Becker.net**

organization is its ability to leverage knowledge and enhance the value of professional services by using knowledge management technologies to capture prior work product and other materials developed by other projects.

Measuring "Hard" Returns

In financial circles, return on investment (ROI) is the most accepted measurement of a company's performance. The formula for ROI can be expressed as follows:

$$\text{incremental gain} - \text{total cost of project} = \text{ROI}.$$

An alternative measurement is known as the "payback period," which is defined as the period required to recover the cost of an investment. Platinum Technology, now part of Computer Associates International, is a good example of how a KMS can save and make real money for an organization. In the late 1990s Platinum Technology undertook an aggressive acquisition strategy, acquiring more than sixty companies. The company used its KMS to communicate information about these acquisitions and the products they brought to the table. This allowed the sales force to move forward much faster with these new offerings, in a very professional and skilled way. The result was a $6 million return on a $750,000 KMS investment—an eight-to-one return on investment.

> **"Most of my work these days is with universities and hospitals and churches, which are three of the biggest knowledge-worker employers, and their productivity is dismal."[7]**
> **—Peter Drucker**
> **Author and consultant**

Projecting Benefits

A KMS creates two types of benefit—hard (financial returns) and soft (intangible benefits). The tangibles are reflected in decreased time to locate required information. By making use of past experience to improve future products and processes, there's no reason to make the same mistakes over again.

> **"There is no substitute for knowledge."**
> **—W. Edwards Deming**

An organization often looks at an investment's effectiveness in generating intellectual capital by measuring how fast the technology expense is converted into valuable information assets. This approach is called "the cost of information." It's calculated by dividing the per-document data cost of a system into the average rate of document and data reuse.

By performing a complete cost-benefit analysis, an organization will understand the value of its KMS. A report written by Mutiran Al-Azmi and Mohamed Zairi, both with Bradford University School of Management, analyzed KMS benefits reported by eight different authors. Figure 7.2 shows the results of their analysis.

Payless Stores is a typical example of how a KMS can improve performance.[8] Payless reduced training time by 30 percent. The company estimates that the system will produce a 3 percent annualized improvement in corporate profits. Payless recovered its $10 million KMS investment in less than twelve months.

Figure 7.2 Knowledge Benefits From Nine Literature Reviews

Authors	Knowledge Benefits
APQC (1996)	1. Greater customer intimacy and satisfaction 2. Improved cycle time and operational excellence 3. Better use of organizational knowledge to improve operations and deliver products and services
Grey (1996)	1. Serve customers well. 2. Reduce cycle times. 3. Operate with minimum fixed assets and overhead. 4. Shorten product development time. 5. Empower employees. 6. Innovate and deliver high-quality products. 7. Enhance flexibility and adaptation. 8. Capture information and create knowledge. 9. Share and learn.
Radding (1998)	1. Prevention of knowledge loss 2. Improved decisions 3. Adaptability and flexibility 4. Competitive advantage 5. Assets of development 6. Product enhancemen. 7. Customer management 8. Leverage investment in human capital
Pervaiz, et al (1999)	1. Reduce loss of intellectual capital from employees who leave. 2. Reduce cost of development of new product/services. 3. Increase productivity of workers making knowledge accessible to all employees. 4. Increase employee satisfaction.
Uit Beijers (1999)	1. Improve efficiency. 2. Improve market position. 3. Enhance continuity of company. 4. Enhance profitability of company. 5. Optimize interaction between product development and marketing. 6. Improve relevant (group) competencies. 7. Provide better foundation for making decisions. 8. Improve communication between knowledge workers. 9. Enhance synergy between knowledge workers. 10. Ensure knowledge workers stay with company. 11. Make company focus on core business and on critical company knowledge.
APQC (2001)	1. Short-cycle internal processes. 2. Cut cost. 3. Operates more efficiently.
Santosus and Surmacz (2001)	1. Foster innovation by encouraging the free flow of ideas. 2. Improve customer service by streamlining response time. 3. Boost revenues by getting products and services to market faster. 4. Enhance employee retention rates by recognizing the value of employee's knowledge and rewarding them for it. 5. Streamline operations and reduce costs by eliminating redundant processes.
Skyrme (2001)	1. Faster and better solutions to customer problems 2. Improved innovation and new product development 3. Early warning of potential market changes 4. Identify new business opportunities through better knowledge management. 5. Minimize duplication of effort and loss of knowledge. 6. Improve alignment between business strategy and technology.

KNOWLEDGE MANAGEMENT CRITICAL SUCCESS FACTORS

Experts have estimated that 90 percent of the success of a KMS involves gaining buy-in from knowledge users and encouraging knowledge sharing. These two points are the most important, yet to share and apply knowledge faster and more effectively than competitors the following critical factors must also be considered:

- Standard flexible knowledge structure
- Knowledge sharing
- Effective knowledge retrieval, usage, and correction
- Creating motivation to share
- Effective organizational change management
- Creative knowledge
- Knowledge ontologies and knowledge repositories to serve as organizational memories in core competencies
- Overseeing content
- Teamwork
- Compelling vision and architecture
- Knowledge leadership
- Internal branding, naming metaphors for internal marketing, and achieving staff commitment
- Intellectual curiosity
- Motivating individuals to share knowledge
- Enhancing process
- Top-management leadership and commitment
- KMS leadership and champions
- Continuous learning
- Clear purpose and language
- Knowledge asset must be nurtured, preserved, and used to the largest extent possible
- Linking economic performance and business imperatives
- Keeping it simple
- Employee training
- Knowing communities
- Appropriate infrastructure
- Technology (networks)
- Organizational constraints
- Systematic knowledge process
- Building on the existing process (i.e., existing e-mail)
- Keeping lines of communications open
- Employee involvement

"KM practitioners have found that a critical success factor in implementation of KM is the creation of a cultural environment that gives confidence to the sharing of information."
—**Thomas M. Finneran**
Former Speaker of the House

- Chief knowledge officer (CKO)
- Technical infrastructure
- Multiple changes for knowledge transfer
- Finding the right people and data
- Availability to collaborators
- Appropriate bottom-line measurements
- Combining knowledge management tasks with daily work tasks and integrating them into daily business activities

> **"Barriers could be either technical, like client-server databases that were too slow and not user friendly, or non-technical, like lack of motivation to share knowledge, resources to capture and synthesize organizational learning, and ability to navigate the knowledge network to find the right people and data."**
> **—S. Trussler, author**

As is evident, many factors can affect the implementation of a KMS. All of them are important and need to be considered.

Major Obstacles

When organizations were asked by The Conference Board what they thought the obstacles to successful knowledge management were, they replied:[9]

- 78%—Perceived need for knowledge management
- 69%—Culture of hoarding knowledge
- 68%—Functional knowledge silos
- 67%—Incentives for sharing
- 46%—Proper technology for sharing
- 46%—Cost and financial support
- 30%—Top leadership
- 29%—Globalization
- 30%—Internal politics

> **"Knowledge is of two kinds— we know a subject ourselves, or we know where we can find information on it."**
> **—Samuel Johnson**
> **English writer**

Why do organizations invest in developing knowledge management systems? A survey of 566 companies already using knowledge management generated the following answers:[10]

- Capture and share best practices—77.7%
- Provide training, corporate learning—62.4%
- Manage customer relationship—58%
- Deliver competitive intelligence—55.8%
- Provide project workspace—31.4%
- Manage legal, intellectual property—31.4%
- Enhance Web publishing—29.9%
- Enhance supply chain management—20.1%

> **"The fundamental mistake that companies repeatedly make is that of equating information and knowledge. While the former can be handled well by information technology tools such as intranet alone, the latter cannot."**
> **—Amrit Tiwana**
> ***The Knowledge Management Toolkit***

SUMMARY

Knowledge management proponents need to think critically when examining industry metrics; they must learn how to recognize bent and twisted numbers. Immodest claims and inflated metrics will proliferate, and perhaps even undermine knowledge management projects, until broader and better understandings emerge about the contributions a KMS can make. Knowledge management is a good idea in its own right, and exaggeration will only devalue it.

Indeed, there is such a thing as knowledge capital—and if calculated correctly, it could explain why the purchase cost of most U.S. firms is greater than their book value (carcass value) that accountants attribute to it as a generally accepted practice. As much as professor Baruch Lev deserves our thanks and appreciation for opening a discourse on placing a dollar value on knowledge capital, his formula still doesn't reflect market valuations. According to Lev's ratio, stocks are either enormously overpriced or knowledge capital is vastly underpriced.

The marketplace isn't excessive in valuing corporate assets in general, useless valuation twisting is standard practice. So this again raises the question of whether one can arrive at reasonable valuations of knowledge capital that are independent of what Strassmann calls "manic-depressive phenomena on the stock exchanges, or the mumbo jumbo of arbitrarily weighted multi-factor indicators." Professors Strassmann and Lev say that this is possible. Sharpening analytic methods will make the differences between theory and reality more compatible and verifiable.

REFERENCES

1. Key, Alan S. "Measuring the Knowledge Deficit," *Knowledge Management,* May–Oct 1999.
2. Paul A. Strassmann, formerly U.S. deputy assistant secretary of defense and vice president of strategic planning for Xerox Corp., is the originator of the "Information Productivity," "Return-on-Management," and "Knowledge Capital" trademarked concepts. He has been the president of a publishing company and adjunct professor at two universities, and has been a regular contributor to *Knowledge Management.*
3. Strassmann, Paul A. "Prices, Finances and Knowledge Capital," *Knowledge Management,* June 2000.
4. This section is based upon an analysis of Paul A. Strassmann's columns in *Knowledge Management* during a two-year period, 1999–2001. Used by permission.
5. McKinley, Tony. "Managing All Information Assets," *Document Management,* July/August 1997.
6. Rubin, Hannele. "How CEOs Get Results—Human Resource Management," *The Chief Executive,* February 2001.
7. Drucker, Peter, and Brent Schlender. "Peter Drucker Sets Us Straight:," *Fortune,* January 12, 2004.

8. A special thanks to Mutiran Al-Azmi and Mohamed Zairi for allowing us to use important quotes and thoughts presented in their paper, "The Knowledge Management Report: A Comprehensive Review and Analysis of KM Critical Factors." Bradford University School of Management, KM report, published August 2003.
9. Dyer, Greg, and Brian McDonough. "The State of KM," *Knowledge Management,* May 2001.
10. Ibid.

CHAPTER VIII

KNOWLEDGE MANAGEMENT EXCELLENCE SUMMARY

"A little knowledge that's acted upon is worth more than a
whole warehouse full of data."

—HJH

WHAT AND WHY

There's no way to stop the knowledge explosion or, for
that matter, even slow it down. In fact, knowledge will grow
even faster. We have more brainpower at work today than
ever before, and every year we're adding more than 88 million people to the job market. That's 88 million more brains
that are better educated. These people are driving a score of
new ideas and concepts. In addition, microprocessor intelligence power is increasing at a
staggering rate. The result is that there are many new concepts in the business world, many
of these impossible just thirty years ago.

> "Knowledge workers cannot
> be supervised effectively.
> Unless they know more
> about their specialty
> than anybody else in the
> organization, they are
> basically useless."
> —Peter Drucker
> Author and consultant

But according to Justin Ewers' article "Is the MBA Obsolete?" (*U.S. News & World Report*,
April 2005), business school critics say it's past time for the vaunted MBA degree to get a new
look: "[C]onventional MBA programs train the wrong people in the wrong ways with the
wrong consequences.... Their classes are focused on analysis and technique instead of clini-
cal experience. Core subjects like finance, accounting, and marketing get disproportionate
attention, Mintzberg argues, at the expense of what he calls crucial 'soft' skills—leadership, teamwork, communication, and the ability to think outside the box of a discipline."
B-school leaders are struggling with how their programs should prepare students to be
effective managers. Some schools have either added segments on leadership, collaboration,
communication, and the like, or moved to a more interdisciplinary approach.

The more knowledge people get, the more they want. The more information is available, the more it's required just to keep up. Today the challenge isn't getting a college
education; that's relatively easy. The real problem is how to keep current. A person just
graduating from college with a bachelor's degree or MBA will see 50 percent of his or her
skills become obsolete within three to five years. With today's fast pace of change and tech-

> **"Within the next decade, education will change more than it has changed since the modern school was created by the printed book over 300 years ago. . . . Education can no longer be confined to the schools. Every employing institute has to become a teacher. The country that is again in the lead is the United States, where employers—business, government agencies, the military—spend as much money and effort on the education and training of their employees as do all the country's colleges and universities together."**
> —Peter Drucker
> Author and consultant

nological advances, people must become perpetual students. After World War II, the public school system provided the population's education. Now, in the Information Age, business spends more money on research and education than the public school system, thus replacing it as the primary supplier of educators.

Knowledge management (KM), in its simplest terms, consists of four processes. They are:

- Creating information
- Collecting knowledge
- Sharing knowledge
- Renewing the knowledge warehouse

We're now living in a knowledge-based economy, and organizations must realize that knowledge management is a required core competency. It's become a critical part of an organization's business strategy, accelerating the ability to take advantage of business opportunities and market challenges while reducing the resource and cycle time required to do the job. Knowledge management makes effective use of the combined talents, skills, and experience of the single resource that sets an organization apart from its competitors—its people. It also helps an organization manage its most valuable asset, its intellectual capital. There's no doubt about it—knowledge management is a business imperative for organizations that want to prosper in the twenty-first century.

> **"There is no substitute for knowledge."**
> —W. Edwards Deming
> Quality guru

Peter Drucker coined the term "knowledge worker" more than forty years ago. Interest over the years has shifted away from the knowledge worker to knowledge management. The term "knowledge management" has generated a lot of buzz in the knowledge age. The knowledge worker created the need for a whole new type of organization, one that's process-based, team-focused, and rich in intellect. Jerry Ash, a senior counselor at the Forbes Group, describes his vision of the future workplace as "an environment without cultural, political, professional, or structural boundaries, where workers and managers at all levels can think together, drawing on the rich and diverse backgrounds, training, and work experience previously confined to information silos and narrowly defined jobs of the former Industrial Age."

"The organization's culture is the major problem. Making information available to all employees is frightening to most managers."

—HJH

Having a successful KMS requires an excellent understanding and application of the following three parts in an integrated framework:

- Information structure
- Technology platform
- Culture aspects (work flow)

"Knowledge takes us from chance to choice."
—Peter Drucker
Author and consultant

All three parts are needed to sustain a successful KMS, but the cultural aspects are the most difficult to implement and maintain. In fact, the biggest component of a successful KMS is the culture of the enterprise that's implementing it. Without a culture that's focused on being a success, the advantages of the KMS will be largely wasted. There's no single KMS that fits all organizations.

Knowledge management is about people, networking, connections, communication, and a culture of sharing and creating new knowledge. It's not a prescriptive technology-driven process. An effective KMS is a carefully balanced mixture of one part technology, four parts culture change, two parts new-reward system, and three parts business focus—all of these in line with an organization's business strategy.

A big challenge related to implementing a KMS is transforming knowledge held by individuals, including processes and behavioral knowledge, into a consistent technology format that can be easily shared with an organization's stakeholders. But the biggest challenge is changing an organization's culture from one that hoards knowledge to one that shares it.

"Brains are in; heavy lifting is out. Hence the development of knowledge is close to job one for corporations."
—Tom Peters

The true standard of success for knowledge management is how people access and implement ideas using knowledge networks. Knowledge networks bring new ideas and/or best practices together in one place where the potential users can readily use and improve them. They also allow new or reassigned workers to access the experience of their predecessors, and to make recommendations based upon personal insight, creativity, and experience.

KM isn't the end of the journey, it's the midpoint that organizations can't go around. Organizations need to evolve through the following four levels:

1. *Organizational memory.* Remembering the past, which includes understanding the organization's values, beliefs, procedures, processes, and traditions. The past often prevents an organization from changing at the rate required to keep pace with its environment.

2. *Organizational learning.* Leveraging the combined experience and skills of an organization's people to improve performance

3. *Organizational intelligence.* An organization effectively using considerations related to its present circumstances and opportunities. This level is where knowledge is enhanced by the creativity of the people within the organization to drive breakthrough improvements in performance.

Profile 8.1 Compaq and Lotus: Hardware–Software Alliance Relies Upon Knowledge Management

Background

You might say that Houston-based Compaq Computer Corp. is learning about knowledge management the hard way. The world's largest computer manufacturer has been trying to absorb some enormous acquisitions: After buying Tandem Computers in June 1997, it merged with Digital Equipment Corp. only six months later. Some five years later, it merged again with Hewlett-Packard.

Retaining both customers and employees depended on getting the right information to the right people quickly and reliably. "As we've seen with all the mergers and acquisitions going on lately, it's very important to have a good information infrastructure," says Sharon Fortmeyer-Selan, director of enterprise solutions marketing at Compaq. "You need to keep the sales force up to speed, and you need to address all the needs of your customers. We've experienced these challenges first-hand."

Knowledge Management Strategy and Structure

This first-hand experience has come in handy for Compaq's latest venture. The company recently announced a new alliance with Lotus Development Corp., to offer customers integrated knowledge management solutions. The alliance counts on Compaq's leadership in the NT server market and Lotus' expertise in collaboration and knowledge management. "Knowledge management is a big market," explains Andrea Ramon, director of strategic alliances at Lotus. "We're looking at how to expand together." By being one of the first to lead and support customers through the entire knowledge management process—from hardware to consulting—they expect the alliance to capture the knowledge management market.

For Compaq, Lotus was a clear choice, because the companies have a large mutual customer base. According to Fortmeyer-Selan, Lotus' applications also fit well into Compaq's knowledge management strategy. Compaq now offers a hardware line that stretches from palmtop and desktop to corporate data centers. Its service network can support business customers with global account management. Lotus provides a single architecture structure for Internet, messaging, knowledge management, and enterprise integration. The alliance aims to make high-performance Web-based collaboration and messaging systems easier to deploy.

Compaq hopes to partner successfully with Lotus as it did with Siebel Systems, a leader in sales information systems. That alliance, started in March 1997, integrated enterprise solutions for sales, telemarketing, and call-center information systems. Compaq became Siebel's preferred deployment platform for Microsoft Windows NT and ended up with nearly 65 percent of that market.

Success Story

Compaq and Lotus kicked off their partnership with two Notes- and Domino-driven knowledge management applications developed by two Lotus premium business partners, Cipher Systems and GlobalServe Corp. The first, Cipher's Knowledge-Works, helps companies process and analyze competitive intelligence. Tapping into employee sources and outside expertise, data are translated into a summary that identifies information sources and rates them according to importance and reliability. The second, GlobalServe's Research Accelerator, helps R&D organizations identify critical knowledge, reduce research redundancy, and facilitate researcher collaboration. It also provides protection for valuable intellectual properties.

Alliance partners Lotus Services Group and Cambridge Technology Partners offer consulting services to guide and advise customers, as necessary. "Our customers want knowledge translated into action," explains Andrew Mahon, senior manager for strategic marketing at Lotus. "They want to look downstream and see immediate benefits that justify their investments."

Today's early adopters of knowledge management tools enjoy quick results because they are predisposed to change, Mahon suggests. Many have experience with discussion databases such as Lotus Notes, that accelerate the sharing of information and expertise. But information sharing is not necessarily knowledge management, Mahon emphasizes. Using the information is what counts. Two employees might pass in the hall, "accidentally" exchange information about their current projects, and elicit help from each other. "Our goal is to make sure these knowledge accidents occur all the time," says Mahon.

(Source: Strategy Associates Inc. Used with permission. For more information, contact Frank Voehl at *fvoehl@aol. com.*)

4. *Organizational excellence.* At this point an organization has developed the ability to anticipate, almost a sixth sense. It's able to foresee future market trends and respond quickly to competitors' maneuvers. At this point stakeholders recognize that the organization has positioned itself ahead of its competition.

KNOWLEDGE MANAGEMENT SYSTEM RESULTS

American National Insurance Company (ANICO) was facing an information overload, a situation that lessened its ability to deliver quality customer service. Field representatives used so many different databases that information was difficult to collect and coordinate. Pegasystems applications provided its single source of business intelligence. ANICO started holding weekly meetings to address common needs and to share best practices. As Gary Kirham, vice president and director of planning and support, put it, "We have captured so much intellectual capital in this system." As a result of using this system, ANICO had the following results:[1]

- $70 million in new business during the first six months
- Premiums increased from $160 million in 1999 to $2.4 billion in 2003
- Response time was reduced by 61 percent.
- Call-abandonment rates dropped by 71 percent.

The following are other typical results of effective knowledge management:

- Dow Chemical saved $4 million the first year and increased revenue from licensing by $100 million.

- Texas Instruments, using internal knowledge and best practices, saved $500 million in the cost of a new plant.
- Kaiser Permanente's transfer of knowledge from one region to a branch resulted in the implementation of an open-access program six to twelve months faster.

> **"Intellectual capital will be the primary way by which businesses measure their value."**
> **—Gartner Group**

- The American Productivity & Quality Center reported that benefits of their KMS included an increase in customer intimacy and satisfaction, improved cycle time and operational excellence, and better use of organizational knowledge to improve operations and deliver products and services.

- Chevron identified and shared best practices, saving millions of dollars each year. Sharing energy-usage best practices saved Chevron $150 million in fuel and power bills in 1996.
- Platinum Technology Inc.'s KMS saved it $6 million the first year. The system paid for itself in a month and-a-half. Productivity in the sales force increased by 6 percent. It reduced Federal Express costs by 15 percent.

> **"It is not good to know more unless we do more with what we already know."**
> **—R. K. Bergethon, author**

- A survey conducted by Teltech Resource Network Corp. of ninety-three KMS projects reported:
  - ☐ Increased revenue—48 percent
  - ☐ Reduced cost—38 percent
  - ☐ Improved customer service—10 percent
  - ☐ Improve quality—6 percent
  - ☐ Improved processes—4 percent

> **"An investment in knowledge pays the best interest."**
> **—Benjamin Franklin**

- Mark Koskinsemi, vice president of human resources at Buckman Laboratories, looked back at what the company's KMS accomplished in an eight-year period. He reported:
  - ☐ Sales per salesperson rose by 49 percent.
  - ☐ Sales per associate rose by 37 percent.
  - ☐ Profits per associate rose by 67 percent.[2]

"The right projects + the right people + the right knowledge
= the right business results."

—HJH

FOUR KNOWLEDGE MANAGEMENT PROFILES

Profile 8.2 Hitachi Innovates Like Nobody's Business

Background

With $6.2 billion in annual profits, Hitachi Ltd. produces nearly 2 percent of Japan's yearly gross national product and 6 percent of its total (R&D) expenditures. Hitachi has 28 factories, 800 subsidiaries, and 320,000 employees. Each year it annually sells $9 billion worth of consumer electronics products, yet it also sells $20 billion worth of power plants, generators, and robots. Its computer chip division annually sells more than Motorola, Intel, and Sun Microsystems combined.

Hitachi is Japan's largest patent holder, and has been at the top of the U.S. patent list for most of the past ten years. Among rivals its own size, including General Electric, Matsushita, and IBM, only Hitachi has interests in more than three of these business areas: computers, chips, software, consumer electronics, power plants, transportation, medical equipment, and telecommunications. In fact, Hitachi is invested in all eight areas and thus capable of undertaking huge projects—such as a national logistics transportation system—that literally no one else could undertake.

Success Story

Hitachi's success story begins with product R&D, but goes beyond new products to include processes in all areas of the firm—processes that help drive costs down, down, down. Facing increased competition and sagging demand in many of its business areas, such as mainframe computers, Hitachi has turned to innovative methods of cost cutting to maintain its market positions. It advances its vision of the future through a sophisticated knowledge management information network, one in which technology often fuses with corporate memory. Sharing knowledge among sister units is seen as paramount to new product development and cost cutting.

Tsutomu Kanai, Hitachi's chairman, is just the nonconformist to lead this firm. His vision for Hitachi's future takes advantage of its diversity in an integrated way. Thus the firm is pursuing integrated complex projects with zeal. Because it has huge cash reserves and has invested in basic businesses that weather recessions well, Hitachi has been able to protect its R&D product stream more effectively than most firms. "Basic science is something we will never sacrifice," says Kanai.

Unlike other Japanese firms, Hitachi has a loose, decentralized management structure. Renegades are encouraged. One such renegade: Yasutsugu Takeda, Hitachi's top R&D administrator at the turn of the 20th century. Undaunted by the fact that none of Hitachi's factory managers were interested in making several products his labs had developed, Takeda created catalogs of these products, lined up customers, then went back to Hitachi to convince managers that they should make these products after all. Decentralization is the name of the game at Hitachi. Its 28 factories operate more like separate businesses. It's often hard to tell exactly who runs the firm. During the past decade there have been ten managing directors and, clearly, Kanai was the boss. But the firm moves in sometimes surprising directions, as a large group of equals might move, more than a pyramidal organization run by a powerful CEO.

Hitachi is now expanding its corporate memory by developing new products that will debut at various points in the future. In the next few years the organization expects to unveil neural networks

(continues)

Profile 8.2 Hitachi Innovates Like Nobody's Business *(continued)*

and multimedia office products, then handheld computers that accept voice commands and exchange data via radio waves. In a decade they expect to produce computers with 100 times the power and 10 times the speed of today's models. And twenty years from now, they expect biocomputers that can organically repair themselves. Knowledge-based innovation is truly the focus at Hitachi.

(Source: Strategy Associates Inc. Used with permission. For more information, contact Frank Voehl at *fvoehl@aol. com*.)

Profile 8.3 Rubbermaid's Simple Knowledge Management Strategy: Innovate

Background

In 1993, after being number two in *Fortune* magazine's most-admired-company contest for five of the previous six years, Rubbermaid finally became number one. The company has maintained a high "admiration" position ever since. Rubbermaid is a veritable juggernaut when it comes to putting out new products—365 a year, for an average of one a day. Headed by Stanley Gault from 1980 to 1991, the company enjoyed unprecedented growth in profits (an average increase of 14 percent a year) and stock appreciation (an average of 25 percent a year). When Gault retired in 1991, only to move on shortly thereafter to become CEO of Goodyear, he was replaced by Walter Williams. CEO Williams, who resigned after 18 months, was replaced by Wolfgang Schmitt.

Knowledge Management Strategy

Rubbermaid excels in making mundane items more interesting and functional, and it also makes them profitably. Each year its knowledge-based approach helps to improve more than 5,000 existing products and creates totally new ones. Its product line includes mailboxes, window boxes, storage boxes, toys, mops, dust mitts, snap-together furniture, ice cube trays, stadium seats, spatulas, step stools, wall coverings, sporting goods, dinnerware, dish drainers, laundry hampers, and endless other utilitarian products. However mundane their products may be, Rubbermaid's knowledge engineers hover over them as intently as General Dynamics engineers faced with an F-111 fighter. This serious approach to knowledge and information in areas others dismiss as trivial has supported Rubbermaid's notable success.

Schmitt and successors have set ambitious objectives for the firm, and have pursued long-established knowledge management innovation strategies to achieve them. Schmitt expected Rubbermaid to enter a new-product category every 12 to 18 months (most recently it has introduced hardware cabinets and garden sheds); to obtain more than 30 percent of its sales from products introduced within the past five years; and to obtain 25–30 percent of its revenues from markets outside the United States by the year 2007, an increase of 10 percent over the current performance.

Success Story

Almost uniquely, Rubbermaid does no market testing, although it does hold focus groups. Management doesn't believe in testing. They don't want their products to be copied, and believe it's not that much riskier to just roll them out. Also, this approach puts pressure on the company to do it right the first time. Product flops do happen occasionally, but the firm has a remarkable 90 percent success rate with new products. The few failures that do occur are tolerated in the name of taking risks.

Most of Rubbermaid's new products come from twenty cross-functional teams, each with five to seven members (one each from marketing, manufacturing, R&D, finance, and other departments, as needed). Each team focuses on the knowledge inherent in a specific product line, so that someone is always thinking about key product knowledge segments.

But Rubbermaid's innovation doesn't stop with its product development teams. Individual employees are encouraged to create new products as well. Rubbermaid encourages its employees to think of new products as flowing from the firm's core competencies—the critically important things it does well. It expects its managers to find out what's happening in the rest of the company, continually mining knowledge from processes and technologies. For example: While running a different Rubbermaid subsidiary, Bud Hellman toured a Rubbermaid plant that made picnic coolers. As he watched the plastic blow-molding equipment, he realized that he could use that same process to make a line of durable, lightweight, inexpensive office furniture. Within a couple of years that line accounted for 60 percent of the furniture division's sales.

Top management contributes its knowledge and ideas as well. When CEO Schmitt and Richard Gates, former head of product development, toured the British Museum in London in 1993, they were fascinated by an exhibit of Egyptian antiquities—and came away from it with ideas for eleven specific new products. As Gates says admiringly of the Egyptians: "They used a lot of kitchen utensils, some of which were very nice. Nice designs."

Also critical to the company's success is Rubbermaid's approach to customer relations. In its customer center, which hosts 110 major retail customers each year—including the largest, Wal-Mart, which accounts for 14 percent of the firm's sales—the pitch is always the same: "Let us help you sell more; we've got what consumers want." At the end of each presentation, the customer sees many new products. Then it's on to the "knowledge war room," where deficiencies in competitors' products are demonstrated. In Rubbermaid's finale, the KMS' "best practices room," retailers experience the best in product mixes and displays. The idea behind the company's customer center is to establish a store within a store—that is, to put a Rubbermaid store inside each retailer's stores.

(Source: Strategy Associates Inc. Used with permission. For more information, contact Frank Voehl at *fvoehl@aol. com.*)

Profile 8.4 Kao Corp.'s Information System Supports Its Knowledge Strategy

Background

Japan's Kao Corp., started in 1890 as the Kao Soap Co., is a diversified company with interests in two primary areas: household products (with divisions for personal care cosmetics, laundry and cleansing, and hygiene) and chemical products (with divisions for fatty and specialty chemicals, and floppy disks). The firm was founded on principles of equality expressed by 7th-century statesman Shotoku, whose philosophy profoundly influenced Yoshio Maruta, Kao's CEO from the late 1970s through the early 1990s. Two of Shotoku's precepts: "Human beings can live only by the Universal Truth, and in their dignity of living all are absolutely equal," and "If everyone discusses on an equal footing, there is nothing that cannot be resolved." Kao's corporate philosophy thus supports individual initiative and rejects authoritarianism.

Knowledge Management Strategy and Strategy

Because work is viewed as flexible and flowing, Kao is designed to be run as a "flowing system" that spreads knowledge and ideas while stimulating interaction. To give free rein to creativity and initiative, organizational boundaries and titles have been abolished. The result is a learning organization in which information sharing is essential and knowledge management systems are critical to the company's success. Every employee at Kao seeks to learn and to help others learn, and every manager embraces Maruta's fundamental assumption: "In today's business world, knowledge is the only source of competitive advantage. The company that develops a monopoly on information, and has the ability to learn from it continuously, is the company that will win, irrespective of its business."

In some U.S. firms, information systems allow only top managers to gain access to key data; at Kao, information extends to everyone in the company. The task of Kao's managers is to take information from the environment, process it, and, by adding value, turn it into knowledge. Every piece of information is valued, because it may offer insight into product positioning, product improvement, or the development of a new product.

Nowhere is the advantage of this philosophy more evident than in Kao's flexible manufacturing program, designed, according to systems developer Masayuki Abe, "to maximize the flexibility of the whole company's response to demand." The firm obsessively collects and distributes information, which is entered into a single system that links together sales and shipping, production and purchasing, accounting, R&D, marketing, hundreds of shopkeepers' cash registers, and thousands of salespeople's hand-held computers. Kao boasts that its knowledge management system is so complete that it can turn out an annual report one day after the end of the year.

Success Story

Kao knows whether a new product will succeed within two weeks of its launch. It does so by using focus groups, consumer calls, and point-of-sale information from hundreds of outlets in a system known as Project Echo. This approach eliminates any need for market surveys. It also helps explain how Kao could enter the highly competitive cosmetics industry in Japan and within ten years become the number two player. Clearly, the company can adjust quickly to meet customer demands. When Mrs. Wanatabe buys a bar of soap, that purchase is instantly recorded. With such detailed information Kao can increase variety while cutting inventory levels. In addition, through its wholesalers, Kao can deliver an order within 24 hours to any of 280,000 shops that, on average, order only seven items at a time. Perhaps no other company in the world can match Kao's flexibility.

(Source: Strategy Associates Inc. Used with permission. For more information, contact Frank Voehl at *fvoehl@aol. com.*)

Profile 8.5 Nippon Steel Steels for Challenging Future— and Innovates

Background

The steel industry faces many challenges. It's a mature industry with more capacity than demand, and plastics and other synthetics are replacing its products. Due to competition from other heavy industries and a downturn in the economy, many steel producers have gone out of business. Yet Nippon Steel of Japan has persevered. Its competitiveness stems from its ability to innovate. Nippon's success can be explored from four perspectives: the challenges the company faces, its approach to technological innovation, its emphasis in innovation management, and the lessons that can be learned from its experience.

Knowledge Management Strategy

Nippon Steel Corp., a creative integrator and innovative supplier, is expanding its business into new technologies by coupling its own assets with external strengths through original development, establishing new firms, and capital participation in or business ties with other firms. This is the essence of its knowledge management strategy.

According to Nippon Steel's management, several major challenges result from the current business environment. They are:

- The need to introduce new products and improve manufacturing processes
- The need to integrate economic functions, such as marketing, design, and operations, to speed product and process innovation
- The need to scan the environment for knowledge about future opportunities and threats, and to use new technologies before others do
- The need to introduce new technologies
- The need to develop new knowledge management systems to cope with rapid change
- The need to change organizational structure and information management systems, and to speed up the CPS process to shorten cycle time between design and manufacturing
- The need for specialization as well as integration
- The need to recover research-and-development costs
- The need for continuous skill development to match new innovations

(continues)

**Profile 8.5 Nippon Steel Steels for Challenging Future—
and Innovates** *(continued)*

Nippon Steel considers knowledge management-based innovation, especially technological innovation, the most critical aspect of its strategy. The company has grouped its technological innovations into seven categories:

- Integrating different steps of a process to reduce delays and waste, and drastically reduce processing time. Example: linking continuous casting and direct rolling into an integrated process.
- Developing new products based on market demand. Example: fire-resistant structural steel.
- Developing new processes and instruments to increase quality, improve a process, or improve monitoring systems. Example: artificial intelligence controls for blast furnaces.
- Assimilating acquired knowledge and technology and transferring it horizontally into new fields. Example: gold bonding wires.
- Developing new construction and fabrication methods. Example: air-inflated double-membrane stainless-steel roof.
- Creating new technologies by fusing knowledge from two diverse technologies. Example: a laser neural network to detect defects in rolling.
- Using joint ventures to develop new technologies and integrate knowledge-based competencies in diverse fields. Example: satellite broadcasting receiver system.

Success Story

The strategy adopted by Nippon Steel indicates that time is the most crucial element of its innovations. Through joint ventures, concurrent engineering, strategic alliances, networking, multifunctional new development teams, and new-product subsidiaries Nippon Steel has been able to rapidly bring about innovative product and process changes. Functional integration, together with a decentralized operation, support organizational innovations. The win-win cooperative strategy adopted by Nippon Steel, including various new subsidiaries established with other firms as partners in competence fusion, has helped its products rapidly reach the market. The approach of Nippon Steel is highly interactive, its strong synergy emphasizing the diffusion of innovations in developing new business.

(Source: Strategy Associates Inc. Used with permission. For more information, contact Frank Voehl at *fvoehl@aol. com*.)

REFERENCES

1. Kay, Alan S. "KM Meets Radical Democracy," *Knowledge Management*, September 2000.
2. Special thanks to Muteran Al-Azmi and Mohamed Zairi for allowing us to use important quotes and thoughts from "The Knowledge Management Report: A Comprehensive Review and Analysis of KM Critical Factors." (This was a white paper presented in 2003 at the University of Bradford, UK.)

APPENDIX A

GLOSSARY

- **Agents (agent technology)**—Software programs that transparently execute procedures to support fathering, delivering, categorizing, profiling information, or notifying the knowledge-seeker about the existence of or changes in an area of interest.
- **Artificial intelligence**—The use of human models for cognition and perception to create computer systems to solve human-like problems.
- **Book assets**—Tangible assets plus financial assets.
- **Browser**—A program that allows users to access documents on the World Wide Web (www), typically using the HTTP protocol. Browsers can be either text or graphic. They read HTML and interpret the code into what we see as Web pages. The two popular browsers in use are Microsoft's Internet Explorer and America Online's Netscape Navigator. Browsers are often used as the primary front-end interface for knowledge management systems that rely on intranet technology.
- **Business operating system (BOS)**—An environment that represents the vast warehouses of knowledge of an organization; the way a business is run, the way people and information come together to add value to a business process. A BOS is a repository comprising a common operating environment, a business process library, and enterprise workflow. The BOS is expressed through a consistent standardized desktop metaphor.
- **Chief knowledge officer (CKO)/chief learning officer**—Oversees efforts to use technology for knowledge capture and distribution. Further, CKOs have three critical responsibilities: creating a KM infrastructure, building a knowledge culture, and making it all pay off.

  The CKO is responsible for enterprisewide coordination of all knowledge leadership. The CKO is typically chartered by the CEO. The CKO's focus is the practice of knowledge leadership, usually solo performer role with no immediate job responsibility. Before a culture of knowledge sharing, incentives, and the basic precepts of knowledge leadership have been acknowledged by the enterprise, the CKO is powerless.
- **Cognition**—The ability to synthesize diverse sources of information in making a decision. Cognition is the aspect of KM solutions used to facilitate decision making. As part of a knowledge map, cognition is the application of knowledge that's been exchanged through intermediation, externalization, and internalization.

- **Communication processes**—The information technology and cultural processes that enable people to share information in an efficient and effective manner. Process, in this case, doesn't describe just the technical process underlying message delivery, but the whole act of communicating. To describe it as a purely technical process would be straying too far away from KM, where the human/cultural side is as important, if not more, than the technological side.

- **Communities of practice**—Groups of virtual or local members with similar specializations. "Communities that form where people assume roles based on their abilities and skills instead of their titles and hierarchical structure." They are sometimes called a community of interest.

- **Competency management**—The ability to use KM to consistently facilitate the formation of new ideas, products, and services that support the core competency of the organization.

- **Competency modeling**—Identifying peak performers and creating profiles and models that specify the skill sets, personalities, values, and other attributes of these employees. Competency modeling is close in spirit to leveraging intellectual assets, but it's more forward-looking, and it focuses on the people aspect.

- **Computer-supported collaborative work (CSCW)**—The shared development of knowledge artifacts. Also called groupware or artifact-based collaboration.

- **Concept-based search**—A form of content-based indexing, search, and retrieval in which the search-engine possesses a level of intelligence regarding semantics and lexicons. In such a system, internalization and externalization can be achieved at a conceptual level, providing results far beyond that of word-based queries.

- **Content directors**—The executive management levels that design, set, and execute strategies on issues for which they provide focus regarding the process of knowledge sharing.

- **Concept mapping**—The educational technique for improving understanding and retention. An aid to writing, a concept map is a picture of the ideas or topics in the information and the ways these ideas or topics are related to each other. It's a visual summary that shows the structure of the material the writer will describe.

- **Conceptual (or "back of the book") indexes**—Map key ideas and objects in a single work. An index is a structured sequence resulting from a thorough and complete analysis of text, with synthesized access points to all the information contained therein. The structured arrangement of the index enables users to locate information efficiently.

- **Content mapping**—The process of identifying and organizing a high-level description of the meaning contained in a collection of electronic documents. Content maps are usually rendered as hierarchical "outlines," but many kinds of more suggestive displays are available through graphical visualization techniques. Content maps are used to facilitate the comprehension of the knowledge base.

- **Context sensitivity**—The ability of a KMS to provide insight that takes into consideration the contextual nature of a user's request based on history, associations, and subject matter experience.
- **Contribution monitoring and valuation**—A method for analyzing the relative value of an individual's knowledge-supporting activities in a KMS, utilizing a variety of metrics, which could include the following electronically based approaches: Numbers of contributions to knowledge forums; numbers of successful problem resolutions associated with an individual's contributions; amount of message traffic targeted to take advantage of an individual's expertise, etc.

  Contribution valuation need not be technology-based or limited to these specific examples, but it must be grounded in agreed-upon KM metrics.
- **Core competency**—The overriding value statement of an organization. Core competency differs from product and market competency in that an organization's core competency outlives (by a significant margin) product lifecycles and market swings. AT&T's core competency, for example, is connecting people, not telecommunications.
- **Corporate memory/institutional memory**—The coherent integration of know-how of (geographically) dispersed groups of people in an organization. This know-how may relate to problem-solving expertise in functional disciplines (e.g., design, testing, and production), experiences of human resources and project experiences in terms of project management issues (e.g., social and organizational aspects related to the project team), innovation and design technical issues (e.g., design rationales, history of solution space explored, and concurrent engineering techniques), and lessons learned. Corporate memory is an unquestioned tacit or explicit understanding of an organization's people, process, or products, and any experts feel that it's one of the keys to continued innovation. Corporations, like individuals, remember the past, including long-standing processes and procedures, along with corporate traditions and values. Memory is strategically important, but it can also become a serious liability if it inhibits an organization from innovating and adjusting quickly to its changing environment.
- **Customer capital**—Customer capital's value is based upon how well the organization understands its customers' needs and expectations.
- **Data**—Raw transactional representations and outputs without inherent meaning.
- **Data mining**—A technique to analyze data in very large databases with the goal of revealing trends, patterns, and converting it into information.
- **Data warehouse**—A storage area for highly structured content. It's a resource of unquestionable value when you need to mine factual data. A data warehouse by itself is devoid of content. It contains clean, structured, and organized data. The size of a warehouse is always large.

- **Digital nervous system**—The computing infrastructure (desktops, servers, networks, and software) used to inform and support the decision-making processes of an organization. KM may be part of a digital nervous system.

- **Discontinuity of knowledge**—A phenomenon that occurs when experienced knowledge workers move from one position to another (inside or outside an organization), without having adequate time or KM facilities to transfer their knowledge to co-workers.

- **Distance learning**—The technology to instruct students at remote locations simultaneously.

- **Distributed and open hypertext systems**—Used to the generation and leveraging of organizational knowledge.

- **Document management**—A system that controls the change level of the documents within the system and includes the ability to develop a database of documents and classify them automatically. Document management standards, like Web DAV and DMA, allow document management solutions to be tightly integrated within the KMS.

  Document management systems provide online access to documents stored as bit-mapped images. Document management is a software system based on an underlying database, in which unstructured objects (i.e., documents) are indexed and tracked. Document-management systems monitor security, log access to files, and maintain a history of file content. If used to track paper documents, maintenance of content isn't provided. Within a KMS, document management can provide an automated approach to externalization and internalization. In more advanced systems, user profiles can be maintained as objects. In these cases, the owners of tacit knowledge are tracked and made available as a known resource through user queries via electronic yellow pages.

- **Electronic yellow page**—A Web-searchable electronic version of skill lists, albeit with a lot more content added to them by past users. It's used as a pointer to the person who actually contributed the knowledge and is used to facilitate knowledge flow. *Electronic yellow pages* are an online listing of personnel, their competencies, and their contact information. Within a KM environment, queries on the profiles will result in a list of known individuals that should possess expert tacit knowledge on the query's subject matter. In heuristic electronic yellow pages the system can infer competencies by observing an individual's behaviors and work product.

- **Explicit (hard) knowledge**—Knowledge that's stored in a semi-structured content, such as documents, e-mail, voicemail, or video media. It can be articulated in formal language and readily transmitted to other people. Also called hard or tangible knowledge, it's conveyed from one person to another in a systematic way.

- **External awareness**—The fourth component of the knowledge-chain, which represents an organization's ability to understand the market's perceived value of its products and services as well as the changing directions and requirements of its markets. When coupled with internal awareness, external awareness can lead to the discovery of successful new markets.

- **Externalization**—The transfer of knowledge from the minds of its holders to an external repository in the most efficient way possible. Externalization tools help build knowledge maps. They capture and organize incoming bodies of explicit knowledge and create clusters of bodies of knowledge. It's one of the four key knowledge management functions.

- **External responsiveness**—The third component of the knowledge chain, which emphasizes the perpetual ability to meet the market on its own terms even when the market can't articulate these. It's a level of responsiveness to environment conditions that's significantly faster and based on better connections between resources and markets.

- **Gatekeepers**—People who control the flow of information that's communicated to a specific part of the organization.

- **Geographic information systems (GIS)**—A technology that involves a digitized map, powerful computer, and software that permits the superimposition and manipulation of various kinds of demographic and corporate data on the map.

- **Help desk technology**—Routing requests for help from information seeker to the right technical resolution person within an organization. The help desk may be internal or serve a customer-support function. It's associated with corporate networking, and it's interaction with internal and external customers can provide a key source of knowledge about desirable characteristics of future products as well as improvements for current products.

- **Heuristic software**—A software solution that learns about its users and the knowledge they possess by monitoring the user's interaction with the system. Thus, over time, its ability to provide users with relevant knowledge should improve.

- **Hubs**—People who collect and share data.

- **Human capital**—The collective value of an organization's know-how. Human capital refers to the value, usually not reflected in accounting systems, which results from the investment an organization must make to recreate the knowledge in its employees. One of three forms of intellectual capital, as defined by Edvinsson and Stewart. The other two are structural capital and customer capital.

- **Hypertext**—A semantic network with [substantial] content at the nodes. But the content itself (the traditional document model) seems to be the driving organizational force, not the network of links. In most hypertext documents, the links aren't semantically typed, although they're typed at times according to the medium of the object displayed by traversing the link.

- **Information**—Data endowed with relevance and purpose (i.e., analyzed data).

- **Information economics**—The study of the tangible value to business enterprises of information holdings.

- **Information mining (or knowledge mining)**—The use of technology to extract additional value from intellectual assets. It begins with finding and managing the right data sources.

- **Information warehouse**—A storage area for the results of data analysis.

- **Information modeling**—Interests itself in precise specification of the meaning in a text, and in making relationships of meaning explicit—often with the objective of rapid and accurate development of new software applications for business requirements.

- **Integrated knowledge environment**—Information technology that supports the flow of knowledge throughout the enterprise.

- **Intellectual assets and intellectual capital**—Also known as intangible assets and invisible assets, an organization's recorded information and, increasingly, human talent itself, often to innovation of patents in particular. The terms reflect the understanding that information is a growing part of every company's assets, and that such information and knowledge is typically either inefficiently warehoused or simply lost, especially in large, physically dispersed organizations. Intellectual capital is intangible assets that can't be measured but are used by the company to its advantages. Intellectual capital can be segmented into three subcategories: human capital, structural capital, and customer capital. Although acknowledged as valuable in most organizations, these assets aren't measured and accounted for in an organization's financial statements other than as goodwill. Many believe these assets form the basis for most equity-market valuations of an organization and are a key to continued innovation and competitive advantage

- **Intermediation**—The brokerage function which brings together knowledge-seekers (questions) with knowledge-providers (answers). Intermediation technologies facilitate the connections between people and the communication of knowledge between seeker and provider.

- **Internalization**—The transfer of explicit knowledge from an external repository (temporary or permanent) to an individual, in the most useful and efficient way possible. There are two aspects to internalization: extraction and filtering. It's one of four key knowledge-management functions. The other three are knowledge mapping, externalization, and cognition.

- **Intranets**—Intra-corporation networks that use the Internet's IP (Internet Protocol) standard. They not only permit sharing of information, but also view the organization's information (including structured resources like relational databases as well as unstructured text) through Web browsers like Netscape Navigator. It's an interesting inversion of the traditional computer interface model, in which computer users run applications like word processors and relational databases in order to view and process information.

- **KQML**—The knowledge query and manipulation language; it's a language and protocol for exchanging information and knowledge. It's part of the ARPA (Address and Routing Parameter Area domain) knowledge-sharing effort aimed at developing techniques and a methodology for building large-scale, sharable, and reusable knowledge bases. KQML is a message-format and message-handling protocol to support run-time knowledge sharing among agents. KQML can be used as a language through which an application program interacts with an intelligent system or through which two or more intelligent systems share knowledge in support of cooperative problem-solving. Information on KQML can be found at *http://www.cs.umbc.edu/kqml/*

- **K-spots**—Represent the knowledge niches on which a company must focus its KM efforts. Based on how the audit process populates the strategic capability framework, you can identify promising processes that stand to gain the most through KM.

- **Knowledge**—Knowledge is a mixture of experience, practices, traditions, values, contextual information, expert insight, and sounded intuition that provides an environment and framework for evaluation and incorporating new experiences and information. It's divided into two major categories: explicit and tacit.

- **Knowledge acquisition**—The process of development and creation of insight, skills, and relationships. Knowledge acquisition is the primary job function of a knowledge engineer; traditionally it consists of "the reduction of a large body of information to a precise set of facts and rules" and is associated with expert systems. Recently, these functions (and this job description) seem to be making a transition from addressing specific project requirements to meeting broad organizational objectives.

- **Knowledge analyst**—Collects, organizes, and disseminates knowledge, usually on-demand. They provide knowledge leadership by becoming walking repositories of best practices, a library of how knowledge is and needs to be shared across an organization. There's a risk that these individuals become so valuable to their immediate constituency that they're not able to move laterally to other parts of the organization where their skills are equally needed.

- **Knowledge artifact**—A specific instance of a knowledge asset.

- **Knowledge base/knowledge warehouse**—The data and "rules of thumb" produced by the knowledge-acquisition and compilation phases of creating an expert system application. It, too, is now broadened to include every imaginable corporate intellectual asset. The knowledge base is the absolute collection of all expertise, experience and knowledge of those within any organization. It's typically used to describe any collection of information that also includes contextual or experiential references to other metadata.

- **Knowledge capital (same as intellectual capital)**—The intellectual material, knowledge, information, property, and experience that can be put to use to create wealth. It's collective brainpower. Knowledge capital is also the present value of all future knowledge earnings, discounted at an appropriate rate.

- **Knowledge-chain**—Corporate instinct, stemming from the flow of knowledge through four definitive stages in this chain: internal awareness, internal responsiveness, external awareness, and external responsiveness.

- **Knowledge deficit**—A " metric that captures the inefficiency and cost associated with intellectual rework, substandard performance, and employee inability to find knowledge resources."

- **Knowledge earnings**—The portion of normalized earnings over and above expected earnings attributable to book assets.

- **Knowledge engineers**—Individuals that reduce a large body of knowledge to a precise set of facts and rules or a new breed of middle managers who "remake reality—or, to put it differently, engineer new knowledge—according to the company's vision." Knowledge engineers convert explicit knowledge to instructions and program systems and codified applications. Effectively, the better knowledge-engineers codify knowledge, the harder it is for the organization to change when their environment demands it.

- **Knowledge half-life**—The point at which the acquisition of new knowledge is more cost-effective and offers greater returns than the maintenance of existing knowledge.

- **Knowledge harvesting**—The work performed by the knowledge engineer. It's the act of selecting, through analysis, information that's new or actionable and should be added to the knowledge warehouse.

- **Knowledge librarian**—An individual who performs custom searches on the knowledge warehouse for individuals within the organization.

- **Knowledge management (KM)**—A strategy that turns an organization's intellectual assets, both recorded information and the talents of its members, into greater productivity, new value, and increased competitiveness. It teaches corporations, from managers to employees, how to produce and optimize skills as a collective entity. It's the leveraging of collective wisdom to increase responsiveness and innovation.

- **Knowledge management experts (strategists)**—Individuals who develop high-level KM strategies.

- **Knowledge management system (KMS)**—A proactive, systematic process by which value is generated from intellectual- or knowledge-based assets and disseminated to stakeholders.

- **Knowledge maps/knowledge mapping/information maps**—Knowledge mapping is finding where information is in the organization, but the term is also used at times to describe concerns with how to structure knowledge. Indeed, maps can range from simple directories of names, titles, and department affiliation, to elaborate online search engines with hypertext links to databases of human expertise, research material, and abstracts of published information. Knowledge mapping is also called knowledge taxonomy. It's the process which provides an organization with a picture of the specific knowledge it requires in order to support its business processes.

- **Knowledge representation**—Explicit specification of "knowledge objects" and relationships among those objects. It takes many forms, with variations in emphasis and major variations in formalisms. Knowledge representation allows computers to reconfigure and reuse information that they store in ways not narrowly pre-specified in advance. Concept mapping, semantic networks, hypertext, information modeling, and conceptual indexing all exemplify knowledge representation, in somewhat different ways.

- **Knowledge segment**—Everything a company's professionals and systems know about a specific domain.

- **Knowledge sharing/information sharing/decision coordination**—Knowledge sharing and information sharing are the precision of expression and access to meet the objective of rapid product development. Information sharing and decision coordination are central problems for large-scale product development. A framework is designed to support information sharing and coordinated communication among members of a product development organization, particularly for the tasks of design knowledge capture, dynamic notification of design changes, and active management of design dependencies. The proposed technology consists of a shared knowledge representation (language and vocabulary), protocols for foreign data encapsulation and posting to the shared environment, and mechanisms for content-directed routing of posted information to interested parties via subscription and notification services. Knowledge sharing involves many dimensions, including the reapplication of lexicons, ontologies, inference syntax, tasks, and problem-solving methods. Principal obstacles to all current work in knowledge sharing involve the difficulties of achieving consensus regarding what knowledge representations mean, of enumerating the context features and background knowledge required to ascribe meaning to a particular knowledge representation, and of describing knowledge independent of specific interpreters or inference engines.

- **Knowledge spiral**—The growth of knowledge based upon the knowledge already present within the organization.

- **Knowledge steward**—Provides minimal, ongoing support to knowledge users in the form of expertise in the tools, practices, and methods of knowledge leadership. The steward is usually an individual who has fallen into the role of helping others better understand and leverage the power of new technologies and practices in managing knowledge.

- **Knowledge topology**—A framework that segments KM into its four key categories.

- **Knowledge transfer experts (practitioners)**—People who extract knowledge from those who have it, reorder it to a form anyone can use, and periodically update and edit the knowledge warehouse.

- **Knowledge transfer™**—a term trademarked by Knowledge Transfer International Corp.; it's the tactical dimension of converting knowledge requirements into working solutions.

- **Learning organization/knowledge-creating organization**—Learning organizations are organizational strategies for creating new knowledge as a competitive advantage; the collective, group, and interpersonal communication, shared visions, uncovering of hidden assumptions that hinder learning ("double-loop learning"), and "new sensibilities" all figure prominently in these approaches.

- **Metadata**—Simply information added to a document (or a smaller unit of information) that makes it easier to access and re-use that content. It's also referred to as simply "data about data." You'll find metadata in many different forms, including key words in a software help system, the document profile information attached to documents in a document management system, and the classification information in a library card catalog. It's data providing context or otherwise describing information in order to make it more valuable as part of a knowledge-management system; most often used to connect information in relevant ways to people, process, or product.

- **Metaskills**—The basic tools of generative learning. These skills are aimed at ensuring three things: skills-adaptability, autonomous decision making, and an emotional aptitude for change.

- **Ontologies (computer-based)**—Computer-based ontologies are formal, structured representations of a domain of knowledge. They're commonly associated with artificial intelligence technology, where they were originally designed to serve as the raw material for computer reasoning and computer-based agents.

  An ontology is a set of definitions of content-specific knowledge representation primitives: classes, relations, functions, and object constants. Ontologies are also crucial for enabling knowledge-level interoperation of agents, since meaningful interaction among agents can occur only when they share a common interpretation of the vocabulary used in their communications. Finally, ontologies are useful in many ways for human understanding and interaction.

- **Organizational change management**—A methodology that analyzes the organization's environment, defines the risks related to change, and defines how to overcome these risks. Organizational change management manages the process of change.

- **Payback period**—Defined as the period required to recover the cost of an investment.

- **Personalization**—Retrieving and structuring knowledge to best meet the preferences and skills set of the knowledge-seeker.

- **Process**—A series of interconnected activities that takes input, adds value to it, and produces output. It's how organizations do their day-to-day routines. Your organization's processes define how it operates.

- **Process-based knowledge mapping (PKM)**—A diagram that visually displays knowledge within the context of a business process. It shows how knowledge should be used within the process and the sources of knowledge.

- **Profiling**—The creation of chronicles that track user interest levels and areas of expertise. In an automated approach, profiles are created by monitoring each user's work submitted; work reviewed, and query habits. Profiling is used to feed agent technology, user-sensitivity systems, and document management systems.

- **Pulse takers**—People who build relationships that keep them informed about what's going on in the organization.

■ **Response/stimuli matrix**—A KM model that plots where memory and knowledge are best used. The matrix indicates that memory is an appropriate vehicle for responding in planned ways to anticipate stimuli. Knowledge is an appropriate vehicle for responding in unplanned ways to surprise stimuli.

■ **Semantic analysis (semiotics)**—the analysis of meaning in text. In the context of KM software, a set of analysis programs which identify concepts in documents and their relative importance to the subject of the document and to each other. These utilities form the basis for accurate search and knowledge-discovery.

■ **Semantic networks**—A technique for representing knowledge. As with other networks, they consist of nodes with links between them. The nodes in a semantic network represent concepts.

■ **Smart networks**—Combine hard and soft networks. This results in effective linking of smart business strategies to every employee throughout the company. Smart organizations are entirely process- and team-based, and use knowledge as their primary asset and are characterized by such smart networks.

■ **Strategic knowledge management**—Links the building of a company's knowledge to a business strategy using a quality function deployment approach. These links are created through knowledge maps.

■ **Structural capital**—The speed that an organization can convert customer capital and intellectual capital into a product or service, and the shorter the cycle time, the greater the value of structural capital.

■ **Suggestive software**—Capable of deducing a user's knowledge needs, and suggesting knowledge associations that the user can't make.

■ **Tacit (soft) knowledge**—Knowledge that's formed around intangible factors embedded in an individual's experience. It often takes the form of beliefs, values, principles, and morals. It guides the individual's actions. It's embedded in the individual's ideas, insights, values, and judgment. It's only accessible through the direct corroboration and communication with the individual that has the knowledge.

■ **Touch points**—The priority areas for the application of KM; typically interactions with customers, suppliers, and employees. Each touch point represents an area of potential process or quality improvement and competitive advantage. Touch points represent areas where human interaction is often most intense.

■ **Workflow**—One of the tools used for the creation of process-assets. A proactive toolset for the analysis, compression, and automation of business activities.

■ **Wrappers**—Scripts and connection modules that allow personal computers and modern networks to access legacy data. Knowledge, query modeling language (KQML), and TCL/TK are often used to write these wrappers.

APPENDIX B

SUGGESTED READING

Allee, Verna. *The Knowledge Evolution: Expanding Organizational Intelligence*. Butterworth-Heinemann, 1997. One of the first full treatments of knowledge management and the broad implications of the field.

Applegate, Lynda M., F. Warren McFarlan, and James L. McKenney. *Corporate Information Systems Management*. Irwin, 1999. The fifth edition of this classic text for IT managers includes a strong focus on technology strategy for senior executives.

Drucker, Peter. *The Age of Discontinuity*. Transaction, 1992. Not one of Drucker's best-known works, but the book contains his first published thoughts about knowledge workers and a future knowledge society.

Gates, Bill. *Business @ the Speed of Thought*. Warner Books, 1999.

Higgins, James. *Innovate or Evaporate*. New Society Publishing, 1995.

Kaplan, Robert. *The Balanced Scorecard: Translating Strategy Into Action*. HBS Press, 1996.

Koulepoulos, Thomas M. and Carl Frappaolo. *Smart Things to Know About Knowledge Management*. Capstone Publishing, 2000.

Koulopoulos, Thomas M., Richard Spinello, Wayne Toms, and Wayne D. Toms. *Corporate Instinct*. Wiley, 1997.

Nonaka, Ikujiro and Hirotaka Taneuchi. *The Knowledge Creating Company: How Japanese Companies Create the Dynamics of Innovation*. Oxford University Press, 1995.

O'Dell, Carla and C. Jackson Grayson. *If We Only Knew What We Know: The Transfer of Internal Knowledge and Best Practice*. Free Press, 1998. This work is based on an examination of the best practices of more than seventy leading companies.

Pearson, Thomas. "Measurements and the Knowledge Revolution," *Quality Progress*, September 1999.

Schwartz, Peter. *The Art of the Long View: Planning for the Future in an Uncertain World*. Doubleday, 1996. A founder of the Global Business Network, Schwartz uses real-world case studies to demonstrate how scenario planning is more useful than applying quantitative predictive models.

Stein, Martin and Frank Voehl. *MacroLogistics Management: A Catalyst for Organizational Change*. CRC Press/APICS, 1998.

Stewart, Thomas. *Intellectual Capital: The New Wealth of Organizations.* Doubleday, 1997.

Svieby, Erik. *The New Organizational Wealth: Measuring and Managing Knowledge-Based Assets.* Berrett-Koehler, 1997. One of the few authors with hands-on experience of running a business, Svieby was among the first to emphasize the importance of the physical office environment and the effect of information overload.

Tiwana, Amrit. *The Knowledge Management Toolkit.* Prentice Hall, 2000.

Tkach, Daniel. "Advances in Knowledge Management," *Knowledge Management,* March 1999. Tkach is the IBM worldwide marketing manager for knowledge management solutions. He serves as technology director at the Institute for Knowledge Management.

INDEX

A

Abe, Masayuki 184
ACollab 79
Acorda Therapeutics 156
action verbs 73
Adams, C. 22
Age of Knowledge 18
agents (agent technology) 187
Agouron Pharmaceuticals 162
Air Products 53
Al-Azmi, Mutiran 168
Allee, Verna 199
Allen, Jim 63
American Home Products 162
American National Insurance Co. (ANICO)
    179
American Productivity and Quality Center
    (APQC) 3
American Society for Quality (ASQ) xxxiv
Ampuero, Marcos 21
analysis process 43
Anderson, Dave A. 146
Annotea 79
Applegate, Lynda M. 199
ARCO 70–71
area activity analysis xxvi
Ark Group 32
Arnold, Dave 92
artificial intelligence 187
as-is status 55

AskMe Enterprise 79
assets, book 19, 187; culture 28; financial
    157; intangible 22, 23, 24; intellectual
    192; knowledge 31, 52, 162
attitude 25
Aurigin Systems 130
AutoSupportDesk 93
availability 40
Avery Dennison (AD) 130
Aviation Industry CBT Committee (AICC)
    41, 42
Axista.com 79

B

Barr Lab 162
Barth, Steve 31
benchmarking 47
Bennet, Alex 166
Bergethon, R. K. 180
Big Three automakers 160
biometrics 40
black holes 107
Bloki 80
Blue Cross Blue Shield 57
Bohn, Roger E. 51, 145
Bohn's Stages of Knowledge 51
book assets 19, 187
Boutelle, Lt. Gen. Steven W. 7
Bradford University School of Management
    168

Briloff, Abraham 18
Bristol-Meyers Squibb 162
British Petroleum 11
Broadhead, Jim 114
Brodeur Porter Novelli 102
browser 187
Buckman Laboratories 4, 133, 180
Buckman, Robert 29, 139
building automation systems (BAS) 88
Burlington Northern Railroad 67–70
burning platform 107
business benefits modeling 136
business intelligence (BI) 96
business operating system (BOS) 187
business plan xxx

C
calculation 46
Caldwell, French 148
Calendars Net 80
Cambridge Technology 103, 108–111, 179
capital, customer 19, 189; financial 25;
    human 25, 191; intellectual 3, 5, 6, 19,
    158, 163, 172, 193; knowledge 12, 19,
    158, 172, 193; structural 19, 25, 125,
    197; worth 19, 21
Carlson, Curtis R. 104
Carnegie, Andrew 155
Carter, C. 36
Cass Information Systems 65–66
categorization 46
centralized content storage 143
CFO 162
change 166; agents 107; current state and
    107; definition of 105; future state and
    107; management of 137; transitional
    state and 107
change management excellence xxii,
    xxviii–xxix

change management plan 142, 147
Chaos Report xxvi
CHEMREG 53
Chevron 180
chief knowledge officer (CKO) 59, 103, 187
Churchill, Winston 3
Clark, John Maurice 1
Clinton-Gore administration 165
coachingplatform 80
cognition 187
Cohen, Ron 156
collaboration management 40, 41
collaborative intelligence layers 144
collaborative platform 143
coMentor 80
commercial portals 97
communication, fog factor and 125–130;
    processes of 188; rules of good writing
    124; simplifying 123–133; verbal 42, 43,
    44, 46
communities of practice 62–64, 188; defini-
    tion of 62
community of interest 62–63
CommunityZero 81
Compaq Computer Corp. 178
competence 25; management of 188; mod-
    eling of 188
comprehensive value 162
computer-aided design (CAD) 88
computer-aided facility management
    (CAFM) 88
computerized maintenance management
    systems (CMMS) 88
computer-supported collaborative work
    (CSCW) 188
ComputerWeekly 161
concept mapping 188
concept-based search 188

conceptual (or "back of the book") indexes 188

condensation 46

Connor, Marcia 132

content 40; directors of 188; management of 136–137; mapping of 188

context sensitivity 189

contextualization 46

continuous improvement, of knowledge management system 148–150

contribution monitoring and valuation 189

core competency 189

corporate memory 189

corporate portals 97; *see also* portals

correction 46

cost 94; recovery of 167

Covey, Stephen R. xxv, 99

Covisint 160

Creative Manager Pro 81

creativity 15

Crosby, Philip 115

cross-functional management 118

cross-functional teams 122

cultural change agent 61

culture assets 28

CU-SeeMe 38

customer xxxii, xxxv; capital 19, 189; needs 117; satisfaction 122

Customer Relationship Management 167

Cuvillier, R. 37

D

Danzig, Richard 14

data 189; mining 189; silos 165; versus information 46; warehouse 45, 189; *see also* information

Davenport, Tom 9, 59, 148

day-to-day experiences 47

Dean, Sarah 135

delivery mechanism 136

delivery style 40, 42

Dello, Michelle 133

Deming Prize 111, 113, 118, 120, 122

Deming, W. Edwards 115, 168, 176

Dennison, Avery 133–134

digital nervous system 190

discontinuity of knowledge 190; *see also* knowledge

disparity in employee value 21; *see also* employees

distance learning, 190; *see also* training

distributed and open hypertext systems 190

diversity 15

document management 190

DocuPortal.net 2004 81

DON IM/IT Metrics Guide for Knowledge Management Initiatives 166

Dow Chemical 14, 179

Drucker, Peter 1, 2–3, 8, 18, 50, 64, 66, 133, 168, 175, 176, 177, 199

Dyer, Greg 51

E

economic profit 158

Edvinsson, Leif 19, 23, 55

eight strategies of knowledge growth 145; *see also* knowledge

Einstein, Albert, 19

electronic data interchange (EDI) 69

electronic yellow page 190

Eliot, T. S. 9

employees, evaluation of 75; intrinsic worth of 162–164

enterprise resource planning (ERP) 88

EPMAC Team Collaboration Portal 81

eProject 81

Ernst & Young 40, 133

eRoom 82

Ewers, Justin 175

expense, internal 167; *see also* cost

explicit (hard) knowledge 10–11, 29, 87, 145, 150, 190; flow of 45; *see also* knowledge

external responsiveness 191

externalization 191

extranet 41

F

face-to-face communication 44, 46; *see also* communication

Federal Energy Regulatory Commission (FERC) 115

feedback measurement systems xxiv

Feigenbaum, Armand V. xxiii

Feigenbaum, Donald xxiii

Financial Accounting Standards Board 1

financial assets, custodianship of 157

financial capital 25

Finneran, Thomas M. 170

five Cs 46

five pillars of organizational excellence xxi, xxxv

five Ps xxi

Flash 41

Flash, Cynthia 59

Florida Power & Light 111–123

Florida Public Service Commission (FPSC) 115

Flypaper 82

fog factor 125–130

Fong, Col. Timothy A. 97, 98

Forbes Group 176

Forehand, Joe W. 5, 64

Forest Labs 162

forms 130–133

Fortune 157, 182

ForumOne 82

four Cs 105

Franklin, Benjamin 180

Frappaolo, Carl 60, 62, 199

G

Gaines, Brian R. 50

Galvin, Bob 104

Gartner Group xxviii, 97, 140, 180

gatekeepers 29, 191

Gates, Bill 1, 52, 79, 199

Gates, Richard 183

Gault, Stanley 182

GE 13

generators 40, 42

geographic information systems (GIS) 88, 191

global village of tomorrow 15

GlobalServe Corp. 178

goal-setting 69, 71, 72, 74

Goodwin, Brad 21

Google Groups 82

Grayson, C. Jackson 199

Greenes, Kent 60

Greenwood, Bill 67, 68, 69, 70, 71, 72, 74

Gregory, John 148

Groove Virtual Office 82

group loyalty and cohesion 17

group thought 15

Gunning Fog Index 125–127

Gunning, Robert 125, 129

H

Haddock, Francine 98

Hamel, G. 37

Hansen, Morten T. 11

hard knowledge *see* explicit knowledge

hard returns, measurement of 168

Health Technology Inc. 112–113

help desk technology 191

Hemre, Anders 97
Hensler, Douglas 155
Herbold, Robert J. xxxiv, 10
heuristic software 191
Higgins, James 199
Highet, Gilbert 46
Hire, Jeff 139
Hitachi Ltd. 181–182
Holmes, Sr. Oliver Wendel 151
HotComm 83
Housel, Tom 2
HTML 41
hubs 29, 191
Hudiburg, John 116, 118, 121
human capital 25, 191
human resource 27
hypertext 191

I

IBM xxvi, 10, 13, 36
IC Audit Model 22
IC-Index 22, 24–25
Industrial Revolution 2
information 191; economics 191; life cycle
    149; mapping 48; mining 191; modeling
    192; sharing 184; sources 48; warehouse
    45,192; *see also* data
information technology (IT), infrastructure
    for 77; for knowledge management
    77–100; system 39
Infowit Creative Manager 83
infrastructure, evaluation of 139–142
innovation management 185
input requirement statement xxiv
intangible assets monitor 22, 23, 24
integrated knowledge environment 192; *see
    also* knowledge
integrated management tools xxvii
intellectual assets 192

intellectual capital 3, 5, 6, 19, 25, 33, 176;
    value of 22; *see also* knowledge people
intellectual property 25, 28
intelligent agents and network mining 49
interest networks 63–64
intermediation 192
internalization 192
International Data Corp. (IDC) 21, 151
International Data Group (IDC) 50
Internet 41, 56
intranet 41, 192
intranets.com 83
ISO 9001:2000 xxv, xxxii, xxxiii

J

job description 75
Johnson & Johnson 162
Johnson, Samuel 171
Juran, John M. 115
just-in-time manufacturing xxv

K

K! New 110–111
Kaiser Permanente 180
Kallan, Richard A. 125, 129
Kanai, Tsutomu 181
Kanevsky, Valery 2
Kansai Electric Power Co. 116
Kao Corp. 184–185
Kaplan, Robert S. 22, 29, 199
Kavi 83
Kennedy, Dennis 94
Kerr Steve 46, 60
key performance indicators 90
Kipling, Rudyard 29
Kirham, Garuy 179
Klasson, Kirk 7
knowledge 193; acquisition of 193; analyst
    61, 193; artifact 193; base 193; benefits

of 169; chain 193; charter 70–71; content 123; conversation 13; culture 29, 31; database 47; deficit 193; definition of 6; discontinuity of 190; earnings 19, 194; enablers 136; engineer 61, 194; evolution of 2; exchange 49; explicit 10–11, 29, 87, 145, 150, 190; four kinds of 9; framework for flow of 48; growth of 145; half-life of 194; harvesting of 194; inputs 150; librarian 194; manager 62; manual 75; mapping 140, 194; moral 9; networks 177; objectives 67; outputs 150; people 3; policy 66–67; professional 9; representation 194; scope of 20; segment 195; sharing 56, 167, 195; silos 144; spiral 7–8, 11, 195; steward 61, 195; system 109; tacit 10–11, 75, 87, 108, 145, 150, 197; tags 145; taxonomy 140; technical 9; theoretical 9; topology 195; total cost of 89; transfer 195; value-added 158; warehouse 45, 47; worker 176

knowledge assets 31, 52, 162; division of 27; six classifications of 27-28; map 22, 27–28

knowledge audit 25; scope of 26; *see also* assets

knowledge capital 12, 19, 158, 172, 193; calculation of 159–162; definition of 13; reasons for measuring, 21; three categories of 12; valuation of 155–158

knowledge management (KM) 119–121, 194; as a strategy 6; benchmark study 143; best practices 101–134; change management and 104; components of 59; cost recovery of 167; critical success factors of 170–171; definition of 6; documents of 75; experts in 194; four processes of 176; goal-setting system for 73; information system (IS) 114; information technology for 77–100; internal expense of 167; introduction to 1–10; life cycle of 35-37; major obstacles of 171; maturity grid, 52; metrics for 164; organization structure 59–76; portals 97–99; process analyses for 90; project 165–166, 172; road map for 138; software for 87–88, 91; spiral 11; strategy 67; technology optimization rollout process steps 89–91; three essential aspects of 7; twelve-level maturity grid for 54, 55; values 155–172; Web tools for 93

Knowledge Management 135, 151, 164

Knowledge Management Consortium International (KMCI) 26

knowledge management excellence xxii, xxix

knowledge management system (KMS) 35, 45, 59, 116, 194; architecture for 49; benefits of 168–169; blueprint 146; budget 151; continuous improvement of 148–150; costs of 94; definition of 6; deployment of 148; design and development 143–146; enablers 39, 151–152; examples of world-class 49–50; five major components of 40–42; implementation methodology 96–99, 135–153; information sources 47–48; infrastructure evaluation 139–142; order of use 51; pilot 146–148; quick assessment of 51, 54, 55; reasons for adopting a 50–51; reason for failure of 88; requirements definition 139; six phases of 137–150; software tools for 78; technical strategy 48–49; top management's tasks for 66; training cycle 147; versus information technology 49;

knowledge-based economy 176

knowledge-sharing culture 75

KnowledgeSpace 57

Koskinsemi, Mark 180
Koslowski, Thilo 161
Koulepoulos, Thomas M. 62, 199
KQML 192
K-spots 193
Kume, Hitoshi 52, 33

L

learning organization 195
Lee, Sai Peck 87
Leibman, Matthias 3
Leighton, Tracy 132
Lesser, Eric 67
Lev, Baruch 19, 160, 172
Levi Strauss & Co. 30
LimeWire 83
Long Island College Hospital 111–113, 133
Lotus Development Corp. 178
Lotus Services Group 179
Lynch, Mike 143

M

Magi Enterprise 84
Mahon, Andrew 179
Malone, Michael S. 19, 23
management, by objectives 117; change 137; collaboration 40, 41; competence 188; computerized maintenance; content 136–137; cross-functional 118; document 190; innovation 185; integrated tools for xxvii; knowledge 119–121; organizational change 61, 104–107, 196; process xxiv–xxvi; resource xxix–xxx; reviews 117–118, 122; strategic knowledge 197; total improvement xxxiii; total quality xxvii–xxxiii
Mantelman, Lee 26
Marcus, Rudolph J. 17, 18
Marr, Bernard 36

Mars Inc. 65–66
Maruta, Yoshio 184
Matsushita, Konosuke 56
McDonald, Marshall 115–117
McDonough, Brian 51
McFarlan, F. Warren 199
McKenney, James L. 199
McKinley, Tony 167
metadata 196; *see also* data
metaskills 196
metrics 90, 164
Microsoft 39
MJI TeamWorks 84
modeling, business benefits 136; competence 188; information 192; performance 136; semantic 96
Mohame, Abdulmajid 87
Moorhead Malting 69
moral knowledge 9; *see also* knowledge
Morrison, Lori 131
Morse, R. 8
Mulcahy, Anne M. 35
Mullich, Joe 146
Murphy, Jim 49

N

Naisbitt, John 45
Neely, Andy 22, 36
Nettles, Patrick H. 19
Nike Inc. 37
Nippon Steel 185
Nohria, Nitin 11
Nonaka, Ikujiro 199
nonverbal communication 44; *see also* communication
Norton, David P. 22, 29
Nuclear Regulatory Commission (NRC) 115, 121

O

O'Boyle, Doug 113
O'Dell, Carla 199
obtaining knowledge 3; *see also* knowledge
online analytical processing (OLAP) 96
ontologies (computer-based) 196
ontology-based knowledge management
   model 87
OPMcreator 84
Oracle 132
organizational change management (OCM)
   61, 104–107, 196; strategies for 108–111
organizational creativity versus innovation
   15
organizational excellence 179
organizational intelligence 177
organizational learning 177
organizational memory 177
outcomes 68–69
output requirement statement xxiv
outsourcing xxxi

P

parietal disgorgement aid (PDA)
payback period 196
Payless Stores 168
Pearson, Thomas 199
Peetz, John 109–110, 133
people, types of 29, 31
PeopleSoft 132
performance and decision modeling 136;
   see also modeling
Perrigo 162
Perry, Erica 167
personal knowledge capital (PKC) 163
personal portals 97; *see also* portals
personalization 196
Peters, Tom 177
Phifer, Gene 99

physical infrastructure 28
Pifzer 162
Pillsbury 86, 133
plan-do-check-act (PDCA) 120
Platinum Technology Inc. 168, 180
Platt, Lew xxi
Platt, Nina 50
policy deployment 116, 118
PopG 84
portals 97–99
PowerPoint 41, 47
practices and routines 28
Prahalad, C. K. 37
problem recognition 68
process xxii, 196; business planning and
   xxx; definition of xxiv; of transformation
   43
process management excellence xxii,
   xxiv–xxvi; macro-level approach xxv;
   micro-level approach xxv
process-based knowledge map (PKM)
   149–151, 196
productivity improvement 167
productivity paradox 164
professional knowledge 9; *see also* knowledge
profiling 196
Project Echo 184
Project Management Body of Knowledge
   (PMBOK) xxvi
project management excellence xxii,
   xxvi–xxvii
project 47; definition of xxvi; manager
   xxvi–xxvii; plan 142
ProjectPlace.com 84
public domain 47
publications portals 97; *see also* portals
pulse takers, 29, 196

Q

quality 69; Web influence on 58

quality technique familiarity versus use
xxxiv

Quorum Tools 84

R

Radicati Group 94

Ramelli, Donnee 2

Ramon, Andrea 178

readability 128–130; index 126

Readability Plus 128

Records Management Quarterly 167

relationships 25

Rembrandt 146

Remez, Shereen 96

renewal and development 25

repository 78

resource management excellence xxiii,
xxix–xxx

response/stimuli matrix 197

Retrieve 91–92, 94

return on investment (ROI), formula for
168

rewards-and-recognition system 146

Roberts, Bill 51

Roelandts, Willem 155

Rooney, John 13

Roosevelt, Eleanor 62

Rubbermaid 182–183

rules of good writing 124; *see also* communication

Rumizen, Melissie 4

Rutgers University 38

S

Saint-Onge, Hubert 31, 139

Salim, Siti Salwah 87

Scarbrough, H. 36

Schaffer, Robert 67

Schiuma, Gianni 36

Schmitt, Wolfgang 182

Schwartz, Peter 199

Schwarz, William J. xxv

scope of knowledge 20; *see also* knowledge

Scrivlet 85

semantic analysis (semiotics) 197

semantic modeling 96

semantic networks 197

Serious Magic Inc. 46

Sharable Content Object Reference Model
(SCORM) 41, 42

Shaw, Mildred L. G. 50

Shewhart's cycle xxv

Siebel Systems 178

Siegrist, Richard 113

Sierhuls, Maurten 77

simple communication cycle 42–44; *see
also* communication

simple language 123–133

six rules for self-examination xxx

Six Sigma xxv, xxxii, xxxiii, xxxiv

Skandia Navigator 22, 23

small-scale teams 67–68

smart networks 197

SmartGroups.com 85

Smith, Fred xxxi

Snell, Don 112

Sockol, Mike 133–134

soft knowledge *see* tacit knowledge

Software Developers 95

solution design 136

Spinello, Richard 199

Sriberg, Dave 133

stakeholder relationship 27

Starr, J. 11, 37

Stein, Martin 199

Stephenson, Karen 29, 31

Stewart, Thomas 200

Stone, Richard 145

Strassman, Paul A. 21, 155, 157, 158, 159, 164, 172

strategic knowledge management 197; *see also* knowledge management

strategic plan, scope of 89, 90

streaming video 41

strengths, weaknesses, opportunities, and threats (SWOT) 90; analysis of 140

structural capital 19, 25, 125, 197

structured query language (SQL) 92

subject matter experts 61

suggestive software 197

Sveiby, Karl Erik 23, 32, 200

T

tacit (soft) knowledge 10–11, 75, 87, 108, 145, 150, 197; flow of 42; *see also* knowledge

Takeda, Yasutsugu 181

Taltech Network Corp. 180

Tandem Computers 178

Taneuchi, Hirotaka 199

team focus 69

Team Workplace 85

technical knowledge 9; *see also* knowledge

Texas Instruments 180

The Conference Board 166, 171

thematic networks 62–63

theoretical knowledge 9; *see also* knowledge

Thomas, Rick 11, 75

Timbuktu Remote 38

Tiwana, Amrit 141, 171, 200

Tkach, Daniel 200

Toms, Wayne D. 199

total cost of knowledge (TCK) 89

total improvement management (TIM) xxxiii

total quality control (TQC) 116

total quality management (TQM) xxxii–xxxiii, xxxiv

total value 25

touch points 197

training, just-in-time 147

transformation process 43

TrioProject 85

Trussler, S. 171

Tucker, Alison 4

Turner, Bob 63

twelve-level knowledge management maturity grid 54, 55

Tyndall, Gene 21

U

U.S. Department of Commerce 164

U.S. Department of the Navy 166

U.S. Department of Transportation 53

U.S. economic growth 164–165

V

verbal communication 42, 43, 44, 46; *see also* communication

vision statement 55–56, 139

Visual Communicator Studio 46

W

W. R. Grace and Co. 16

Wal-Mart 183

Washington Research Center (WRC) 16

Welch, Jack xxx, xxxv

Williams, Walter 182

Wilson, Linda 18

Wilson, Woodrow 108

wisdom filters 8–9

Woolard, E.S. xxi

workflow 197

workplace neural network (WNN) 39

WorldJam 10
World Bank 106
wrappers 197
Wurman, Richard Saul 3
Wysocki, Jennifer 102

Y
Yahoo! Groups 85
Young, Wise 38, 60

Z
Zack, M. H. 9
Zaiti, Mohamed 168